"I had a 'first-draft paperweight' on my desk for months. With Pilar's help, my scripts have transformed from desk clutter into calling cards. I've been hired by Warner Bros., signed with ICM, and am a new member of the WGA. I can honestly say that I wouldn't be in the position I am today if it weren't for Pilar."

— Bill Birch, writer of *Shazam*, Warner Bros.

"Pilar's techniques not only fine-tune your draft but serve as lessons that stick with you and make you a better writer overall. I highly recommend her if you want to take your writing to the next level!"

— Monica Macer, staff writer *Prison Break* and *Lost*; former creative executive Disney Studios.

"Sometimes it's astonishing how much there is still to learn. But then Pilar is an astonishing teacher who sent me off fizzing with ideas to inject life into what I thought was a moribund idea."

— Simon Rose, writer of *The Flying Scotsman*, Scion Films.

"Everyone has 10 minutes to spare, and this book maximizes that time with a treasure trove of clever tips and exercises guaranteed to improve your script. There are so many great lessons for writers of all skill levels ... It's quite possibly the most complete step-by-step system for taking a screenplay from rough concept to polished final draft that I've ever seen."

— Trevor Mayes, *scriptwrecked.com*

"The genius of Pilar's book isn't that she tells you how to write quickly — it's that she provides invaluable exercises and questions to help you focus on each individual element of your script: act breaks, character motivations, emotional arcs, individual scenes, lines of dialogue, etc. She breaks the entire process into short, digestible bits designed to push you forward swiftly and determinedly, whether you have 10 minutes or 10 months."

— Chad Gervich, writer/producer – *Wipeout, Reality Binge, Speeders, Foody Call*; author, *Small Screen, Big Picture: A Writer's Guide to the TV Business*

" ... A collection of lessons that will hone your craft and turn you from a hobbyist into an authority. It's a definitive and deceptively simple book that has boiled out all of the irrelevant minutia and pretense and bites deep into the bone of what makes a screen play work."

— Paul Linsley, writer – *Pangea, Bobby Stellar: Space Kid*

"I loved *The Coffee Break Screenwriter*! For many writers, facing the prospect of writing a feature-length screenplay is formidable and sometimes unnerving. Pilar Alessandra breaks the task into short, sensible bites, and before you know it you've conceptualized and written the entire draft — with or without coffee!"

— Mary J. Schirmer, screenwriter, instructor, *screenplayers.net*

"An entertaining and practical manual for getting it done! Leads you step-by-step through the process, with worksheets and examples to get your juices flowing. Even if you have only 10-minute chunks of time in which to write, this book will help you on your way to a finished script in record time!"

— John Dart, *storypros.com*

"With *The Coffee Break Screenwriter*, Pilar Alessandra has demolished a writer's most cherished excuse — now you can never say you don't have time to write! Get the book and get to work!"

— Ellen Sandler, co-executive producer — *Everybody Loves Raymond*; author, *The TV Writer's Workbook*

"*The Coffee Break Screenwriter* is an asset for both producers and screenwriters. It provides clarity on story and structure, works for developing characters, and is a great help on any project."

— Beau St. Clair, producer — *The Thomas Crown Affair* (1999), *Laws of Attraction*, *The Matador*

"Awesomely inspiring! Through her book, Pilar is your mentor, your muse, and your time keeper. She takes you right into your story every time, making the most of all those precious writing moments of yours, and proves that you can — or rather, *must* — balance organization with creativity to really succeed as a writer."

— Deborah S. Patz, filmmaker; author, *Film Production Management 101*

"This is a unique and highly useful guidebook that provides valuable practical advice for both the aspiring and working screenwriter. While it's true that 'writing is easy but thinking is hard,' Pilar has made the 'thinking' part that much easier."

— Herschel Weingrod, writer — *Trading Places*; producer — *Falling Down*

"Anyone who's listened to her podcast or taken her class will tell you — Pilar knows screenwriting. At last here's the book we've been waiting for! If you don't live in L.A., it's the next best thing to having Pilar give you notes while you write."

— Robert Grant, *Sci-Fi-London*

"Pilar brings amazing passion and technical skill to prepare writers for a professional career. I have been bringing her in to work with our writers in the Disney ABC Writing Program for years and have seen her methods in action. With Pilar's help, writers brainstorm on the spot, prepare outlines efficiently, and learn to deliver pages under tight deadlines. Now through this important book, she brings her unique writing tools and techniques to everyone."

— Frank Bennett Gonzalez, program director, Disney ABC Writing Program

The Coffee Break Screenwriter:

 **Writing Your Script
Ten Minutes at a Time**

Pilar Alessandra

MICHAEL WIESE PRODUCTIONS

Published by Michael Wiese Productions
12400 Ventura Blvd. #1111
Studio City, CA 91604
(818) 379-8799, (818) 986-3408 (FAX)
mw@mwp.com
www.mwp.com

Cover design by MWP
Cover photo by Zoltan Tischler, www.bookpictures.eu
Interior design by William Morosi
Printed by McNaughton & Gunn

Manufactured in the United States of America
Copyright 2010

Library of Congress Cataloging-in-Publication Data

Alessandra, Pilar
 The coffee break screenwriter : writing your script ten minutes at a time / Pilar Alessandra.
     p. cm.
 ISBN 978-1-932907-80-3
 1. Motion picture authorship. I. Title.
 PN1996.A48 2010
 808.2'3--dc22

                                                2010018798

Printed on Recycled Stock

Mixed Sources
Product group from well-managed
forests and other controlled sources
www.fsc.org   Cert no. SW-COC-002283
© 1996 Forest Stewardship Council

FSC

This book is dedicated to the writers of the *On The Page* weekly writing groups, each one deserving of a three-picture deal.

This book is also dedicated to my storytelling daughters, Sara and Rita, and to my husband, Pat, who said: "You should start your own class!"

Contents

Introduction

You've got ten minutes. No, really, that's all you've got. After all, you had to use your lunch hour to feed yourself. You had to get to that meeting. You had to make that phone call. You had to get the kids in the bath. There were things to do, and no time to do it!

But now you've crammed your lunch in, sat through the meeting you don't know why you took in the first place and cleaned up the kids. You've managed to take a deep breath and sit down for a second and focus … perhaps for ten whole minutes. Perhaps, even on your screenplay.

Remember your screenplay? That wonderful, visual story that you've been dying to finish … or just start. The one you keep nagging yourself to write every time you leave a movie theater and think, "I can do that!"

You think you need days, weeks, years that you don't have. You think you need to study theory, create long outlines and carefully pick each word before it even hits the page. You think you'll never have the time to even consider an idea, let alone write it. And, you've only got ten minutes. Ten lousy minutes.

Good enough.

If only every screenwriter were as lucky as you. Ten minutes gives you the "ticking clock" every writer secretly needs: a deadline.

As a screenwriting instructor, I'm an advocate of in-class writing work that gets people writing in the moment. I give students ten minutes to write entire scenes, and they often create masterpieces. I've also seen what can happen when I give writers the additional five minutes they beg for: they overwrite. They think too much. They fix what ain't broke, and they write themselves into a corner.

Fortunately, *you* only have ten minutes. You have no choice but to create work that's spontaneous and fresh. You just need some help to learn to use that time well.

How to Use This Book

This book will help you use your stolen ten minutes of time to make real progress on your screenplay. Each chapter focuses on a different phase of the writing process: THE STORY, THE STRUCTURE, THE OUTLINE, THE CHARACTERS, THE FIRST DRAFT, THE DIALOGUE, THE REWRITE, THE CRAFT, THE FINAL EDIT, THE PRESENTATION, and THE OPPORTUNITY.

Within these chapters there are subsections to help you work through each phase. As you move through, you'll also see "Take Ten" writing tools and exercises. These have been created to help you move through the writing process quickly and efficiently, ten minutes at a time. When a "Take Ten" exercise comes up, try it out. Not every tool is going to work for every writer. But you should be able to find at least one new thing that will help you to brainstorm, outline, expand or polish your script.

At the end of each "Take Ten" exercise, you'll see a summary of "What You've Accomplished." This should remind you that you actually have moved forward in your story — despite the short amount of time in which you've worked. "You've finished something," they'll say. "So don't go back and make it perfect. Turn the page and do something else!"

And, from time to time, you'll also come across a "Ten-Minute Lecture." These are meant to quickly distill and demystify current screenplay theory or common screenwriting language.

If you're just beginning a new project, I'd suggest following along chronologically, using the book to build your story from concept to finished script. Even if you've already written a screenplay, you'll find outlining tools and writing tips that will streamline your process.

If you're a writer who only needs help with certain areas of your script, feel free to jump from chapter to chapter. Even skipping around, you should find a writing tool that will work for you.

It's up to you. All I can tell you is that time is wasting, so start writing! You've only got … well, you know!

CHAPTER 1

The Story

This chapter will help you to brainstorm your idea, shape it into a story, and hone it into something movie-worthy. We're going to build from character flaw, nail the hook of your movie, make decisions about the middle, experiment with the ending, and then see what happens when we put it all together. Not every brainstorming tool will be the one that cracks your story open. But at least one of them will. And, when it does, keep working from there!

Getting Past Brain Freeze

So you've carved out that ten minutes, but now your brain is frozen. What was it you were going to write again? It was about that guy who did that thing in that place, right?

Well, believe it or not, that's a start!

 TEN-MINUTE LECTURE:

THE KEY INGREDIENTS OF EVERY MOVIE

A movie is usually about a MAIN CHARACTER with a PROBLEM who engages in an ACTIVITY with STAKES hanging in the balance.

END OF LECTURE

While you have ten minutes, let's put these elements in order and see what you come up with.

TAKE TEN:
THE OVERVIEW

MAIN CHARACTER
What kind of person is he?

PROBLEM
What difficult situation occurs?

ACTIVITY
What does he do about it?

STAKES
Ultimately, what does he have to lose if he doesn't succeed?

WHAT YOU'VE ACCOMPLISHED
By listing some central elements, you've begun to figure out a movie's story. Add a couple of other ideas into the mix and you'll see it take a clearer shape.

Emotion Tells the Story

Every screenwriting teacher has a theory about story.

Here's mine: Action triggers emotion. Emotion triggers action.

Honestly, that's it. In screenplays, you can't have one without the other. And it's important, as you go through these tools and build your screenplay, that you keep in mind how married these two things are. After all, who cares about a major event in a movie like a bomb going off or a car chase or a haunting or a wedding unless we get a chance to see how that bomb, chase, haunting or wedding affects a character?

And how can we invest in what a character is actually feeling if we haven't been privy to an event that drove her to that emotional place?

Action shows us the story. Emotion pushes the story forward.

(10) **TAKE TEN:**
EMOTION + ACTION = STORY

Start your main character off on an active, emotional journey by asking the following questions:

In the beginning of my story, this event occurs: *2009* _____.

It makes my main character (MC) feel this way: _____.

So he does this: _____.

But that makes someone else do this: _____.

That event makes MC feel: _____.

So MC does this: _____.

Keep asking these questions and see how much story you can invent in your ten minutes.

Character Flaw Tells the Story

Don't you wish you had someone who could just tell you what your script is going to be about? Someone who could come up with plot points and scenes and save you all of that planning work? Fortunately, you do. You've got your main character (who we'll call the MC). With the right questions and exploration, that main character can often reveal its own movie story.

That's why we're going to start the writing process by taking a hard look at the person you think may be your main character. We're going to figure out what that person is like before he hits page one, what his flaws are, how those flaws can launch a story, and how his personal rules might pay off in interesting plotting and scenes.

So, let's start with your main character — "that guy who did that thing." If that guy is at all interesting, it's because he is human, fallible … *flawed*. Oh, your character doesn't have a flaw? Well, mess him up. Get his hands dirty. Perfect characters are boring. Flawed characters are like us, and that's what viewers respond to.

Flaws don't have to be "fatal" – they can simply be human. Anger, arrogance and selfishness are flaws that often start a character off on an intriguing rocky road. But sweetness, humbleness and charity carried out to the extreme can also be flaws.

What would *It's A Wonderful Life* be like if the MC wasn't restless? What would the movie *Erin Brockovich* have been like if the MC wasn't demanding? What kind of a journey would *Sophie's Choice* have taken if the MC wasn't in denial? What would *Sideways* have been like if the MC wasn't a drinker?

In *Cast Away*, William Broyles Jr. wrote a story about a man ruled by time. He even gave the man a flaw-related job: FedEx supervisor. Then he simply stranded this man on an island, an island where he had all the time in the world.

Instant movie.

Let's see what trouble your flawed main character can get into and out of. Answer the following questions and see what movie develops.

TAKE TEN:
THE MAIN CHARACTER FLAW BRAINSTORM

First, determine the flaw of your character. Then, discover his story by asking the following questions:

1. Keeping your main character's flaw in mind, what's the WORST SITUATION he could find himself in?

2. What is the FIRST ACTION your MC would take?

3. How might that action BACKFIRE?

4. Who is the LEAST LIKELY PERSON who might help the MC or team up with him?

5. What NEW ACTION might that person push the MC to take?

6. Who or what might GET IN THE WAY of this new activity?

7. How might the flaw of the MC turn into a SKILL?

8. What SURPRISING FINAL ACTION could be taken that is the least-likely thing your character would have originally done?

WHAT YOU'VE ACCOMPLISHED
You may have just structured your entire movie!

Character-driven Structure

How did you structure your entire script by answering a few questions about your character's flaw? Well …

Questions 1- 3

Act 1 usually ends when a character creates a problem or makes an existing one worse. It's not just that something terrible happens *to* him. The way that flawed person takes action as a result of that event is usually the more interesting act break. He makes the wrong choice and, ultimately, his adventures within the movie lead him to a better one.

Question 4

In the first part of Act 2, the main character often works directly or indirectly with a supporting character. This builds a relationship, creates a B-story, and gives the MC someone to interact with. Making that character the "least likely" choice builds tension. Will these two characters be able to achieve a goal, while also managing their personal conflict?

Question 5

The supporting character is often the outside influence that causes the main character to take a new action or begin to change. She's not there just to support; she's there to change the game. She pushes, she comes up with new ideas, she influences. The new action may also force your character to confront his flaw and start thinking differently.

Question 6

In the second part of Act 2, an opposing force often shakes things up by trying to prevent the main character from achieving a goal. This is the antagonist … the bad guy. But sometimes it's a force of nature, or even the MC's own flaw. Sometimes it's a mixture of all three! The key to this act is remembering to use the antagonistic force to create a challenge for the MC. Keep us worrying and wondering!

Question 7

Now we're in Act 3. So, how will your character ever get out of this situation? Well, your character always had a distinguishing characteristic: his flaw. Perhaps that could actually be of use and translate into a skill. Selfish = survivor. Loose cannon = risk taker. Obsessive = knowledgeable. The goal in a movie is not to abandon what makes your MC interesting, but to use those traits to help. Looking for a key to character development? There it is.

Question 8

By movie's end, your MC has learned from his journey not to make the same mistakes he made the first time. In short, to do the least-likely thing he would originally have done. Here, we see him make the correct choice, instead of the wrong one he made at the Act 1 break. With this new approach, he finally solves his problem.

Concept Tells the Story

So, now that you know who your character is and what trouble he gets into ... exactly what *is* your movie about?

Most writers try to reach for the stars when asked this question.

"It's about man's inhumanity to man," they answer.

"It's about the universal search for love."

"It's about the need to put others first."

No, really, what is it *about*? What's the big idea? In short ... what's the *log line*?

What's that perfect, one-line synopsis that will make studios throw money at the movie and have audiences lining up at the theaters?

Drawing a blank? Here's a trick, and it's actually going to take *less* than ten minutes. Just ask yourself one question: What's the "what if" question of my movie?

"What if" a lawyer, paid to lie for a living, couldn't lie for one day?

"What if" an out-of-work actor gets the gig of his life ... as a female soap star?

"What if" a group of over-the-hill friends decided to relive their youth by starting their own fraternity?.

"What if" a man ages backward, growing younger as the love of his life grows older?

Of course *Liar Liar, Tootsie, Old School* and *The Curious Case of Benjamin Button* are high-concept movies, meaning that they can often stand on concept alone to bring in the big bucks. But the "what if" can also be found in smaller character-driven and "slice-of-life" movies as well. If it's really a movie, there's a big idea in there somewhere. In fact, you probably began this project because you imagined something that no one else has imagined.

"What if" a respected mathematician's top-secret government project is really a schizophrenic delusion?

"What if" the midlife crisis of a suburban father leads to murder?

With *A Beautiful Mind* and *American Beauty,* we think high drama rather than high concept. Yet, in each case, the writer has found the big idea within the story and exploited it.

A Beautiful Mind, for example, could have just been about a noble mathematician who struggles against a mental illness. But would it have gripped audiences? By focusing on the imagined top-secret project, the writer creates both a suspense movie and a character play.

American Beauty was also wise to frame its story as a thriller. A midlife crisis movie on its own, but pitch it as only that and you're going to have a producer falling asleep in his sushi. Add the twist that this crisis actually leads to the character's untimely death, and you'll start a bidding war.

So, let's find your "big idea," the special premise that makes this story worthy of being on the big screen. It's there!

Come up with your own "what if" question for your movie. Remember to focus on the hook. What makes your story unique? Is it the clash of two opposite characters? Is it the unconventional approach the character uses toward solving a problem? Or is it the problem itself — a situation never before seen on the big screen?

Thinking.

Thinking.

You may be dwelling on Act 1 when you try to find your hook. But you should also feel free to explore other areas of your script. "I see dead people," for example, wasn't revealed until the midpoint of *The Sixth Sense.* And that *was* the hook, without question.

Got it? Good. Here goes:

TAKE TEN:
FIND YOUR LOG LINE

What if _____?

See the big movie in that one sentence? Didn't think you could boil it down like that, did you?

Now, scratch off the "what if" so you turn your statement into a workable *log line*.

~~What if~~ _____.

WHAT YOU'VE ACCOMPLISHED
The log line is the cornerstone of your script. By defining the big idea of your movie — the hook — you've given yourself something to build on. From here, you can take your idea and run with it.

Secondary Characters Tell the Story

It's been said that every character in a movie thinks the movie is about them. The first time I heard that, I thought, "Of course! Why should characters in movies be any less self-centered than we are?"

A villain doesn't know he's the villain — he thinks he's the hero. He believes some good-looking guy with more screen time is simply getting in his way. A romantic interest doesn't know she's just "the girl" — she thinks she's running the show.

Modern-day kids' movies are often based on this idea. Turn the typical bad guy in a children's story into a hero by looking at the story from his point of view and you've got an instant hit. *Shrek* follows the Ogre's point of view in a princess story; *Monsters, Inc.* looks at the story of the monsters who scare children.

Pixar, in particular, has a great way of building entire worlds from even the most seemingly minor character's point of view. It thinks: "What if" the toys in children's rooms came alive? (*Toy Story*) "What if" insects had a society of their own where humans and birds were obstacles? (*A Bug's Life*)

Turning a story around from a secondary character's point of view makes for great grown-up films as well. *My Best Friend's Wedding* is told from the point of view of a bridesmaid. *The Queen* looks at the story of

Princess Diana's death from the point of view of her mother-in-law. *The Departed* is so rich because it focuses equally on the lives of two men on opposite sides of an undercover mob sting.

By discovering the "movies" of your supporting and opposing characters, you'll discover their character arcs and find new depth in your screenplay. You may even find a better screenplay idea. You're still in the brainstorming stage, so it's worth taking ten minutes to try it.

TAKE TEN:
YOUR SECONDARY CHARACTERS' LOGLINE

What if _____ ?
     Love interest log line

What if _____ ?
     Mentor log line

What if _____ ?
     Best friend/family member log line

What if _____ ?
     Antagonist log line

WHAT YOU'VE ACCOMPLISHED
By seeing the movie through the eyes of the other characters, you've seen them as richer individuals with their own stories. If, indeed, you've found out that the more exciting story to tell is that of another character, don't worry. It's early enough in your writing process to make a new choice.

Complication Tells the Story

A well-written log line pushes the reader or listener to want to know more about your script. The inevitable follow-up question is: "And then what?" What happens next? Where do you take the story from here?

So, I put it to you:

And then what?

You don't know? Time to brainstorm the major *complication* of your story. If your log line is "a troubled therapist discovers that his twelve-year-old patient sees dead people," the "and then what" would focus on what problems occur as a result of this power. In the case of *The*

Sixth Sense, problems occur when the dead people threaten the boy's sanity and the case threatens the therapist's marriage. Notice that these "problems" all stem from the antagonist: the "dead people."

Ask yourself what problems occur for characters once you've set up the premise and you'll probably discover that they're created by your *antagonist*, a.k.a. your bad guy. Who might want to prevent your hero from doing what he wants to do? What villainous steps would he take? That's your complication. And it's also the answer to "and then what?"

Sometimes, of course, problems can occur because of the intrusion of your supporting character. Falling in love can be a positive complication, but it's still a complication. In *When Harry Met Sally*, problems occur when Harry sleeps with Sally, then panics, causing her to cancel their friendship altogether. In *Juno*, complications occur when Juno becomes attached to the couple that intends to adopt her baby.

Sometimes, problems occur because of the flaw of your main character. And that's a good thing. That flaw is only really useful if it comes back from time to time to shake things up. In *The Silence of the Lambs*, problems occur when Hannibal Lecter forces Clarice to confront her psychological demons, causing her to weaken in the face of the serial killer. In *(500) Days of Summer*, main character Tom Hansen's romantic nature and obsession with falling in love cause him to continually push to make a failing love affair work.

It's time to find your own story complication. By doing so, you'll find the climax of your second act and spin it in such a way that it propels you from the first half of Act 2 into the second half of Act 2, giving your screenplay that extra "oomph" it needs to reinvest the reader and the audience.

TAKE TEN:
DISCOVER COMPLICATION

Find the big complication of your movie story:

Problems occur when _____.

Now heighten it.
Don't be afraid to go to extremes.
What's the worst thing that could happen?
What's the most emotional thing that could happen?
What's the most genre-worthy thing that could happen?

Problems occur when _____.

List two more complications. Don't forget to think about your supporting characters and what they're going through.

Problems occur when _____, _____, and _____.

WHAT YOU'VE ACCOMPLISHED
You've thrown a wrench into your character's story and forced her to deal with new problems that heighten the second act. By dealing with clever complications, characters earn their happy endings. If the journey is easy, it isn't a movie.

Synopsizing Tells the Story

Thanks to your brainstorming from character, you have a sense of your story. Creating a log line has helped you find the hook and creating complication has expanded that idea into a movie.

But we've done this all in pieces. Now, we want to see how the story feels when we describe it briefly with a simple beginning, middle, and end.

Use the Brief Synopsis template to get you there. Notice that the "Solution" section presents different options. Feel free to use one or more of these.

TAKE TEN:
BRIEF SYNOPSIS

PREMISE WITH HOOK: (What if) _____.

COMPLICATION:　　Problems occur when _____.

SOLUTION:　　　　This leads to the discovery that _____.

　　　　　　　　OR

　　　　　　　　Fortunately, _____.

　　　　　　　　OR

　　　　　　　　Tragically, _____.

Use descriptive, active language to help you see your movie. Characters don't just feel, they do! Use verbs!

Example: *The Sixth Sense*
(what if) A troubled therapist discovers that his twelve-year-old patient "sees dead people." Problems occur when the dead people threaten the boy's sanity and the case threatens the therapist's marriage. Fortunately, the therapist learns that the ghosts simply need attention from the boy. Tragically, he learns that he himself is dead.

Example: *The Wizard of Oz*
(what if) A restless girl is hurled by a tornado into a magical world and discovers that the only way she can get home is to seek help from a powerful wizard. Problems occur when an evil witch sabotages her and her new friends: a brainless scarecrow, a cowardly lion, and a tin man without a heart. Fortunately, the group melts the witch, proving that they have the brains, courage and heart to solve their own problems.

WHAT YOU'VE ACCOMPLISHED
A beginning, middle and end are nothing to sneeze at. In movie terms, those are your first, second and third acts.

Resolution Tells the Story

In your screenplay, you know that your sweethearts get married, your cop gets the robber, and your good guy defeats the bad guy. Now you just need to figure out *how* all that happens.

Remember that audiences invest their interest and their money in a movie in order to discover *how* a character will solve a big problem. Wimp out with that solution and they'll demand their money back.

Many writers do know what the big discovery will be for their character, they just don't know how to get there. Often, the answer can be found in the small, clever details — what I call the *trigger moments* — that lead to the big revelation.

In *Willy Wonka and the Chocolate Factory*, the entire story is turned around by one honest moment in which Charlie returns the top-secret new candy he's been asked to steal. His act of honesty triggers the third-act reward.

In *Casino Royale*, James Bond is asked about funds he was supposed to transfer, triggering his realization that the love of his life has betrayed him.

In *Eternal Sunshine of the Spotless Mind*, main character Joel Barish is given the cassette tape that talks about his former girlfriend, triggering him to reclaim his memories.

In *Primal Fear*, a supposedly innocent defendant casually reveals he knows something he shouldn't, causing his lawyer to realize he's been played. Again, one small moment, in this case a slip of the tongue, triggers an "a-ha!" moment which leads to the answer.

Discover your script's big trigger by working backward from the big revelation.

TAKE TEN:
WORK BACKWARD TO FIND YOUR ENDING

1. Start with the *final reveal*: What does the character discover that is most painful, shocking, surprising, or delightful?

2. *Where* did that person discover it?

3. What *physical clue* led her to that place?

4. What *was said* that triggered the character to search for that clue?

5. What *event* occurred that caused that character to speak the line?

6. What *problem* occurred that created that event?

7. How did the main character's *own actions* create that problem?

8. What *goal* did the main character have that caused her to behave badly enough to create this problem?

9. What *circumstances* in the main character's world inspired that goal?

WHAT YOU'VE ACCOMPLISHED

By asking these questions, you should have at least one new way of moving toward your big revelation.

A sequence of clever details that push a character toward a truth is a much more interesting journey than one in which she simply trips on the answer, or worse, is just told!

Plot and Character Elements Tell the Story

Use ten more minutes to review your elements by putting them on one page. Use this page as a constant reference tool to remind you of your original intentions for your project.

TAKE TEN: INTENTION SHEET

Use this sheet to sum up your "take-ten" exercises so far.

Main Character Flaw _____

Log Line _____

Secondary Character Logline _____

Major Complication _____

Third-Act Trigger _____

Fortunately/Unfortunately Ending _____

WHAT YOU'VE ACCOMPLISHED
You've created a guide that will keep you on track as you outline, write and expand your script.

You Tell the Story

All of the work you've done — finding your character-driven story, creating your structure, using a "what if" question to find your hook, building on the hook to find the complication, and working backward to find your ending — should have helped you to create a real movie story in your mind.

Additionally, as a veteran moviegoer, you already have a story sense that helps you as a writer. And as a person who tries hard not to be boring, you've become a master storyteller. You relate funny events to your coworkers, reminisce with your loved ones, and tell bedtime stories to your kids.

In fact, the next template uses the language and simple beats of a bedtime story to help you tell your movie story. You don't need fancy film terms to create an outline, just a rich beginning, middle, and end.

This template is somewhat long since it works through your entire movie. To deal with it in ten-minute increments of time, it's been divided into four sections to equal *acts* (we'll get into those in the next section).

If you get stuck on a blank, just move on to the next section. Or, it may mean that there's an obstacle or activity that's missing from your movie. Make something up and see what happens!

TAKE TEN:
DESCRIBE YOUR MOVIE LIKE A BEDTIME STORY

10 Minutes:
ACT 1

Once upon a time, there was a _____
main character

who was _____.
character flaw

When _____ happened, she _____.
obstacle   *flaw-driven strategy*

Unfortunately _____.
screw up

So she decided _____
goal

and had to _____.
action that begins a new journey

WHAT YOU'VE ACCOMPLISHED
You've set up the character by describing her as a flawed (translation: human) person. You've also triggered a big, movie-worthy problem by having your own main character make an unwise choice. This helps move her into Act 2.

10 Minutes:
ACT 2A

In order to take this action, she decided to _____.
strategy

Unfortunately _____ happened, which caused
obstacle

_____!
complication

Now she had to _____ or risk _____!
new task   *personal stake*

WHAT YOU'VE ACCOMPLISHED
You've set goals for the MC with potential to lead to a variety of interesting adventures. Then, by the midpoint, you've created a major complication that forces the audience to reinvest in the character and her story.

10 Minutes:
ACT 2B

Where she once wanted to _____
old desire

she now wanted _____.
new desire

But how could that happen when _____?
obstacle

Filled with _____, she _____.
emotion   *new action*

But this only resulted in _____.
low point

WHAT YOU'VE ACCOMPLISHED

You've used your antagonist to mess things up for your main character and fooled the audience into thinking that there's no way out. This will make Act 3 — when your main character solves the problem — feel like even more of a victory.

10 Minutes:
ACT 3

Fortunately, this helped her to realize _____!
the solution

All she had to do was _____!
action using new lesson

Using _____ , _____, and _____
other characters   skills   tools from journey

she was able to _____.
victorious action

Unfortunately, _____.
final hurdle

But this time, she _____!
clever strategy

This resulted in _____.
change in situation

WHAT YOU'VE ACCOMPLISHED

You've drawn from your MC's journey, using the characters, skills and resources obtained along the way, to help solve the problem. Just to make sure it doesn't end too neatly, you've added a final hurdle, a staple of modern film structure, to give the screenplay one last hitch.

To get here, you made up a story on the spot — filling in the blanks as you went. If any of the beats don't work for you, just replace a word. Doing so may change the whole story!

16

■ TEN-MINUTE CHAPTER REVIEW: STORY

1. Brainstorm the central ELEMENTS and EMOTION of the story.

2. Find a CHARACTER-DRIVEN STRUCTURE through the character's FLAW.

3. Commit to concept by creating a "WHAT IF" LOG LINE.

4. Discover the second act by creating a COMPLICATION.

5. Decide on a beginning, middle and end by writing a BRIEF SYNOPSIS.

6. BRAINSTORM BACKWARD from the reveal to "trigger" the solution in your third act.

7. Get a sense of the flow by describing your movie like a BEDTIME STORY.

CHAPTER 2

The Structure

Structure is simply the organization of story beats. That's it. The placement of an event and the amount of time it takes up on screen determines the "structure" of a story. Where it all gets kind of crazy is when writers, teachers and other industry folk try to determine exactly *what* events have to be included and where.

Books have been written about it. Theory has been developed about it. Debate has gone into it. And writers either feel that they have to follow every single rule they read or that they should abandon structure altogether and commit themselves to artistic aimlessness.

Like many other people who write books about screenwriting, I've provided some guidance about what *tends* to take place in critically — and commercially — successful movies and will continue to do so throughout this book. Our character-driven structure, for example, suggests a pattern that flawed characters fall into when they're pushed out of their comfort zone. Later, I'll point out more patterns that take characters from the lows to the highs as they move through a story.

But this is only a guide; a reminder that a story changes as characters make new choices. You don't have to create story in exactly the way it's laid out here. Instead, once you've determined the beginning, middle and end of your story, feel free to play.

To get started, and to keep your story as clear as possible, I'm going to take you through the steps of creating a linear structure for your script.

Yes, I said linear. Stay with me, structure rebel! I promise that, after you've gotten a sense of your linear structure, you can then change that structure and tell your story any way that you want. As long as your writing is clear, you can jump back and forth in time. You can tell your story from several points of view. You can tell your story backward. But, none of that's going to make any sense unless you first come up with a simple beginning, middle, and end.

Organizing Your Story

As mentioned, screenplay structure doesn't have to be a set of rules that one either follows or rejects. It's simply story organization.

Imagine that all of the ideas for your movie are written on tiny scraps of paper. Imagine that there are tons of these scraps of paper. And imagine that they are everywhere! (I have a feeling that some of you may know too well exactly what I'm talking about.) You could throw the pieces up into the air, see where they land and hope for the best. You could hand them over to audience members and tell them to come up with the movie on their own. Or, you could organize the scraps into a cohesive story that makes sense, entertains, and is all your own. This organization of ideas is your "structure."

To better help with the organization process, I'm going to get you familiar with some terminology so that we're all speaking the same language. Consider it a ten-minute crash course in ACTS, SEQUENCES, and SCENES.

 TEN-MINUTE LECTURE:

ACTS, SEQUENCES AND SCENES

Imagine those pieces of paper again — the ones with the ideas written on them. Imagine sweeping those ideas into three or four big piles. Those are the ACTS. Now imagine dividing those piles into a series of events that add up to each act. Those are your major SEQUENCES. Now go through each sequence pile and look at each piece of paper. Imagine that each piece has a character moment or activity on it. Those are the SCENES.

To review:

Big picture piles of story are ACTS.

Divide them up to get SEQUENCES.

Divide them up even further to see the individual SCENES.

END OF LECTURE

The Structure Sheet

The Structure Sheet is a one-page table that will help you "see" the big, structural picture of your screenplay. Just follow each step and watch your story build.

Step 1: Divide Your Story into Four Acts

Let's start with those big "piles" of ideas — your acts. In this book, we're going to make structure simple by dividing your script into four sections: Act 1, Act 2A, Act 2B, and Act 3.

Replacing the traditional three sections with four means that we're dealing with *four equal parts*. Dividing Act 2 in half also prevents that act — the longest of the three — from becoming repetitive and eventually flat-lining. We're also going to break from the traditional notion of 30 pages (first act), 60 pages (second act), 30 pages (third act) and make each section 25 pages instead. After all, most scripts these days average 110 pages. One hundred and twenty pages is "going long."

Think about screenplay structure this way:

Act 1:	pages 1-25
Act 2A:	pages 25-50
Act 2B:	pages 50-75
Act 3:	pages 75-100

When we get to the actual page-writing part of this book, you'll find that writing 25 pages in an act is much less intimidating than writing up to 60. Average two pages per workday and you'll cruise through your script!

If you're writing a one-hour drama, which tends to be written as five and six acts, you can still group your major beats into four sections.

Think 12-15 pages per segment. (Page count and act breaks vary in one-hour. But, remember that this is all about organization.)

Act 1:	12-15 pages
Act 2:	12-15 pages
Act 3:	12-15 pages
Act 4:	12-15 pages

Half-hour, multi-camera TV shows conventionally have two or three acts, but commercial breaks still create four segments. Think about eight *single-spaced* pages per segment if it's single-camera (*The Office, Entourage*) **or** 10 *double-spaced* pages per segment if it's multi-camera (*The Big Bang Theory, Two and a Half Men*).

Act 1A:	8-10 pages
Act 1B:	8-10 pages
Act 2A:	8-10 pages
Act 2B:	8-10 pages

Working with four segments allows you to see each part equally. There's no vast wasteland of "middle" anymore. But now that you're thinking in four separate segments, you need to brainstorm the story that each segment will tell.

Step 2: Title Your Acts

In each act the MC is at a different place physically and emotionally. So, think about how you might build your story in four parts and then title each section based on the main event or activity that occurs in that chunk of time. *The Wizard of Oz*, for example, might look like this:

Act 1	Kansas Restlessness
Act 2A	Oz Problems
Act 2B	Wizard Challenges
Act 3	Witch Showdown

As we know, Dorothy experiences conflict with Miss Gulch, gets yelled at for being in the way at home, and wishes she were "Over the Rainbow" in the first quarter of her movie. That's why we're labeling that part "Kansas Restlessness."

"Oz Problems" occur in the second quarter when she lands in Oz, accidentally kills a witch, angers the victim's wicked sister, and has to protect friends on the yellow brick road.

But, once she does get to the Emerald City, "Wizard Challenges" get in her way. She has to doll up to get into the castle, then can't get in at all, then is given a seemingly impossible task by the Wizard: Bring him the broom of the Wicked Witch!

Faced with that task, a "Witch Showdown" inevitably happens in the fourth quarter. The Witch kidnaps Dorothy, forcing her friends to go undercover as guards to rescue her. This attempt incites the Witch to set the Scarecrow on fire. Dorothy's quick thinking in dousing the Witch with water actually "liquidates" the Witch, leaving only her broom behind and earning the whole group their wizardly rewards.

One movie. Four quarters.

But what if we didn't want to tell the story in this order?

Shifting an act completely restructures your movie.

Act 1	Oz Problems
Act 2A	Wizard Challenges
Act 2B	Witch Showdown
Act 3	Kansas Restlessness

Look at our new story. By simply re-sorting the titles, we have a different movie. Dorothy gets back to Kansas but isn't so happy to be there. "There's no place like Oz," she might cry.

Continue to make structural changes by switching the acts around. Each act shift tests out a new story.

Changing the title of an act helps you to brainstorm completely new changes in the plot.

Act 1	Wizard Challenges
Act 2A	Witch Showdown
Act 2B	Dorothy Discovers Wizard Is a Fraud
Act 3	Dorothy Takes Over

Here, we lose Kansas entirely and set the movie completely in Oz. In this story, Dorothy delivers the broom as ordered, but discovers, in Act 2B, that she's been duped by a faux Wizard! Now, the third act contends with that complication and shows how Dorothy takes over as the *new* Wizard of Oz.

So, try anything at this point, knowing that you can mix and match until you find the story and structure that work for you.

TAKE TEN:
FIND YOUR FOUR-PART ACT STRUCTURE

"Title" each segment by summarizing the theme or event in a short sentence. You're just marking structure right now, trying to get a sense of "the big picture."

———————	———————	———————	———————
Act 1	Act 2A	Act 2B	Act 3

Be daring. It's only four sentences. Re-sort your sentences, or even replace one with a new title, and see what happens to your story.

WHAT YOU'VE ACCOMPLISHED
You've created a structural timeline for your script, boiled down to four phrases.

Step 3: Add a Reveal

Now that you roughly know where you're going, you can expand your story, asking yourself "what happens" and "what's revealed."

You may know what you want to cover per segment, but it's equally important to know what new thing is discovered or happens at the end of each segment that pushes you into the next one. An MC may think she knows what's going on, but something usually forces her to look to the next segment for answers.

At the end of segment one for *The Wizard of Oz*, for example, Dorothy learns that she must seek help from the Wizard to get home. Subsequently, she heads out onto the yellow brick road ... and her "Act 2" begins.

The Wizard of Oz, with only titles and the big "reveal" of each act, looks like this:

Act Titles:

KANSAS RESTLESSNESS	OZ PROBLEMS	WIZARD CHALLENGES	WITCH SHOWDOWN
Reveal Dorothy must seek the way home from Wizard.	**Reveal** Dorothy arrives at Emerald city, but can't get in.	**Reveal** Dorothy must bring back broom of the witch in order to earn rewards from Wizard.	**Reveal** Dorothy can only be transported back when she realizes, "there's no place like home."
Act 1	Act 2A	Act 2B	Act 3

TAKE TEN:
ADD A "REVEAL"

You've titled each segment. Now, drop down to the bottom of each column and describe the personal or physical discovery – the "reveal" – of that section of the movie. If you don't have one, make one up!

Title	Title	Title	Title
Reveal	**Reveal**	**Reveal**	**Reveal**
Act 1	Act 2A	Act 2B	Act 3

Step 4: Add Event

You know what's revealed at the end of each segment. Now you're going to figure out what happens *within* the segments that build to that reveal. What sets it up? Are there obstacles along the way? Remember that your act titles suggested a focus or theme. What events reflect that?

In *The Wizard of Oz*, Dorothy runs away and gets caught in a tornado, demonstrating some of the "restlessness" implied in the *title* of the act. But, she also kills a bad witch and becomes an enemy of that witch's sister. Those events drives us to the *reveal* that she must now go home and has only one way to do it.

Act Titles:

KANSAS RESTLESSNESS	OZ PROBLEMS	WIZARD CHALLENGES	WITCH SHOWDOWN
Key Event(s)	**Key Event(s)**	**Key Event(s)**	**Key Event(s)**
1. Dorothy runs away and gets caught in Tornado. 2. She lands in Oz, killing the Wicked Witch of the East and inciting Witch of West's anger.	1. Dorothy makes three friends on the yellow brick road. 2. Dorothy and friends brave scary forest and field of poison poppies.	1. Dorothy and friends welcomed by city and meet with Oz. 2. Witch threatens them. "Surrender Dorothy."	1. Dorothy is kidnapped and her friends have to save her. 2. They fight with Witch and melt her. 3. They return to Oz for reward.
Reveal	**Reveal**	**Reveal**	**Reveal**
Dorothy must seek the way home from Wizard.	Dorothy arrives at Emerald City, but can't get in.	Dorothy must bring back broom of the Witch in order to earn rewards from Wizard.	Dorothy can only be transported back when she realizes, "there's no place like home."
Act 1	Act 2A	Act 2B	Act 3

TAKE TEN:
ADD EVENT

Expand your segments by building on the segment titles to include the *key event* or events of that segment. These events also lead to the "reveal."

Title	Title	Title	Title
Key Event(s) **Reveal**	**Key Event(s)** **Reveal**	**Key Event(s)** **Reveal**	**Key Event(s)** **Reveal**
Act 1	**Act 2A**	**Act 2B**	**Act 3**

WHAT YOU'VE ACCOMPLISHED

You've built on your titles to include story events and major twists. Now you can see the big picture on one page. Looks like you may have a movie on your hands!

■ TEN-MINUTE CHAPTER REVIEW:
STRUCTURE

1. Break your story into FOUR ACT SEGMENTS: Act 1, Act 2A, Act 2B, and Act 3.

2. TITLE each segment so that it covers a different event or theme.

3. To test all of the structural possibilities, SHIFT and RENAME your titles.

4. Create a big REVEAL at the end of each segment that twists the story in a new direction.

5. Flesh out each segment by adding the KEY EVENTS that build to each reveal.

6. Review your completed STRUCTURE SHEET to see the BIG PICTURE on one page.

CHAPTER 3

The Outline

I f you're still feeling like you don't have all of the pieces together, don't worry. This section, "Outlining," will help you discover more activity and possibilities.

An outline helps you to brainstorm more story ideas, forces you to make clever scene choices, and – most importantly – keeps you on track as you write your screenplay pages. The challenge lies in making sure that the outline doesn't take up more pages or writing hours than the actual screenplay.

Ask any writer about the outlining process and you'll see the headache written all over her face. Perhaps this is because she thinks an outline isn't complete unless it's twenty-five pages long and contains every scene moment. But that doesn't leave much room for change once the writing begins. And so much is discovered during that process!

For that reason – and because outlining can be a pain in the butt – we're going to do it the easy way.

The Eight-Sequence Beat Sheet

A good screenplay outline simply needs to lay out the broad beats of the screenplay and provide a guide for the writer. It should also be a tool that is malleable, one that can change as the story changes. For these reasons, you're going to focus the majority of your outline on a simple *eight-sequence beat sheet*.

The term "beat sheet" can mean different things to different people. And even the term "beat" can be confusing. For the purposes of this book, we're going to refer to a beat as a distinct section of story. We're going to divide our script into eight of those beats/sequences and use the details of the beat sheet to develop story and character.

Divide Your Four Act Segments into Eight Sequences

So, to write your beat sheet, you're going to find eight sequences – roughly two per act. Remember our four-part act structure? Well, we're simply going to divide those acts in two.

SEQUENCE 1	SEQUENCE 2	SEQUENCE 3	SEQUENCE 4	SEQUENCE 5	SEQUENCE 6	SEQUENCE 7	SEQUENCE 8

| Act 1 | Act 2A | Act 2B | Act 3 |

Now we're going to turn that table on its side so that you can more easily write down the page:

ACT 1
    SEQUENCE 1
    SEQUENCE 2

ACT 2A
    SEQUENCE 3
    SEQUENCE 4

ACT 2B
    SEQUENCE 5
    SEQUENCE 6

ACT 3
    SEQUENCE 7
    SEQUENCE 8

And that's all that you're going to have to fill out. Here's how to do it …

Describe Your Sequences Using Three Sentences

It's not math that determines a "beat" – it's story. To better define your beats, ask: At what point does the story twist or heighten? At what point does your character come to a new emotional place or make a new choice? That's your new sequence or "beat." Don't think in terms of scenes, think in terms of grouping of scenes. So, your "beat" of story may be ten to fifteen pages.

Now that you have a sense of what the beat might be, we're going to describe it using three simple sentences. Each sentence will cover the GOAL, ACTIVITY and COMPLICATION of each sequence.

Simply put: You're telling a small story every ten to fifteen pages or so.

 ## TEN-MINUTE LECTURE:

GOAL, ACTIVITY, COMPLICATION

GOAL: What your main character wants.

ACTIVITY: What your main character does.

COMPLICATION: What gets in your main character's way.

Character GOALS fuel and motivate a screenplay, inciting new activity. Character goals change and grow as complications are dealt with and new obstacles appear.

Rather than simply long for something, a character engages in an ACTIVITY and does something to get what he desires.

A COMPLICATION is a major obstacle that gets in the way of the activity and threatens to prevent the character from meeting his goal.

Story moves forward as a character now has to create a **new** *goal to overcome the complication, followed by a new activity, etc.*

END OF LECTURE

Here's an example of the first act of *The Wizard of Oz* written in two sequences and described as "Goal, Activity, Complication."

Act 1 of *The Wizard of Oz*:

SEQUENCE 1

GOAL: Dorothy wants to get away from Miss Gulch.

ACTIVITY: Dorothy runs away from home with Toto.

COMPLICATION: A fortune-teller reveals that Aunt Em is sick with worry, so Dorothy rushes home.

SEQUENCE 2

GOAL: Dorothy wants to get back to Aunt Em.

ACTIVITY: Dorothy is caught in a twister and forced to take refuge in the house.

COMPLICATION: The house lands in Oz, killing an evil witch and turning her sister, the Wicked Witch of the West, into a mortal enemy.

In six sentences, we've landed Dorothy in Oz and driven her into Sequence 3, the start of Act 2A. See? Easy.

Now it's your turn. Since you only have ten minutes, I've broken the beat sheet into four parts: Acts 1, 2A, 2B, and 3, so that you can focus on one segment at a time. If this is a television script, each segment should still have two beats in it to keep the script moving in a new direction.

TAKE TEN:
BEAT SHEET

10 Minutes:

Act 1 Tips: I know you feel there's a lot to set up in Act 1. But leave the smaller character moments for later. For now, focus on the big picture and keep driving your main character forward.

Hit Sequence 2 hard since it's your act break and will include the event that's going to spin you into an adventure in Act 2.

ACT 1

SEQUENCE 1

GOAL: _____

ACTIVITY: _____

COMPLICATION:_____

SEQUENCE 2

GOAL: _____

ACTIVITY: _____

COMPLICATION: _____

10 Minutes:

Act 2A Tips: Often this first part of the second act is a training period for the main character as he is thrown into a new situation or world. Your supporting characters can help.

In Sequence 4, you've hit your midpoint. This is an opportunity to heighten your second act and keep it from flat-lining. Make this a big, story-twisting complication — something that helps the audience reinvest in the movie. Your antagonist plays a role!

ACT 2A
SEQUENCE 3
GOAL: _____

ACTIVITY: _____

COMPLICATION: _____

SEQUENCE 4
GOAL: _____

ACTIVITY: _____

COMPLICATION: _____

10 Minutes:

Act 2B Tips: This section deals with the new complication introduced in Sequence 4. So it tends to be even more exciting. As the villain gets closer and the relationships become more intense, the stakes rise. Sometimes, all of this momentum results in a Sequence 6 low point. Don't be afraid to let your main character fail. It will be all the more fun to get him back on his feet and victorious in the third act.

ACT 2B
SEQUENCE 5
GOAL: _____

ACTIVITY: _____

COMPLICATION: _____

SEQUENCE 6
GOAL: _____

ACTIVITY: _____

COMPLICATION: _____

10 Minutes:

Act 3 Tips: A screenplay feels complete when the main character uses the lessons and skills he has learned along the way to accomplish his goals. Pay off those minor characters, pull from second-act information, turn a first-act flaw into a skill, and solve the problem!

ACT 3
SEQUENCE 7
GOAL: _____

ACTIVITY: _____

COMPLICATION: _____

SEQUENCE 8
GOAL: _____
ACTIVITY: _____
COMPLICATION: _____

WHAT YOU'VE ACCOMPLISHED
You've "beat" out your entire movie. It's the big picture, plus some! After a quick beat-sheet rewrite to make sure you have the movie you're going for, you'll be ready to hit the scenes.

The Beat-Sheet Rewrite

Congratulations! You've actually "beat out" your story from beginning to end. But now it's worth a few more ten-minute sessions to revise and tighten that beat sheet so that it truly meets your story intentions. Doing so will force you to be more original and specific right out of the gate — and save you lots of "what do I do now" time in the long run.

Beat-sheet Story Development Rewrite

I have to admit that I'm not big on telling any writer what *has* to take place in certain sections of a movie. But when recently challenged by one of my students to define each section, I did notice a certain rhythm.

 TEN-MINUTE LECTURE:

STORY DEVELOPMENT IN EIGHT BEATS

Though each beat tells its own story, it is always connected to the next one in order to reveal the big picture. Each beat tends to "trigger" the next. And, by doing so, the story is pushed forward. Here's a common pattern:

1. CHARACTER FLAW triggers CONFLICT

2. CONFLICT triggers PROBLEM

3. PROBLEM triggers STRATEGY

4. STRATEGY triggers EMOTIONAL EVENT

5. EMOTIONAL EVENT triggers MAJOR ACTION

6. MAJOR ACTION triggers MISSTEP

7. MISSTEP triggers BATTLE

8. BATTLE triggers FINAL CHALLENGE

An example from The Wizard of Oz might look like this:

1. CHARACTER FLAW triggers CONFLICT

Dorothy's rebelliousness against Miss Gulch triggers Miss Gulch to take Toto.

2. CONFLICT triggers PROBLEM

The theft of Toto triggers Dorothy to run away, get caught in a tornado, and end up hurled into Oz.

3. PROBLEM triggers STRATEGY

Dorothy's need to leave Oz triggers her to seek out the Wizard with the help of the Scarecrow, the Tin Man, and the Cowardly Lion.

4. STRATEGY triggers EMOTIONAL EVENT

Dorothy and friends' arrival in the Emerald City triggers upset when the witch threatens her publicly.

5. EMOTIONAL EVENT triggers MAJOR ACTION

Fear of the witch triggers the Wizard to insist that Dorothy bring him the witch's broom as payment.

6. MAJOR ACTION triggers MISSTEP

Attempt to steal the broom triggers the witch to kidnap Dorothy.

7. MISSTEP triggers BATTLE

Dorothy's kidnapping triggers Dorothy to escape and, in a struggle to protect her friends, melt the witch.

8. BATTLE triggers FINAL CHALLENGE

Return of witch's broom triggers fraudulent wizard to find a way to truly return Dorothy to her home.

END OF LECTURE

TAKE TEN:
BEAT-SHEET STORY DEVELOPMENT REWRITE

If the pattern I've described doesn't completely match with your beat sheet, don't worry. What's important is that there's a flow and a sense of movement from one beat to the other. So try it out. Define the story development in your beat sheet by looking at how one event "triggers" another. If you're not seeing a flow from one to the other, correct it by adjusting a goal, activity, or complication.

1. _____ triggers _____
2. _____ triggers _____
3. _____ triggers _____
4. _____ triggers _____
5. _____ triggers _____
6. _____ triggers _____
7. _____ triggers _____
8. _____ triggers _____

WHAT YOU'VE ACCOMPLISHED
In eight lines you've strengthened your story development and prevented it from reading as too episodic or disjointed.

Beat-sheet Supporting Character/Antagonist Rewrite

I asked you to follow the path of the main character when creating the beat sheet in order to create a strong spine for your story. But that doesn't mean that your antagonist and supporting characters aren't involved. In fact, they're the people that inspire new goals, aid with activity, and create complication.

TAKE TEN:
BEAT-SHEET SUPPORTING CHARACTER/ANTAGONIST
REWRITE

In an effort to bring other characters into the rewrite, try one of the following:

1. Use the MC's feelings for a supporting character to create a NEW GOAL.

2. Use the skills of a supporting character to create a more interesting ACTIVITY.

3. Make a COMPLICATION more interesting by allowing the antagonist to connect in some unexpected way to the MC or supporting character.

WHAT YOU'VE ACCOMPLISHED
You've made your story richer through the involvement of additional characters. This rewrite might also bring out an important story layer or subplot.

Beat-sheet Complication Rewrite

I'm often surprised that so many scripts I read play it safe. When I point this out, the writer will often explain that "real life" doesn't work that way. But great movies aren't real life. They don't rely on "what is." They play out "what if."

After she runs away from home with Toto, the Sequence 1 complication has Dorothy discovering that Aunt Em is sick with worry. But what if ...

SEQUENCE 1

GOAL: Dorothy wants to get away from Miss Gulch.

ACTIVITY: Dorothy runs away from home with Toto.

COMPLICATION: Miss Gulch chases after Dorothy with a machete. (WORST)
-OR-
Dorothy becomes an icon for the animal rights movement. (BEST)

Change the complication of that sequence by going to extremes and you breathe a different life into the next beat.

TAKE TEN:
BEAT-SHEET COMPLICATION REWRITE

Go to extremes. Ask of every sequence, "What's the best or worst thing that can happen?" and replace the complications accordingly. Use the genre. If this is a horror movie, what's the most frightening thing that can happen? If this is a comedy, what's the funniest?

SEQUENCE 1
Complication (best) _____
Complication (worst) _____
Complication (genre) _____

SEQUENCE 2
Complication (best) _____
Complication (worst) _____
Complication (genre) _____

SEQUENCE 3
Complication (best) _____
Complication (worst) _____
Complication (genre) _____

SEQUENCE 4
Complication (best) _____
Complication (worst) _____
Complication (genre) _____

SEQUENCE 5
Complication (best) _____
Complication (worst) _____
Complication (genre) _____

SEQUENCE 6
Complication (best) _____
Complication (worst) _____
Complication (genre) _____

SEQUENCE 7
Complication (best) _____
Complication (worst) _____
Complication (genre) _____

SEQUENCE 8
Complication (best) _____
Complication (worst) _____
Complication (genre) _____

Beat-sheet Midpoint Rewrite

Does your beat sheet start to run out of steam in the second half? Are sequences repeating each other? Perhaps the big event in the middle of the movie, the *midpoint*, needs some reinvention.

In *The Wizard of Oz*, big problems occur in the middle of the movie when Dorothy gets to the Emerald City only to be told that she has to kill the Wicked Witch of the West. Were we to change that midpoint complication, everything else would have to change as well.

Instead of being sent on a new mission by the Wizard, perhaps …

CRIME DRAMA: Dorothy discovers that the Wizard's been kidnapped and has to follow the clues to find him.

HORROR: The Emerald City has been taken over by zombies and Dorothy and friends must destroy them all.

ROMANCE: Dorothy falls in love with the "man behind the curtain."

Change the midpoint; change the movie.

TAKE TEN:
BEAT-SHEET MIDPOINT REWRITE

Try rewriting the midpoint of your beat sheet using one of the following options and see if it helps your story.

1. Have your MC engage in RISKIER ACTIVITY.

2. Have your antagonist make his BIG MOVE.

3. CREATE EMOTIONAL INVOLVEMENT with a supporting character.

4. PAY OFF something seemingly mundane from Act 1 or 2A.

5. Establish an ULTIMATUM or TICKING CLOCK that ups the pace.

WHAT YOU'VE ACCOMPLISHED
You've saved yourself major rewrite work by covering all of the midpoint possibilities now, and by doing so, have possibly steered your entire story in a new and more interesting direction.

Beat-sheet Structure Rewrite

The beat sheet is the best tool for helping with your structure because it allows you to see — on one page — where your story slows down, cuts corners, or repeats. And the verbs you've chosen often hint at the pace. Use the beat sheet to tighten your structure at this point and you'll have less editing to do later.

TAKE TEN:
BEAT-SHEET STRUCTURE REWRITE

Try out one or all of the suggestions below to see if your beat sheet could benefit from a structure rewrite.

1. ELIMINATE SEQUENCE 1 and see if it helps or hurts the pace of your script. You may find that doing so cuts the fat and helps you to hit the ground running.

2. COMPRESS SEQUENCES 1 THROUGH 4, changing them into two. Do you get to your movie quicker? Some writers take too much time setting up and don't realize that their movies should have begun twenty minutes earlier.

3. ADD MORE ACTIVITY TO SEQUENCES 5 AND 6. Cut the talk and up the activity. Sentences that begin with "they discuss" or "they plan" are red flags that your Act 2B is too slow.

4. CHANGE THE GOAL OF SEQUENCE 8. Take a hard look at that sequence. Did you speed up your third act by simply writing Sequence 8 as a wrap up? Instead, look to it as a "final hurdle" and create a final physical or emotional goal that has to be accomplished. That will give your third act the heft it needs.

WHAT YOU'VE ACCOMPLISHED

Instead of wrestling with a rewrite of your 110-page script, you've used your one-page beat sheet to make important changes to story and structure before you hit page one.

Beat-sheet Rewrite: Nonlinear Structure

Hey, structure rebel, remember how I promised that you could eventually create a nonlinear structure for your screenplay? Here's your chance. And by playing around with structure in the beat sheet, you'll get a chance to see how some of those more "out-of-the-box" structural risks might play out should you choose to go that route.

TAKE TEN:
BEAT-SHEET NONLINEAR STRUCTURE REWRITE

Instead of restructuring your entire script after it's written, you can use your beat sheet to mix and match sequences. Try one or more of these options and see if a nonlinear method of storytelling will work for you.

1. REVERSE YOUR SEQUENCES: See what happens if you move backward from Sequence 8 to Sequence 1.

2. INSERT PART OF SEQUENCE 8 INTO SEQUENCE 1: Set a Sequence 1 goal by leading with a "flash" of Sequence 8. Then you can build back up to 8 again. By the time we get to the event we started with, we'll have an entirely new perspective.

3. JUMP TIME: Mix and match sequences to create nonlinear jumps in time and place. (Just read it over when you're finished to make sure that the story still tracks.)

4. CHANGE MAIN CHARACTERS PER SEQUENCE: If this is an ensemble movie and you want to switch character point of view per sequence, try it here and see how it reads.

5. CREATE PLACES WHERE CHARACTERS CONVERGE: If you do choose to branch off into different directions, eventually bring your key characters together at key places in your beat sheet (act breaks or sequence breaks) in order to show a physical or thematic connection between them.

WHAT YOU'VE ACCOMPLISHED
You've tested different structural possibilities. One of them may work to help tell your story in a way that challenges the reader and audience to "Think Different."

Beat-sheet Rewrite: Emotion

So now you've taken enough ten-minute rewrite passes at your beat sheet to be clear about your story and structure. But is your story emotional? What does it mean for the main character or for other characters? Remember that you're not really telling your story unless you convey the emotional impact of the events.

TAKE TEN:
BEAT-SHEET EMOTION REWRITE

Write the key emotion experienced by the MC in every sequence.

SEQUENCE 1 EMOTION _____

SEQUENCE 2 EMOTION _____

SEQUENCE 3 EMOTION _____

SEQUENCE 4 EMOTION _____

SEQUENCE 5 EMOTION _____

SEQUENCE 6 EMOTION _____

SEQUENCE 7 EMOTION _____

SEQUENCE 8 EMOTION _____

Write the resulting emotional arc.

Example: Fear to bravery. Loathing to love.

EMOTIONAL ARC: _____ to _____

If this arc doesn't meet your original intentions for the development of your character, look into the events that are creating that emotion and revise.

WHAT YOU'VE ACCOMPLISHED

Even at the beat-sheet level, you've taken your MC on an emotional, movie-worthy journey.

Adding Scenes

We've taken the beat sheet through so many revisions that it's almost a complete outline on its own. But to make sure we've got a map that will be easy to follow and turn into pages, we're going to add even more to it … your scenes.

Scene invention is the fun part of the script-planning stage. This is where you get to "see" the script and make up dramatic, funny ways for the characters to bring your beats to life.

 TAKE-TEN LECTURE:

THE DEFINITION OF A SCENE

All those little scraps of activities and character moments that are in your head? The ones we separated into big-picture piles of acts and then subdivided into sequences? Those scraps are your scenes.

A scene tends to take place at a fixed point in time, in a single place. That's why we write …

INT. PLACE – TIME OF DAY

… in a scene heading.

When the location or time changes, a new scene takes place.

Scenes capture public events, personal relationship moments, or private emotion. They can include many people or no one. They can be as short as an eighth of a script page or as long as several pages.

A series of scenes adds up to a sequence.

END OF LECTURE

The Scene List

With your beat sheet you have a general sense of what your characters want, do and battle per sequence, but *how* you show them wanting, doing and battling is where the scenes come in. The next part of the outlining phase, the *scene list*, expands your beat sheet so that a blueprint of your screenplay emerges.

(10) TAKE TEN:
WRITE A SCENE LIST

When creating your scene list, take ten minutes to work on each beat. Build from your beat sheet, putting synopsized scenes under the goal, activity and complication of your sequences. Your outline will eventually look something like this:

SEQUENCE 1

Goal: Dorothy wants to get away.
Activity: Dorothy runs away from home.
Complication: A fortune-teller tells her that Aunt Em is sick with worry, so Dorothy rushes back.

> 1. EXT. PIGPEN
> Dorothy pleads for help from farmhands, but ends up falling in the mud and looking silly.
>
> 2. EXT. FARM
> Dorothy tells Toto that she wishes she could be over the rainbow.
>
> 3. INT. HOUSE
> Miss Gulch dognaps Toto.
>
> 4. EXT. ROAD
> Toto gets away and Dorothy runs off with him.
>
> 5. EXT. FORTUNE-TELLER'S WAGON
> Dorothy wanders into a fortune-teller's wagon.
>
> 6. INT. FORTUNE-TELLER'S WAGON
> Via crystal ball, a fortune-teller shows Dorothy problems at home.
>
> 7. EXT. ROAD
> Dorothy runs off into the storm to return to Auntie Em.

Only *synopsize* your scenes. And don't get hung up on finding every one. More scenes will come to you later. You have spaces here for eight scenes per sequence. Feel free to write less if that's all that's coming to you for now, or more if the scenes start to spill out.

Ready to begin? The passages above each section guide you through it, or *ignore* and write as many scenes as come into your head as quickly as you can within the ten minutes!

10 Minutes:
SEQUENCE 1 SCENE TIPS: Here's where you get to include those smaller character moments you've been dying to write. What are the one or two scenes that show the character's first act goal? Is he at home when he shows us how he feels? At school? Work? And what's the scene that shows us he may not be handling his life very well? Any scenes pointing to potential relationships down the road? How about a scene showing brewing conflict with a potential antagonist?

ACT 1
SEQUENCE 1
GOAL: _____

ACTIVITY: _____

COMPLICATION:_____

Scene_____

Scene_____

Scene_____

Scene_____

Scene_____

Scene_____

Scene_____

Scene_____

10 Minutes:

SEQUENCE 2 SCENE TIPS: You can stop setting up flaw in Sequence 2 and instead switch focus to the activity that gets your character into trouble. Show the scene where something happens that triggers a complication. Does someone challenge the MC? Does the MC go where he shouldn't or do something questionable? And when that complication does occur, whether it's a terrible slip of the tongue or a giant disaster, make sure that it's there, on the page. By the end of the sequence, create a scene that suggests a way out; a new goal for the MC to pursue and even a strategy toward doing this.

ACT 1
SEQUENCE 2
GOAL: _____

ACTIVITY: _____

COMPLICATION: _____

Scene_____

Scene_____

Scene_____

Scene_____

Scene_____

Scene_____

Scene_____

Scene_____

10 Minutes:

SEQUENCE 3 SCENE TIPS: Consider a scene that reflects the character's new goal by showing him developing a plan and attempting to execute it. Does he educate himself by learning about a new environment? Does he train in some way, gather a team, investigate, track? What's the scene where his plan works ... or doesn't work?

The supporting character may show her worth at this point by bringing up an important question, showing a skill that can be useful, testing the main character's emotion, or pushing the MC into a new activity. A pivotal scene dealing with the antagonist or antagonistic force is also suggested at this point to make the audience worry or wonder about what will happen next.

ACT 2A
SEQUENCE 3

GOAL: _____

ACTIVITY: _____

COMPLICATION: _____

Scene_____

Scene_____

Scene_____

Scene_____

Scene_____

Scene_____

Scene_____

Scene_____

10 Minutes:

SEQUENCE 4 SCENE TIPS: Your MC may be so invested in his current situation that he forgot what his original story goals were. No worries. Let him fall under someone's spell, get too involved with a plan or discover clues that reveal an even bigger problem ahead. By the end of this sequence, the "complication" may be the fact that your MC simply can't turn back. He's invested in his story ... and so are we.

ACT 2A
SEQUENCE 4

GOAL: _____

ACTIVITY: _____

COMPLICATION: _____

Scene_____

Scene_____

Scene_____

Scene_____

Scene_____

Scene_____

Scene_____

Scene_____

10 Minutes:

SEQUENCE 5 SCENE TIPS: No more setup needed! You've picked out all of your Lego pieces. Now, play! Let your MC apply one of his newfound skills to a scene. Let him take a risk. Let's see a fight or chase that we've never seen before. Horror movie? Give us a fright! Romance? Kiss the girl! The supporting character's own story may be deepening. What's going on behind the scenes with her that only we see? And don't forget those intense scenes of trouble. The antagonist may be moving closer, fighting harder, or creating a trap for our MC.

ACT 2B
SEQUENCE 5

GOAL: _____

ACTIVITY: _____

COMPLICATION: _____

Scene_____

Scene_____

Scene_____

Scene_____

Scene_____

Scene_____

Scene_____

Scene_____

10 Minutes:

SEQUENCE 6 SCENE TIPS: This can be a very emotional sequence as the ride we were on in Sequence 5 threatens to break down or collide. The more risks our MC takes, the closer he gets to slipping up. Create scenes for the character in which his flaw returns or he shows personal doubt. The lower the moment, the more victorious we'll feel when the MC wins in the end.

ACT 2B
SEQUENCE 6

GOAL: _____

ACTIVITY: _____

COMPLICATION: _____

Scene_____

Scene_____

Scene_____

Scene_____

Scene_____

Scene_____

Scene_____

10 Minutes:

SEQUENCE 7 SCENE TIPS: Something happens here to help your MC refocus and solve his problem. Think about a scene that pays off a seemingly mundane line, event, or action in an unexpected way. Think about creating an "a-ha!" moment that then triggers the MC into taking the right action. Write a scene that gives us a sense of his strategy for Act 3. Think about a scene where the supporting character makes a choice at this point, too. And, at sequence end, invent a scene where the antagonist has one last trick up his sleeve.

ACT 3
SEQUENCE 7

GOAL: _____

ACTIVITY: _____

COMPLICATION:_____

Scene_____

Scene_____

Scene_____

Scene_____

Scene_____

Scene_____

Scene_____

Scene_____

10 Minutes:

SEQUENCE 8 SCENE TIPS: The final showdown takes place in this sequence, so consider paying off your minor characters and bringing them in to help with the battle. Create a scene where a learned skill or piece of knowledge (something gained on the movie's journey) pays off to help physically or emotionally conquer the antagonist. And remember that the MC's original "flaw" can be reworked as a skill to help at this point, too. A final scene to show how the events have affected our MC and others will help create "closure" for your movie. Or, tag the sequence with an additional small scene that makes us wonder about the future. Sequel, anyone?

ACT 3
SEQUENCE 8

GOAL: _____

ACTIVITY: _____

COMPLICATION: _____

Scene_____

Scene_____

Scene_____

Scene_____

Scene_____

Scene_____
Scene_____
Scene_____

WHAT YOU'VE ACCOMPLISHED
You've outlined your movie scene by scene. And you've done so without writing a 20-page document that reads like a novel.

Scene Brainstorming

You may take a look at your outline and feel that it's missing something. You feel there's more to the story, but don't exactly know what. To add to your scene list, try out one or all of the options below for finding additional scenes or replacing existing ones.

Character Flaw = Scene Activity

Great scenes are born out of great character activity. To find this activity, simply go back to the thing that made your character interesting to begin with ... the flaw.

Even in the most traditional setting, a flawed character can bring entertainment and drama into a moment, simply by being herself.

Imagine a character is at a supermarket. Think of the normal things she'd have to do:

1. Get a cart

2. Shop for items

3. Check out

Boring, right? Not necessarily.

A competitive character might engage a hapless fellow customer in a race for the best cart.

An obsessive-compulsive character might have to feel and smell every fruit and vegetable in the whole store.

A selfish character might cut in line or sneak five extra items into the "ten items or less" line.

In the TV show *Friends*, Phoebe was the "free spirit" of the group. Her "flaw" might be described as behaving inappropriately in public – compared to "normal" people. During one episode, Rachel and Phoebe go jogging together. Phoebe sprints, swinging her arms and legs in all directions as she goes, much to Rachel's embarrassment. But Phoebe was simply being true to herself — putting freedom and joy above societal norms.

Similarly, the lead character in *Monk* is obsessive-compulsive. Not only does he solve crimes, he cleans as he does so. Annoying to others, funny to the audience, and true to character.

This next exercise helps you bring activity into a scene based solely on the flaws of the characters.

TAKE TEN:
CHARACTER FLAW CREATES SCENE ACTIVITY

Build a scene answering these questions:

1. Where does your scene take place? _____

2. Who are the characters? _____

3. What are their flaws? _____

4. List the traditional things that each character would have to do in that setting: _____

5. Add complications by applying their flaws to those activities: _____

6. What entertaining or dramatic moments emerge? _____

7. How might this scene further the story? _____

WHAT YOU'VE ACCOMPLISHED
Not only have you created entertaining activity, you've built an entire scene. And, if you've been able to answer the last question, you've found a way to tie that scene to the plot so that it pushes the story forward.

External Obstacles = Scene Activity

Just as internal obstacles — character flaws — create scene activity, so do external obstacles. In short, "sh*t happens." Make it happen to your character, and you'll find scene opportunities at every turn.

Again, let's start with the ordinary. If a woman needs to get to work, the ordinary steps might be:

1. Get ready

2. Ride subway

3. Enter building

Another dullard.

But, complicate it at every turn by throwing an obstacle in her way, and you'll have a movie. Add a *genre obstacle,* and you'll have a big movie!

Here's the woman's morning using external obstacles:

1. Get ready
   a. Obstacle: Apartment floods, shorting out alarm clock, soaking clothes, and drenching hair.
   b. Thriller Genre Obstacle: There's a dead body in her closet.

2. Ride subway
   a. Obstacle: There's a power outage and the subway breaks down.
   b. Horror Genre Obstacle: The passengers on the subway turn into vampires.

3. Enter building
   a. Obstacle: New security clearance needed; they don't believe she's who she says she is.
   b. Action Genre Obstacle: Everyone in the building's been taken hostage, and it's up to her — a mountain climber in her off-hours — to scale the building and rescue her coworkers.

10 **TAKE TEN:**
CREATE EXTERNAL OBSTACLES FOR YOUR CHARACTERS

Find great scenes by throwing obstacles in your character's way.

1. Establish your character's goal for the scene:

CHARACTER GOAL: _____

2. Create three ordinary steps for meeting this goal.

STEP #1 _____

STEP #2 _____

STEP #3 _____

3. Add obstacles to each step. Don't be afraid to make them big!

STEP #1 OBSTACLE _____

STEP #2 OBSTACLE _____

STEP #3 OBSTACLE _____

4. To find more story or scene potential, try and solve the problem caused by each obstacle. Knowing your character's flaw, as well as the skills she's learning from her journey, what would she do?

STEP #1 SOLUTION _____

STEP #2 SOLUTION _____

STEP #3 SOLUTION _____

WHAT YOU'VE ACCOMPLISHED
You've created great scene activity by complicating the ordinary. By doing this, you've grounded the scenes in reality, then spun that reality so that it feels movie-worthy.

Finding Scenes through Setup And Payoff

Pay off a setup and you not only find a new scene, you make audience members happy. Why? Because they've been tracking all of the information you've thrown at them. They've taken notice of the props you focused on, the behavior you pointed to, and the lines you gave your characters. Bring back these details, *pay them off*, and you'll reward your audience for paying attention. Or, better yet, you'll surprise them by cleverly paying off something they thought wasn't very important at all.

The payoff accomplishes so many things for your script. One of its most effective uses is in helping you find your third act.

Think about your favorite movie and ask yourself, "What was drawn from the first half and paid off in the second? What was a seemingly meaningless piece of information that paid off to great effect at story's end?"

Think of the Three Musketeers question in *Slumdog Millionaire* or the way that the simple act of reading out loud pays off again and again in *The Reader*. We have an "a-ha!" moment when Rosebud is revealed in *Citizen Kane* and share the victory when a bowl of grits pays off in *My Cousin Vinny*.

Object Payoff

Movies allow the writer the luxury of pointing out even the smallest detail through a close-up. And that small detail could be the very thing that cracks the movie wide open. Remember the dropped ring in *The Sixth Sense*?

Sometimes, the most seemingly mundane objects travel through a movie and tell their own story. In the movie *Up In The Air*, main character Ryan Bingham carries a small, efficient suitcase that symbolizes his ability to leave at a moment's notice and his refusal to be attached to anything or anyone. The suitcase pays off throughout the movie. We see him lug it through the airport, alone in Act 1. In Act 2A, he forces a work colleague to trade in her large piece of "baggage" for a travel suitcase herself. And in Act 2B, we see him bonding with a love interest when their suitcases travel side-by-side.

Travel Club cards also pay off in this movie. Ryan collects them, meets his love interest by comparing them, and is presented with a prized card at story's end, symbolizing how much he's traveled … and how little he's lived.

Traveling along with him is yet another object: a cardboard cutout of his sister and future brother-in-law. It symbolizes the personal relationships he so desperately wants to leave behind, and a story is told simply by his relationship with the cutout: He reluctantly throws it in his suitcase. He makes his business partner hold it. At a low emotional point, it causes him to fall into the water. And he has an epiphany as he sees all of the cutouts on a bulletin board at his sister's wedding. It's their "wish list" for travel. They want what he's experienced.

TAKE TEN:
FIND SCENES THROUGH OBJECT PAYOFF

1. List all of the objects set up in Act 1 or 2A. It can be anything that you know or imagine for your story.

2. "Match" the list with payoffs in Act 2B and Act 3.

Object payoff in *Up In The Air* could look something like this:

ACT 1	ACT 2A	ACT 2B	ACT 3
Ryan shows pride in his travel suitcase.	Ryan forces business partner to buy a suitcase like his.	Ryan bonds with love interest as their matching travel suitcases move side-by-side in airport.	
Ryan woos love interest with club card comparison.	Ryan's many cards create confusion when trying to get into hotel rooms with love interest.		Ryan is finally given the club card he's always wanted, but it's meaningless now.
Ryan is forced to take cardboard cutout of sister on travels. It almost doesn't fit in travel suitcase!	Ryan's business partner questions his philosophy when he insists on taking photos with the cutout at major airports.	Ryan, in an emotional state, loses his balance while trying to take photos with cutout and falls in a river.	Ryan has a new understanding of his sister when he sees a billboard filled with photos of her cutout, standing in front of all of the places she wishes she could visit.

Now you try it:

ACT 1	ACT 2A	ACT 2B	ACT 3

WHAT YOU'VE ACCOMPLISHED
You've found fresh new scenes and moved story by paying off ordinary objects.

Event Payoff

A character may do something in the early part of a movie that reveals character or adds life to the act. But when that small event pays off in an unexpected way later, it's even more rewarding.

In Act 2A of *One Flew Over The Cuckoo's Nest*, main character Randle McMurphy urges his fellow inmates to use a heavy water fountain to bust a window and escape. The inmates are reluctant to try, including a supporting character, Chief Bromden, who stands silently by.

In Act 3, Nicholson's character has been given a lobotomy. And, too late to help him, the Chief has found his voice. Determined not to make the same mistake twice, he single-handedly lifts the water fountain out of its base, hurls it through the window, and escapes to freedom.

Watching the earlier water fountain scene, we feel that it's just a small event that reveals character. Randle shows his will to leave, in contrast to the ensemble's reluctance to take a stand. By Act 3, we've almost forgotten about it … and that's exactly why the moment pays off so well. Sadly, we realize, had Chief actually listened to Randle in the first place and moved that fountain to begin with, tragedy could have been prevented.

TAKE TEN:
FIND SCENES THROUGH EVENT PAYOFF

1. List the events — big and small — set up in Act 1 and Act 2A.

2. "Match" the list with payoffs in Act 2B and Act 3.

Event payoff in *One Flew Over The Cuckoo's Nest* could look something like this:

ACT 1	ACT 2A	ACT 2B	ACT 3
	Randle tests the inmates by challenging them to throw a water fountain through a window. Randle tries and fails to do this himself. No one helps.		After Randle is given a lobotomy, the Chief's anger and grief motivates him to hurl the fountain through the window and run from the asylum.

Now you try it:

ACT 1	ACT 2A	ACT 2B	ACT 3

Line Payoff

"Do you feel lucky?"

"You complete me."

"We're on a mission from God."

We remember certain lines in movies, not only because they have music to them, but because each scene in which they were uttered gives them new meaning. They don't mean one thing; these lines mean everything!

In *The Dark Knight,* The Joker, knife pointed, asks the question of his victims: "Wanna know how I got these scars?"

It's a rhetorical question, and every time he asks this, he gives that person a different answer. He reveals that his father abused him when he tried to defend his mother. Later, he changes his story and says that he stuck razors in his mouth in sympathy with his scarred wife. By story's end, we know that he'll change his story to fit the listener. But, we also feel that one of these stories — or a combination of all of them — may actually be true. In this example, the question pays off each time by helping us learn more about the central villain. It also pays off as a threat. Whenever The Joker starts to ask that question, we know that someone is about to be hurt.

In the movie *Toy Story,* Buzz Lightyear's signature line is: "To infinity and beyond!" He utters this while "flying" around a room and winning the favor of the toys while being met with disdain from Woody. "That isn't flying," Woody states. "That's falling with style!"

By movie's end, though, as the two main characters hurl through the air in an attempt to return to their owner, Andy, Woody has to admit that, "We're flying!"

"This isn't flying," Buzz Lightyear replies. "This is falling with style!" To which Woody responds (you guessed it): "To infinity and beyond!"

In this example, a simple line payoff in which the two characters *switch* lines is the key to showing their relationship arc. Trading lines means that they "get" each other. A friendship is formed. A sequel can take place.

TAKE TEN:
FIND SCENES THROUGH LINE PAYOFF

1. List a line or lines a character may utter in Act 1 or Act 2A.

2. In Act 2B and Act 3, pay off that line by showing it uttered in a new situation. Take note of how the line's meaning changes.

Line payoff for *Toy Story* could look something like this:

ACT 1	ACT 2A	ACT 2B	ACT 3
While demonstrating his flying techniques, Buzz crows, "To infinity and beyond!" Woody remarks, "That isn't flying, that's falling with style!"		Buzz hears "To infinity and beyond" on a commercial, revealing that he is a toy. He shouts this in the same scene, in a test of his flying abilities, only to fall.	Inspired to save their friends and return to Andy, Buzz and Woody strap a rocket to their back. When Woody remarks that they're "flying," Buzz reminds him that they're "falling with style." Woody crows, "To infinity and beyond!"

Now you try it:

ACT 1	ACT 2A	ACT 2B	ACT 3

WHAT YOU'VE ACCOMPLISHED
You've added to your scene list by paying off objects, events, and lines of dialogue. What was once a throwaway becomes real story.

TAKE TEN:
ADD TO THE SCENE LIST AND COMPLETE YOUR OUTLINE!

You found new scenes in your setup/payoff tables. Now go through your scene list and *add those scenes* to the correct sequences.

WHAT YOU'VE ACCOMPLISHED

You've fleshed out your scene list and added to your detailed beat sheet. Your outline is finished!

■ TEN-MINUTE CHAPTER REVIEW: THE OUTLINE

1. Divide your act segments into two, revealing EIGHT SEQUENCES of STORY BEATS.

2. Describe each story beat in three sentences focusing on the GOAL, ACTIVITY and COMPLICATION of each beat.

3. REWRITE your beat sheet, concentrating on the SUPPORTING CHARACTERS, the EMOTION, the COMPLICATIONS, the MIDPOINT, and the STRUCTURE.

4. Add SYNOPSIZED SCENES to each beat to create a SCENE LIST.

5. Find ADDITIONAL SCENES by using FLAW and OBSTACLES and by PAYING OFF established OBJECTS, EVENTS, and LINES.

6. Add new scenes to the list to complete your OUTLINE.

CHAPTER 4

The Characters

Congratulations! Expanding your beat sheet into a scene list has created an *outline* — a screenplay blueprint from which you can begin writing.

Before you start writing in screenplay format, however, take some time to focus on *character*. Doing so will help you to find even more scenes and to "channel" your characters as you write so that you know what they'll do or say in every scene.

In this chapter, you'll learn who your characters are and find clever ways to showcase their personalities. Doing so will help fend off the dreaded producers' note: "Your characters need more development!"

Character Biography

Writers are often urged to come up with a character biography before they begin writing — a diary of sorts going into a character's childhood, family, personal issues, etc. My experience has been that this only keeps writers mired in their characters' backstory and creates exposition problems later on.

Better to reveal character *within* the story, by showing the small details and allowing the camera to go close-up. After all, film affords us that luxury. We can pick up on the minutia of a character and, by doing so, get to know him in an intimate way.

Consider this next ten-minute tool to be an update of a more traditional character biography. By answering these questions, you'll get to know your character better. By paying off the answers, you'll find new scenes.

TAKE TEN:
CREATE A CHARACTER BIO THROUGH SETUP AND PAYOFF

Ask the following questions of your character(s):

What does the character always wear? _____

How does that pay off later? _____

What object does the character carry around? _____

How does that pay off later? _____

What personal habit does the character have? _____

How does that pay off later? _____

What secret does the character try to protect? _____

How does that pay off later? _____

What is the character's favorite hiding place? _____

How does that pay off later? _____

What joke, exclamation or phrase does the character always use? _____

_____

How does that pay off later? _____

What or who is most important to the character? _____

How does that pay off later? _____

WHAT YOU'VE ACCOMPLISHED
You've created a small biography of your character. Feel free to add more details about your character to this list as you discover them — and ask yourself how these details might pay off. In doing so, you've found story and potential character arc in the small things you thought were just simple character setup.

Character Makes An Entrance

Too often, writers don't take advantage of the first appearance of a character. They forget that first impressions are everything and that the audience will judge a character from the first moment they see him. For that reason, bring your character into your script in an active way. In short: Give him something to do that gets our attention.

In *Pirates of the Caribbean: The Curse of the Black Pearl*, Jack Sparrow sails in on what looks like a grand ship, but it turns out to be nothing more than a sinking dinghy.

In *The Hangover,* one of the first images we have of our ensemble of heroes is the group of them passed out in a Las Vegas hotel room while a tiger prowls in the bathroom.

In *The Devil Wears Prada*, Miranda Priestly strides in, slams her coat and bag down on her assistant's desk, and sends the office into a state of instant flux.

Notice that all of these powerful introductions tell an immediate story. In this way, we cut entire scenes of first-act setup and exposition.

In one-hour dramas, combining a strong first impression with an opening teaser can sell a pilot:

Meredith Grey wakes up with a stranger in *Grey's Anatomy*.

In *Prison Break,* Michael Scofield holds up a bank *on purpose* in order to get thrown in the same jail as his brother.

In the teaser of *Breaking Bad,* lead character Walter White recklessly drives a Winnebago while dressed only in a gas mask and white underpants.

Character voice is also established with the initial line that comes out of the character's mouth. So forget the small talk and think of that *one-liner* that will get noticed.

In *A Beautiful Mind*, the main character's first line shows his obsession, social awkwardness, and eccentricity. "You know," John Nash tells a colleague, "there's a mathematical explanation for how horrible your tie is."

In *The Devil Wears Prada*, Miranda Priestly asks, "How hard is it to confirm an appointment?" Then states, over her assistant's excuses and apologies: "The details of your incompetence do not concern me."

Now, find that powerful "introduction" for your main character.

TAKE TEN:
CHARACTER INTRODUCTION

Create memorable entrances and introductions for your main character and others:

Main character first action:

_____

Main character first line:

_____

Supporting character first action:

_____

Supporting character first line:

_____

Antagonist first action:

_____

Antagonist first line:

_____

WHAT YOU'VE ACCOMPLISHED
You've done some editing work already by cutting the fat from some of your first-act setups and instead coming in on strong, revealing moments.

Character Rules

You might know what your characters want from your script and have some idea of their point of view. But how do you know what to do with them scene-by-scene?

To get to know your characters and to find interesting things for them to do, you need to figure out their _rules_ — the things they tend to always do — or in some cases, never do. _Iron Man_ cracks jokes. _Wall-E_ cleans. _Juno_ listens to music. Elle Woods from _Legally Blonde_ knows haircare.

You have rules.

We all have rules.

Think about a recent family dinner. Couldn't you count on your mom to make a certain comment, your dad to do a certain thing, your brother to embarrass you in a certain way, or a grandparent to tell a certain story?

Character rules are abundant in the dinner scene in the first act of *Little Miss Sunshine*:

MOM'S RULE: Act like a mom no matter what.

SO SHE … reminds people to "eat their salad," even though she's serving fried chicken and sets the table with plastic cups.

DAD'S RULE: Apply his personal self-help program, the "Nine Steps," to everything.

SO HE … refers to "winners" and "losers" even when learning about his brother-in-law's attempted suicide.

GRANDPA'S RULE: Always tell the truth, no matter how painful.

SO HE … openly complains and swears right in front of his young granddaughter.

THE SON'S RULE: Refuse to talk until he makes it as a test pilot.

SO HE … writes sarcastic remarks on a pad.

THE DAUGHTER'S RULE: Ask questions.

SO SHE … innocently inquires as to why the uncle would try to kill himself in the first place and makes everyone uncomfortable in the process.

THE UNCLE'S RULE: Focus only on himself.

SO HE … tells every sorry detail of his story.

By everyone applying their rules to the scene — their habits, personal references, likes and dislikes, quirks, and ways of communicating — they let us get to know them quickly and also learn some much-needed information about how they all ended up together. There's a lot of information that comes out in the scene. But the character rules distract from the exposition. It's just funny.

Your screenplay is one big family dinner, and every character in it brings habits and quirks — their rules — to the table.

TAKE TEN:
CREATE A CHARACTER RULE

Write down one rule for every character you know in your screenplay.

MC _____

LOVE INTEREST _____

FRIEND _____

RELATIVE _____

COWORKER _____

ANTAGONIST _____

OTHER CHARACTER _____

OTHER CHARACTER _____

OTHER CHARACTER _____

WHAT YOU'VE ACCOMPLISHED
You'll never need to ask yourself "what would my character do in this scene?"

Three-dimensional Characters

Of course, we want our characters to be fully realized and dimensional. But how do we show all sides of them without going into long monologues about what they feel or think about everything?

Well, if you think about the kinds of scenes we see on-screen, they're usually *public scenes* out in the world or workplace, *personal scenes* that focus on one-on-one relationships, or *private scenes* that take place when a character doesn't think anyone else is looking.

So, if you just invent three rules for your characters — things they *always* do in their public, personal and private lives — you'll have a guide to their actions throughout the screenplay. And when you come up with those rules, you'll see that they may be very different from each other. Bottom line: You'll find three dimensions of a character.

TAKE TEN:
CREATE CHARACTER RULES

Come up with three rules for a character:

1. PUBLIC LIFE: What does the character always do out in the workforce or in the world?

2. PERSONAL LIFE: What does the character always do in one-on-one relationships?

3. PRIVATE LIFE: What does the character always do when he thinks no one else is looking?

Use your ten minutes to find rules for as many characters as possible.

WHAT YOU'VE ACCOMPLISHED

By creating three major rules of behavior, you're showing the different sides of a character to the audience, allowing them to get the full picture.

Character Rules = Entertainment

Learning a character's rules, and then seeing how she applies those rules to a situation, is the fun of any movie or television show.

The entertainment in *As Good As It Gets* rides almost solely on Melvin's unlikable compulsions. He refuses to step on cracks in a sidewalk, brings plastic cutlery to a restaurant, and throws a dog down a garbage chute. His verbal rule gets in the way as well. A habitual truth teller, he rarely lets people like him.

In *The 40-Year-Old Virgin,* Andy Stitzer's rule of being sexually awkward drives the movie, but the rules of the supporting characters make the scenes even funnier. A coworker, Jay, believes in making time with everyone. A friend, David, can't talk about relationships without getting mournful about his old girlfriend, and Trish, the woman Andy loves, will do anything to actually get him to make a move!

Often we invest in a television show just to see how the characters apply, or are forced to break, one of their own rules. The classic sitcom *Seinfeld* was a show "about nothing" other than its characters' weird habits and strident rules. Jerry was phobic about germs. Kramer was an inventor. George was cheap. Elaine was selfish.

Throw this ensemble into a parking lot they couldn't get out of, or a restaurant they couldn't get a table at, and you had a half-hour of big laughs and major Emmys.

In *Lost*, a show that is about, well... *everything*, the character rules actually bring order to the extreme moments. No matter whether a smoke monster is chasing them or "The Others" are spooking them, Jack will lead, Kate will act, Sawyer will joke, and Locke will philosophize.

We invest so heavily in the rules of our favorite television characters, in fact, that we tune in each week just to see those rules applied to a new situation.

(10) TAKE TEN:
CHARACTER RULES CREATE ENTERTAINMENT

Create situations within your script and apply your character rules to them to find comedic or dramatic moments.

In public, this character always _____ .
rule

Later, this rule is applied when _____ .
new situation

The entertaining activity that results is _____ .
specific scene

In personal relationships, this character always _____ .
rule

Later, this rule is applied when _____ .
new situation

The entertaining activity that results is _____ .
specific scene

In private, this character always _____ .
rule

Later, this rule is applied when _____ .
new situation

The entertaining activity that results is _____ .
specific scene

WHAT YOU'VE ACCOMPLISHED
Natural comedy or drama has occurred because you've applied a character rule to a situation.

Character Rules = Complication

In *The Dark Knight,* Batman's self-imposed rule is not to kill. Does this create complications for him? You bet it does. In *The Wrestler,* Randy's signature move in the ring is the very move that threatens to kill him. In the dark, comedic-action movie *In Bruges*, Harry's insistence that those who kill kids must die results in his having to kill himself!

TAKE TEN:
CHARACTER RULES CREATE COMPLICATIONS

Find moments in your script where a character's own rules result in major complications.

In public, this character always _____ .

Later, this rule creates problems when _____ .

In personal relationships, this character always _____ .

Later, this rule creates problems when _____ .

In private, this character always _____ .

Later, this rule creates problems when _____ .

WHAT YOU'VE ACCOMPLISHED
No more contrived complications!

Breaking Character Rules = Change

The breaking of character rules is a great way to telegraph change and transition without resorting to "on the nose" dialogue. Imagine, in Act 3, a man who couldn't dance, refused to dance, or was afraid to dance suddenly grabbing the hand of the woman he loves ... and dancing the tango. Clearly, whatever he experienced throughout the film has triggered a change in him. And we see that change only when he *breaks his own rule.*

In *When Harry Met Sally,* Sally shows she's lightening up when she reenacts a faked orgasm in the middle of a diner.

In the television drama *Dexter,* Dexter's desire to lead a normal life leads him to take on familial responsibilities — causing him to break his homicidal code.

In *Knocked Up,* main character Ben Stone shows he has dad potential by reading a pile of baby books he'd previously avoided.

In *Baby Mama,* tightly wound Kate lets her trashy surrogate Angie make her over and take her dancing. By breaking her own rules and trying to follow Angie's, Kate shows us she is really changing.

TAKE TEN:
BREAK CHARACTER RULES

Find one rule to *break* for each character — something that will show they've changed or been affected by their journey.

MAIN CHARACTER

This character always _____ .

Later, this character breaks this rule by _____ .

SUPPORTING CHARACTER

This character always _____ .

Later, this character breaks this rule by _____ .

ANTAGONIST

This character always _____ .

Later, this character breaks this rule by _____ .

WHAT YOU'VE ACCOMPLISHED

You're showing full change and character development without resorting to unnecessary exposition.

Character Rules = Great Scene Moments

Remember that the more specific you can be with your rules, the more interesting your character moments will be. It's not just that a character always feels shy at a party; it's that she always hides in the coat room. It's not that a character lets go in his private life; it's that he always sings opera in front of the mirror.

TAKE TEN:
DISCOVER YOUR CHARACTERS THROUGH THEIR RULES

Create a rule sheet for a character, listing things he or she would always or never do in a certain situation.

At a funeral, my character would always _____ .
At a funeral, my character would never _____ .

At a wedding, my character would always _____ .
At a wedding, my character would never _____ .

At a high school reunion, my character would always _____ .
At a high school reunion, my character would never _____ .

In an elevator, my character would always _____ .
In an elevator, my character would never _____ .

At a family dinner, my character would always _____ .
At a family dinner, my character would never _____ .

While driving, my character would always _____ .
While driving, my character would never _____ .

Come up with new situations to discover new character rules.

WHAT YOU'VE ACCOMPLISHED
The more you know about a character, the more scenes will unfold for you. Put two characters together with contrasting rules, and you have a huge opportunity for conflict and comedy.

Relationship Rules

Just as characters follow their own personal rules, they tend to also work with rules when it comes to the relationships in their lives. Think about it: Your best friend may act differently when she's with you, versus when she's with her husband. And her relationship rule may change again when she's with her kids, again with the neighbors, again with her boss, and so on.

The movie *Away From Her* opens on an elderly husband and wife who've clearly been with each other for years. They ski silently together. They watch the sunset. They share a laugh over dinner. Then, while putting the dishes away, the wife puts the frying pan in the freezer. She looks confused for one moment, then leaves. The husband looks sad — but he doesn't point out her mistake. Instead, he calmly opens up the freezer and puts the pan in a cupboard.

Her character rule is that she forgets. (We'll soon discover that she has Alzheimer's.) His rule is that he remembers for her. Their *relationship* rule is that this problem is not to be discussed or dealt with. And, when she chooses to break that rule and talk about it at the end of act one, the movie story begins.

The great lovers and buddies of American cinema have all had well-defined relationship rules. In *Adam's Rib,* the two attorneys, Adam and Amanda Bonner, are vicious in the courtroom, but have a weak spot for each other in private.

In *Sex and the City*, Carrie, Samantha, Charlotte and Miranda have different rules of behavior when they're in a group of four than when they're coupled off in groups of two. And they certainly have different relationship rules when they're with their male friends.

Showing an MC's new character rule when she's with her family, her spouse, or her friend will show us yet another side of her character and reveal personal history.

TAKE TEN:
RELATIONSHIP RULES

With her mother, my character always / never _____ .

With her father, my character always / never _____ .

With her spouse or partner, my character always / never _____ .

With her friend, my character always / never _____ .

With her children, my character always / never _____ .

With authority figures, my character always / never _____ .

WHAT YOU'VE ACCOMPLISHED
By having a character always act a certain way with a particular person, you're educating the audience in the backstory of that relationship. We don't have to hear about history; behavior reveals it all.

Creating Great Antagonists

Great antagonists steal the show when they truly believe that the movie goal they're pursuing is the correct one.

Assuming that the evil Joker in *The Dark Knight* believes the movie to be his, his log line might read: "A merry prankster rids a city of its hypocrites and liars as he gets closer to defeating the masked man who threatens to ruin all of the fun."

In *Michael Clayton,* executive Karen Crowder orders the death of a central character, but she believes she's just doing her job. Her log line might read: "A dedicated executive sacrifices her career and conscience when she engages in illegal attacks in order to protect her company."

Even Anton Chigurh, the cold-blooded assassin in *No Country For Old Men,* believes he's killing for the right reason. As he interrogates a clerk about his isolated gas station, we see Anton choke on the realization that the clerk "married into it." When he makes the decision to kill this character, it's because of his belief that he's putting the man out of his misery. Fortunately for the clerk, Anton's own "rule" of flipping a coin — determining whether or not he actually goes through with the kill — ends up saving the poor guy's life.

If antagonists clearly pursue their own movie goals, we leave the script feeling that we understand them. We may not like them or want to be like them, but they read as fully realized characters — not just characters who exist to get in the way.

TAKE TEN:
HUMANIZE YOUR ANTAGONIST

Ask the following questions of your antagonist and find the person underneath.

1. How does your antagonist believe he is helping people or doing a greater good? _____

2. Other than hate, what are the feelings the antagonist has for the main character? _____

3. Who does the antagonist love? _____

4. What's your antagonist's greatest skill? _____

5. What's your antagonist's biggest weakness? _____

WHAT YOU'VE ACCOMPLISHED
By taking ten minutes to humanize your antagonist, you've made a major step in breaking away from bad-guy cliché.

■ TEN-MINUTE CHAPTER REVIEW: THE CHARACTERS

1. Create a CHARACTER BIOGRAPHY through habits and behavior.

2. Create a MEMORABLE ENTRANCE for your central characters.

3. Discover CHARACTER RULES in PUBLIC, PERSONAL and PRIVATE scenes.

4. Apply character rules in situations to create ENTERTAINMENT.

5. Use character rules to create COMPLICATIONS.

6. BREAK character rules to show transition and change.

7. Determine the RELATIONSHIP RULES of your script.

8. HUMANIZE your antagonist by discovering his POINT OF VIEW.

CHAPTER 5

The First Draft

You've brainstormed, homed in on a concept, outlined your broad beats, added the scenes to demonstrate those beats, and discovered the character moments that make those scenes richer. This means that we're going to stop planning now and start writing.

In this chapter, you hit the pages running and move quickly through a *speed draft*, roughing it out by working around the main intentions of your scene. Then you build out, honing the scenes and adding more until you have a solid *first draft*.

But how much writing can one possibly get accomplished in ten minutes?

For now, let's go for one scene.

Remember that scenes can be as short as one-eighth of a page, so this doesn't have to be overwhelming. Just focus on one scene at a time, working around the intentions of that scene, and you'll nail it.

Scene Intention

By scene intention, I mean what has to happen on a physical, verbal, emotional and story level to make the scene work. Writing solely around these intentions will help you get to the heart of your scenes and keep you from meandering or overwriting.

TEN-MINUTE LECTURE:

SCENE INTENTION

Your PHYSICAL INTENTION focuses on activity. What has to happen in the scene? What do we have to see someone do?

Your VERBAL INTENTION focuses on dialogue. What has to be communicated with words? Since you'll hone the scene in the rewrite, give yourself permission to write "on the nose" dialogue if you need to at this point.

Your EMOTIONAL INTENTION focuses on how a character within the scene is affected. Or, how the audience should be emotionally affected.

Your STORY INTENTION is possibly the most important element on this list. How does this scene move the story forward? If it doesn't, delete it from your scene list.

END OF LECTURE

Writing Scenes Around Intention

Never written a screenplay? No worries. When you break down a scene element by element, it's really pretty simple.

Look at how the following scene from *Sideways* is written. It's short, simple, and works solely around intention, and yet it is a key scene in an Academy Award-winning script.

1. The writer creates a *scene heading* to show whether a scene is taking place inside or outside, what location it's in, and what time of day it is:

```
EXT. PARKING AREA - DAY
```

2. The writer adds *scene direction* in order to meet the *physical intention*.

```
Maya leads the way toward the Saab.
```

3. The writer adds *dialogue* that conveys the *verbal intention*.

```
                    MAYA
      Were you ever going to say anything?
```

```
                    MILES
          Of course I was. I mean, just now I
          could have made up some story, but I
          didn't. I told you the truth.
```

4. The writer adds *an action line* that shows what is really going on in the scene in order to reveal the *emotional intention*.

```
Maya turns to confront Miles with a look of "Give
me a break." Miles reaches out to touch her.
```

5. The writer adds a *button* to the scene that brings closure to the moment, while also pushing the story forward, thereby achieving the *story intention*.

```
                    MILES
          Maya.

                    MAYA
               (jerking away)
          Don't touch me. Just take me home.
```

From Sideways, *written by Alexander Payne & Jim Taylor, 2004.*

Here's another example, written by writer Matt Harris. Notice how this scene accomplishes all of its intentions in eight simple lines.

```
INT. ANCHORAGE AIRPORT TERMINAL - LATER

An empty lounge.

A man, JEFF, stands over her.

                    JEFF
          Charlotte?

                    CHARLOTTE
          Yes?

                    JEFF
          I thought so. I'm, uh … Jeff.

Charlotte stares mystified; hard to say who's more
nervous.

                    JEFF
          Your dad.
```

From Bloodborne, *written by Matt Harris, 2007.*

Write a Scene

You've only got ten minutes. And the goal is simply to write a scene. Don't try to make it perfect!

Write quickly, only focusing on getting a super-rough-scratch-it-out scene on the page.

Reference your scene list, pick a scene, and go.

TAKE TEN:
WRITE A SPEED DRAFT OF YOUR FIRST SCENE

```
SCENE HEADING

Scene direction.

                    CHARACTER
        Dialogue.

Action line with revealing physical/emotional
moment.

                    CHARACTER
        Dialogue that brings out emotional
        intention.

Action button that brings closure and pushes the
story forward.
```

WHAT YOU'VE ACCOMPLISHED

Congratulations. You wrote your first scene. And you did it without stressing or overwriting!

Quicky Format

Still intimidated by the form? You only need to know a couple of terms. Honest. We'll talk about formatting tricks and trends as you expand and rewrite, but for now, just concentrate on the essentials:

TEN-MINUTE LECTURE:

FORMAT BASICS

A SCENE HEADING, also referred to as a SLUGLINE, tells you whether or not you're inside or outside, what place you're in, and what time of day it is. It should be capitalized, with interior or exterior referred to as INT. or EXT. and have a dash between the place and time of day. It looks like this:

```
INT. OFFICE — DAY
```

An ACTION LINE, also referred to as SCENE DIRECTION, gives a visual description of scene activity. It is written in sentence form and looks like this:

```
Mary writes.
```

DIALOGUE is what we call the words spoken aloud by characters. Before a line of dialogue, the name of a character appears, capitalized, above it. Dialogue is centered on the script page and looks like this:

```
                MARY
     Only one hundred pages to go.
```

Put together, scene heading, action lines and dialogue look like this:

```
INT. OFFICE — DAY

Mary writes.

                MARY
     Only one hundred pages to go.
```

END OF LECTURE

How Screenwriting Software Can Help You

Want to spend your ten minutes indenting, capitalizing, and generally putting your head through a wall? Then don't get screenwriting software. If you want to press a key and have it done for you, *do get screenwriting software*. I like *Final Draft*, but they all work.

The Speed Draft

The goal of the speed draft is to finish. It's not to make every scene perfect. It's not to find the perfect line or trailer-worthy moment. It's simply to put your scenes in the order you've decided on in your outline. And to write those scenes in a format that looks like a movie.

To get started, look at a scene on your scene list and write a quick scene around its main intentions. Once you've met those intentions, move on!

Don't worry about word choice, character nuance, scene direction detail, etc. Just write. Try and bang out a scene per ten minutes. Maybe you'll get so good at this that you'll write two!

Now, if you do get on a roll and feel that "writer's rush" that happens when a scene is simply writing itself, by all means, go for it! Don't limit yourself to strictly writing around the main intentions. *But*, the minute you start laboring over a word, deleting and rewriting, or stopping to look up something on the Internet, go back to writing around intention again, using the speed draft as a shortcut to get you moving forward.

If you get stuck, mark the scene for now and move on. Even writing "Hero does something cool to make lady love him" is enough to push the story ahead. Keep marking scenes until the scene direction and dialogue come to you again.

Your mantra is: "This is a speed draft. It does not have to be perfect."

When you're finished, we'll use more of those stolen ten minutes to craft and rewrite. But for now, take ten minutes whenever you can to get your scenes out of your outline and onto the page.

TEN-MINUTE
SCENE-WRITING CALENDAR

Keep writing quickly, roughing it out to the end.

DAY ONE
10 minutes: Set the alarm clock ten minutes early — write a scene
10 minutes: Office coffee break — write a scene
10 minutes: Back early from lunch — write a scene

DAY TWO
10 minutes: Drinking morning coffee — write a scene
10 minutes: Baby napping in chair — write a scene
10 minutes: Older kid doing homework — write a scene

DAY THREE
10 minutes: Arrived at class early — write a scene
10 minutes: Riding the train — write a scene
10 minutes: Waiting for bath to run — write a scene

WHAT YOU'VE ACCOMPLISHED
In three days, catching three breaks of ten minutes per day, you could be done with the first sequence of your movie. Only seven more sequences to go. At this rate, you'll be done with your speed draft in less than a month. Double your work time and make it two weeks!

TAKE TEN
WRITE YOUR SPEED DRAFT

You've stolen moments and written your first sequence. Keep pushing forward to the end!

1. Write quickly, working around intention and roughing it out to the end.

2. Don't stop to think.

3. Don't go back to fix.

4. Mark it where you don't know it.

5. Keep writing where you do.

6. Stuck? Make it up!

7. It doesn't have to be perfect!

WHAT YOU'VE ACCOMPLISHED
You wrote to the end! And you did it by working around the main intentions of the scene. You didn't stop to nitpick because you just didn't have the time. And your time limitations have actually forced you to write more efficiently and from the gut.

Speed Draft to First Draft

You wrote to the end! Celebrate.

Finished? Good.

Because you've got more work to do.

You see, since this is only a speed draft, it's going to be short, rough and meet your original concept and story intentions only halfway. That means that your next step is to go *back through the script and develop it*, turning it into a clean first draft that delivers on story.

Script Development: Add New Scenes

You worked, as you should, off of the scene list from your outline. And those were the scenes that were put together to form your rough draft. But, no matter what anyone tells you, not every scene can be planned out ahead of time. So, in expanding your rough draft into a solid first draft, the first thing to do is see *what scenes are missing*.

You don't have to completely redo. Just add scenes to make story connections. Fill in the story gaps. Add to the relationships. Create powerful introductions. Create trailer scenes. Below, we'll cover some of the ways to do that.

Remember that the goal here is to add scenes that expand your speed draft into a solid first draft. And we'll then take that through a rewrite as well. All this to say, once again, that it doesn't have to be perfect.

Trigger Scenes

Taking a hard look at your story, you might notice that some of the sequences just don't add up. In the planning stage, they looked OK. But it turns out you need more.

By writing a scene around *the event that triggers a new beat* in the story, you're filling in a necessary gap and bringing in extra activity.

In the animated movie *Up,* the writers could have shown their character evicted from his home, and the assumption could have been that it was because of the land development going on around him. But instead, they had him bonk a land developer over the head in anger, *triggering* the eviction.

Sometimes a trigger is subtle; something small witnessed or experienced that adds to a character's motivation. A great trigger scene can be the emotional glue that helps us understand a character's choice later on.

In *Juno*, Juno's observation of Vanessa interacting with a child *triggers* her decision to give Vanessa her baby. We see the moment she "gets it." Without that scene, her choice would have seemed to have come out of nowhere.

In *Up In The Air*, Ryan needed to see that bulletin board full of places his sister hadn't gone to in order to *trigger* him to give her his miles later on. Yes, he could simply have given them to her, but that trigger scene helped him recognize the problem.

For other trigger scenes, think about …

The event or moment that triggers a character to explore.

The event or moment that triggers a character to take a risk.

The event or moment that triggers a character to quit.

The event or moment that triggers a kiss.

The event or moment that triggers a proposal.

The event or moment that triggers a murder.

TAKE TEN:
ADD A TRIGGER SCENE

Write in a trigger scene wherever a character makes a new choice. Add it to your scene list, and then work it into your draft.

CHOICE _____

TRIGGERED BY _____
new scene

CHOICE _____

TRIGGERED BY _____
new scene

CHOICE _____

TRIGGERED BY _____
new scene

WHAT YOU'VE ACCOMPLISHED

The audience has now witnessed, firsthand, the moment where the MC is actually motivated to take action. You've avoided the note, "but why is he doing that?"

Relationship Scenes: Supporting Character

You claim your script is a love story. But did you write the scene where the characters actually commit to that love? Your script is a buddy movie. But did you show the friends working as a team? Your script is an action adventure. Did you reveal the moment where the hero emotionally connects with the person he's going to save?

If we don't see the connection, we don't buy the stakes. A character may crow about his love for someone else, but unless the audience witnesses it, it rings as untrue. And friends may say they'd die for each other, but unless we've seen a moment where they bond, we'll never feel the impact when they actually make that sacrifice.

These connections don't have to be hugely dramatic or overly emotional. Backstory does not have to be shared. Tears do not have to be shed.

These connections could be made with …

A joke.
A look.
A promise.
A secret.
A compliment.
A kiss.
An accusation.
A threat.
An argument.

TAKE TEN:
EMOTIONAL CONNECTION WITH SUPPORTING CHARACTER

Create new scenes showing an emotional connection between your MC and the supporting character. Add it to your scene list and then work it into your draft.

ACT 1

Emotional connection with supporting character _____ .

new scene

ACT 2A

Emotional connection with supporting character _____ .

new scene

ACT 2B

Emotional connection with supporting character _____ .

new scene

ACT 3

Emotional connection with supporting character _____ .

new scene

WHAT YOU'VE ACCOMPLISHED
You've enriched your story and strengthened your character development. The audience will feel more attached to your MC's journey, now that we're caught up in his relationship with someone else.

Relationship Scenes: Antagonist

And, when making those emotional connections, don't forget your antagonist! Bad guys need attention too! Or, I should say, bad guys need to show the audience that they get under the skin of the main character ... and vice versa! Sometimes villains are most interesting when they connect with a main character in a positive way. There's the famous "I didn't kill my wife!" line uttered by the hero in *The Fugitive*, followed by the marshal's response: "I don't care!"

In that moment, we see the main character and his antagonist connect in a way that communicates that they're both just doing what they have to do. It's a small but powerful break in the action, connecting them on a human level before plunging us back into the action.

The movie *Heat* is remembered most for the scene where cop and thief stop chasing each other to hash it out over a cup of coffee in a diner. Again, there's a mutual understanding. At one point, thief says to cop: "I do what I do best. I take scores. You do what you do best — trying to stop guys like me."

But negative connections can be just as powerful. In *The Lovely Bones*, the father of a slain girl has an in-person meeting with a neighbor. Though there's nothing he can do to stop him in this moment, the father knows, through their interaction, that this is the man who killed his daughter. The neighbor, in turn, realizes that the father is onto him. In this moment of personal connection, they both recommit to their movie goal: the father wants, more than ever, to put this man away; the neighbor knows that he must avoid getting caught at all cost.

(10) TAKE TEN:
EMOTIONAL CONNECTION WITH ANTAGONIST

Create new scenes showing an emotional connection between your MC and the antagonist. Add it to your scene list, and then work it into your draft.

ACT 1

Emotional connection with antagonist _____ .
new scene

ACT 2A

Emotional connection with antagonist _____ .
new scene

ACT 2B

Emotional connection with antagonist _____ .
new scene

ACT 3

Emotional connection with antagonist _____ .
new scene

WHAT YOU'VE ACCOMPLISHED
You've added a new layer to the classic good-guy / bad-guy relationship. If you want to make your MC hate the antagonist, your new connecting scene will strengthen that. If you want to make him see a different side of the antagonist, your scene has the potential to do that as well.

The Teaser

If you're a fan of one-hour crime shows, you're familiar with the teaser. It's an opening scene that focuses on a startling event: A threat! An abduction! A murder! And a good teaser is there for more than shock value alone. Often, the subject of the teaser turns out to be the murder we're investigating that week or the key puzzle piece in a mystery.

Contemporary films also use the trick of a teaser to entice us and lure us into a film. Here's one from a feature spec that instantly got my attention:

FADE IN:

EXT. REMOTE BEACH - DAY

Sea oats sway in a brisk morning breeze.

A YOUNG BOY (5) emerges carefree and happy, a true king of
the hill. Up ahead, he sees--

A WHITE DIAMOND KITE

loom high above him, tethered behind another dune.

> MOTHER'S VOICE (O.S.)
> Stay close by, sweetie.

The Boy turns towards his family playing along the shore.

> MOTHER
> Come back this way, okay.

But the kite proves irresistible. With a mischievous smile,
he takes off towards the kite.

LARGER DUNE - MOMENTS LATER

The downed kite flutters about the ground.

The Boy's fingers strum along the fly line leading up to the
kite spool buried deep in the sand.

He drops to his knees and digs at the spool. The deeper he
digs, the deeper his frustration. He grabs the fly line and
heaves forth to the surface--

A SEVERED LEFT HAND

of a young woman, cleaved mid-forearm, relatively fresh,
still loosely clutching the kite spool.

On the hand, an elegant tattoo of wild scarlet roses spirals
around the appendage, cut off by the amputation and extending
down across the back metacarpals.

THE BOY

falls back, his eyes transfixed upon the hand. Frightened,
he runs off.

From The Wild Rose, written by Stephen Cowan, 2007.

Though the boy himself will never figure into this scene again, his adventure sets the tone for the rest of the story and also establishes the murder evidence that we'll be following throughout the movie. When I first read this scene, I was caught up by the journey of the small boy: that carefree moment, the search for the kite, the gruesome discovery. By the end of the page, I was sold. A severed hand on page one? What would happen next? That's how a good teaser grabs the reader (and the audience).

Great teaser scenes don't always have to be scary — at least not in the conventional sense of the word. In *The Hangover*, the first scene slams us into the heart of the problem. A best man calls a worried bride from the middle of the desert. His car is a wreck. So is his face. His friends look like death warmed over. And, worst of all, the groom is nowhere to be found.

When we cut to the next scene in this movie, it's forty hours earlier. The movie *really* begins there. But that teaser is stuck in our head, reminding us that no matter how safe the characters feel now, they're in for a heck of a ride.

Teasers don't always have to be over-the-top. In *The Ice Storm*, we begin the movie with an icy-cold, pre-dawn train ride. Nothing terrible happens: A boy rides. A family picks him up. The train doesn't crash. Yet the scene is filled with cold and darkness, giving us a sense of dread that lingers through much of the story.

TAKE TEN:
WRITE A TEASER

Use one of the choices below to create a provocative opening scene. Add it to your scene list, and then work it into your draft.

1. Focus on a dramatic physical event that takes place deeper into the movie. Hint: Show us only one part of this scene. Save the full scene for later!

2. Show a dreamlike event that turns out to be reality later on.

3. Come up on an antagonist involved in his evil work.

4. Focus on an intense, private moment filled with emotion — something that will be explained later.

5. Write a genre-specific opening. A scare if it's a horror movie. A silly moment if it's a comedy. A battle if it's a war movie.

WHAT YOU'VE ACCOMPLISHED
Adding a teaser strengthens your story, lures the reader in and sells it on page one.

Set Pieces

"Set piece" is one of those weird industry terms like "best boy" and "key grip" that doesn't always mean what it says. Some writers hear the term set piece and think "setting." So, when asked to come up with more set pieces, they throw in a library, a beach, or a skyscraper. Actually, the term means something completely different.

 TEN-MINUTE LECTURE:

SET PIECE

A set piece, as it applies to a script, is an active, visual, trailer-worthy scene that uses a setting or world in an original way. Let's take our library, beach, and skyscraper. In our library, books suddenly fly off shelves and knock out a bad guy. A placid beach day turns into a nightmare when a tidal wave hits. Lovers have a picnic on the ledge of the skyscraper.

In Close Encounters of the Third Kind, *an obsessed father builds a mountain, first out of the mashed potatoes on his dinner table, then out of the mud and bushes in his backyard. The mountain, the mission, and the emotion as his family looks on in horror are all shown to us in those active moments.*

A great set piece multitasks. Not only does it do something new and visual by taking advantage of the script's world, it also uses that world to ...

SERVE THE GENRE: Such as the fight scene through the treetops in Crouching Tiger, Hidden Dragon.

BUILD CHARACTER: Check out the upside-down kiss in Spider-Man.

CREATE A PROBLEM: As in the stuck zipper scene in There's Something About Mary.

Or it can do all of the above: The FAO Schwartz "Chopsticks" scene in Big *is a terrific example. In it, Josh, a twelve-year-old trapped in the body of a grown man, teaches his stuffy boss a little something about playtime by jumping up and down on a giant keyboard and playing "Chopsticks."*

This scene:

A: Takes advantage of its toy-store SETTING.

B: Brings home the "child in us all" THEME through its activity.

C: Honors its CONCEPT and character by having the grown-up-looking Josh behave like a twelve-year-old. And ...

D: Moves the STORY forward by earning Josh a promotion.

END OF LECTURE

TAKE TEN:
WRITE A SET PIECE

Use one of the choices below to create a memorable set piece. Add it to your scene list, and then work it into your draft.

GENRE SET PIECE _____
new scene

CHARACTER-DRIVEN SET PIECE _____
new scene

STORY-BUILDING SET PIECE _____
new scene

CONCEPT SET PIECE _____
new scene

THEME-SPECIFIC SET PIECE _____
new scene

WHAT YOU'VE ACCOMPLISHED

Adding set pieces to your script makes it stronger and more saleable. Adding a key set piece can also breathe new life into a standard story moment.

Script Development: Build On Existing Scenes

You zipped through your speed draft by writing scenes built solely around their main intentions. That's great, because it allowed you to focus on what the scene was really about, instead of meandering until you found the point.

But, now that you're expanding from rough draft into a real first draft, it's fine to look at the scenes that you do have and see if they need more.

Scene Expansion

The following is a scene written around its most basic intentions by writer Suzanne Keilly. Follow her choices as she starts small and builds out:

INT. BOBBIE AND MINA'S TRAILER

Mina tosses her knapsack on the floor and plops into a chair at the table. Bobbie puts a cereal bowl in front of her.

> MINA
> I wanted eggs.

> BOBBIE
> We ran out.

> MINA
> Whatever. I'll just get something unhealthy. They sell donuts at school.

Bobbie reaches into her purse.

> BOBBIE
> I'll give you some money.

The scene, written around intention alone, is straightforward and gets across the central idea.

But the writer wanted more. For one thing, she wanted to create a better sense of *place*. So she added more detail up-front, just enough to stage the scene:

INT. BOBBIE AND MINA'S TRAILER

Bobbie stands in the kitchenette part of their trailer pouring Frosted Flakes into a bowl. A lit cigarette sits in an ashtray on the counter.

The writer also wanted to talk about marital problems between Bobbie and her husband, so she decided to *add more dialogue*:

> MINA
> I wanted eggs.

> BOBBIE
> We ran out.

> MINA
> (rolling her eyes)
> Uhhh. Well, can I have milk at least?

> BOBBIE
> We don't have any.

```
                    MINA
          Did you chuck the carton at dad?

                    BOBBIE
          I'll buy some more today.

                    MINA
          Whatever. I'll just get something
          unhealthy at school.
```

She also wanted to establish Bobbie's lifestyle contradictions. By doing this, she created a *new beat* in the scene:

```
Bobbie takes a drag on her cigarette.

                    BOBBIE
          No. We're both gettin' healthy from now
          on. We talked about that.

She exhales a lungful of smoke.

                    MINA
          With what? You throw everything edible at
          dad.
```

Then the writer created a *tonal shift* by showing a softening within the scene, a chance for Bobbie to try a new tactic with her daughter:

```
Bobbie stubs out the cigarette. Turns to face her
daughter.

                    BOBBIE
          I'm sorry. I am. Things will be better
          soon.

                    MINA
          When?
```

Finally, the writer wanted to make sure that it was clear that the daughter "won" this particular round with her mother. To do that, the writer changed course again with a key piece of *emotional scene direction*.

```
Mina sulks and grabs her backpack.

                    MINA
          They sell donuts at school.

Bobbie reaches into her purse.
```

```
                    BOBBIE
                  (sighing)
        I'll give you some money.
```

The final scene looked like this:

```
INT. BOBBIE AND MINA'S TRAILER

Bobbie stands in the kitchenette part of their
trailer pouring Frosted Flakes into a bowl. A lit
cigarette sits in an ashtray on the counter.

                    MINA
        I wanted eggs.

                    BOBBIE
        We ran out.

                    MINA
                  (rolling her eyes)
        Uhhh. Well can I have milk at least?

                    BOBBIE
        We don't have any.

                    MINA
        Did you chuck the carton at dad?

                    BOBBIE
        I'll buy some more today.

                    MINA
        Whatever. I'll just get something
        unhealthy at school.

Bobbie takes a drag on her cigarette.

                    BOBBIE
        No. We're both gettin' healthy from now
        on. We talked about that.

She exhales a lungful of smoke.

                    MINA
        With what? You throw everything edible at
        dad.

Bobbie stubs out the cigarette. Turns to face her
daughter.
```

> BOBBIE
> I'm sorry. I am. Things will be better soon.
>
> MINA
> When?

Mina sulks and grabs her backpack.

> MINA
> They sell donuts at school.

Bobbie reaches into her purse.

> BOBBIE
> (sighing)
> I'll give you some money.

From Three Days, Three-Thousand Miles, *Written by Suzanne Keilly, 2009.*

TAKE TEN:
DEVELOP YOUR SCENES

Working one scene at a time, go through and develop your scenes by asking the following questions. Remember, though, that you may need to add only one element. Don't do everything, or you'll overwrite!

1. Do you need to give the scene a better sense of PLACE?

2. Would your scene benefit from MORE DIALOGUE?

3. In order to change the rhythm should you try out a TONAL SHIFT?

4. Do you need to add a NEW BEAT to the scene?

5. Would a piece of EMOTIONAL SCENE DIRECTION help you to tell the story?

WHAT YOU'VE ACCOMPLISHED
You've fleshed-out your scenes and met your emotional and dramatic intentions.

Scene Division

Rather than expand every scene, sometimes what's actually needed is to chop them up. A long conversation or action scene may be necessary for your script, but it's going to look like a bunch of talking heads if you keep your characters in one place for a long time.

A flirtatious scene between a man and woman may be charming, but if it's five pages in one place, it's going to grow old quickly. We can chop it up, though, so that it starts at a pool table, moves to the bar, then ends in the parking lot. In this way, we keep the characters on their feet and hold the attention of the audience.

So, look to your scene list and then to your scenes themselves. Did you write only one long, meandering scene, when it could have easily been two or three shorter ones?

TAKE TEN:
DIVIDE YOUR SCENES

Starting from the scene list, look at your scenes and see where you can split locations to create additional scenes.

Look for ...

1. Talky scenes: If all of the information is important, stretch it out over different locations.

2. Fight scenes: If the action is moving, your characters are probably pursuing each other from place to place.

3. Party scenes: Move our eye to the different mini-locations in the room. One group may be at the food table, while another is on the balcony.

4. Chase scenes: It goes without saying that the characters are probably chasing each other from location to location. Make sure your scenes reflect that.

WHAT YOU'VE ACCOMPLISHED
Your script was longer, and you didn't even know it! Just by splitting locations, your script is looking less like a play and more like a movie.

Show Don't Tell

It's the oldest rule in screenwriting, and it's the best one. Who needs talk when you can show the audience what's going on? Yet, in your haste, you may have come up with scenes where people simply talk about what's going on, rather than show it. Replacing those talky scenes with activity will quickly turn your speed draft into the real thing.

TAKE TEN:
SHOW IT

Take your speed draft to the next level by replacing talky scenes with active moments.

STEP 1: Look at your scene list and note where you've described a scene with words like *convinces*, *talks to*, and *asks about*. Replace with verbs that force your character into an action — not a conversation.

STEP 2: Focusing on your new activity, rewrite the scene. If a character *overheard* the truth before, for example, in your developed scene she may *discover* it.

WHAT YOU'VE ACCOMPLISHED
You've made your script more interesting and active. We'll now feel that we're experiencing events, rather than just hearing about them.

Script Development: Add Your Voice

Speeding through a draft is a great way to get to the end, but not necessarily the best approach for bringing out your individual writer's voice. By adding personality to the words, you create the correct mood and tone for your genre.

Word Choice and Tone

Your writing style and choice of words is all yours. But keep in mind the genre.

You may want to add beauty and thoughtfulness to your pages: In *A Beautiful Mind*, we literally get inside main character John Nash's mind by tracking the way he thinks:

```
Nash's gaze carries the floating geometry across
the crowd to find the rainbows on the bar top.
```

Or, you may want wording that suggests magic and surprises. In *The Lord of the Rings: The Fellowship of the Ring,* an action line reads:

```
Bilbo materializes as he pulls a plain gold ring
off of his finger. He finds Gandolph looming over
him.
```

Note that Bilbo doesn't just appear, he "materializes." Gandolph doesn't stand, he "looms."

Or, you may have the kind of scene direction that's as straightforward as its characters. At a key emotional point in *Little Miss Sunshine*, the action line simply reads:

```
Silence. Everyone avoids everyone else's eyes.
```

Expanding your scenes means choosing the words that stir up emotion in the reader. If this is a thriller, we should feel anxious. If this is a comedy, we should smile.

Jude Roth, a client of mine, has the amazing ability to write in almost any genre. For this reason, I asked her to take a script with a strong voice and adapt it to several different genres.

She chose the screenplay for *L.A. Confidential*. Here's the opening paragraph of the original script.

```
EXT. L.A. SKYLINE - SUNSET

Palm trees in silhouette against a cherry sky.
City lights twinkle. Los Angeles. A place where
anything is possible. A place where dreams come
true. As the sky darkens, triple-Klieg lights
begin to sweep back and forth.
```

From L.A. Confidential, *written by Brian Helgeland, from the novel by James Ellroy, 1997.*

"Palm trees in silhouette," "cherry sky," "lights twinkle," "a place where dreams come true." With this kind of word choice, the writer has gone out of his way to make us experience old Los Angeles at its heyday.

So, what if it was written as a different genre?

ACTION-ADVENTURE:

```
EXT. L.A. SKYLINE - SUNSET

A Maserati RACES along Mulholland Drive. High
above the glittering city lights of Los Angeles.

The car's speed arches the silhouetted palm trees
as it whips by. A BOB SEGER SONG blasts from
within.
```

Klieg lights sweep back and forth. The Maserati SWERVES just in time to miss SLAMMING into an oncoming pickup truck.

ANIMATION/CHILDREN:

EXT. L.A. SKYLINE - SUNSET

Palm trees sway under a red and pink sky. The city lights twinkle far, far below as the GOOD PEOPLE bustle with activity. In and out of toy stores. And arcades. And costume shops.

This is LITTLE ANGELES, the magical city where only kids are allowed. A place where dreams come true.

Just as the dark night comes a'knockin', thousands and thousands and thousands of Klieg lights begin to sweep back and forth, keeping daytime — and playtime — alive.

DRAMA:

EXT. L.A. SKYLINE - SUNSET

Palm trees stand proud in silhouette against a cherry sky. Lights glimmer in the sweeping city of Los Angeles. A place where anything is possible. A place where dreams come true.

But as the sky darkens, Klieg lights begin to sweep back and forth. Night in the city is a different matter altogether.

SUPERHERO:

EXT. L.A. SKYLINE - SUNSET

Palm trees sag in silhouette against a cherry sky. A few city lights blink peaceably until …

CRACK. SMASH. SPLAT!

SOMEONE — an evil someone — HURLS rocks at the street lights, sending glass shattering to the cement.

This is Los Angeles. A place where nothing good happens anymore. A place where dreams become nightmares.

BUT WAIT. As the sky darkens, TRIPLE KLIEG LIGHTS begin to sweep back and forth. What could it be? Who could it be? Is it? Yes, it is! It's STARLET GIRL!

COMEDY:

EXT. L.A. SKYLINE - SUNSET

Palm trees. Sparkling lights. This is L.A. A good place. A place where dreams come true. Unless, that is, you're …

NORBERT SCOWLER, the unluckiest scumbag to ever walk the earth. Just as Norbert galumphs by, a KLIEG LIGHT falls off a roof and knocks him out cold.

The end to just another run-of-the-mill day.

ROMANCE:

EXT. L.A. SKYLINE - SUNSET

Palm trees stand majestic in silhouette against a sumptuous cherry red sky. The city lights below quiver and announce a place where anything is possible. A place where dreams come true. Where love reigns supreme.

The most romantic city in the world. Los Angeles.

As the cashmere night descends, spotlights begin to sweep softly back and forth.

SCI-FI/FANTASY:

EXT. L.A. SKYLINE - SUNSET

TITLE: SOMETIME IN THE 22ND CENTURY

Chrome palm trees stand out against a black cherry sky. City lights blind.

Welcome to Los Angeles. A place where still anything is possible. A place where dreams come true.

The only catch. None of it is real.

As the sky darkens, triple-Klieg lights begin to sweep back and forth. Looking for no one. Illuminating nothing.

HORROR:

EXT. L.A. SKYLINE - SUNSET

Palm trees in silhouette against a blood cherry sky. City lights quiver frantically.

Los Angeles. A place where anything is possible. A place where dreams come true.

But not tonight.

As the sky darkens, triple-Klieg lights begin to sweep back and forth.

The MADMAN is on the run.

Genre rewrites by Jude Roth, 2008.

So, as you're expanding, feel free to let your voice come out and bring energy to the page. If it's too much, we can always scale you back in the rewrite. But, for now, play.

TAKE TEN:
ADD PERSONALITY

Working ten minutes at a time, use word choice to adjust the tone of your scenes and create the right mood.

1. COMEDY — Keep your descriptions straightforward, almost dry. Let the humor add the color.

2. THRILLER — Work down the page, building suspense moment by moment.

3. HORROR — Try out some poetry in your most horrific moments. It'll make your scenes even creepier.

4. SCI-FI — Work in descriptions of futuristic devices and new rules as they actually impact the story.

5. PERIOD PIECE — Point us to the emotional undercurrent in your scenes with loaded looks and whispered moments.

6. SUPERHERO — Give your scenes comic-book color by punctuating sounds and action moments.

7. ROMANCE — Work emotion into action. But don't feel you have to get too flowery. (They may stare a moment too long, but that stare doesn't have to "smolder.")

WHAT YOU'VE ACCOMPLISHED

By writing to the genre and putting your own stamp on your script, you've made it more involving and readable. The clearer your writing voice, the more executives and producers are going to want to hire you.

■ TEN-MINUTE CHAPTER REVIEW: THE FIRST DRAFT

1. Write a SPEED DRAFT by writing scenes only around the MAIN INTENTIONS.

2. DEVELOP STORY by adding TRIGGER SCENES and EMOTIONAL MOMENTS involving your supporting character and antagonist.

3. Make your script cinematic by writing a TEASER and strong SET PIECES.

4. Develop scenes by giving them a sense of PLACE, adding DIALOGUE, creating TONAL SHIFTS, bringing in NEW BEATS and using EMOTIONAL SCENE DIRECTION.

5. DIVIDE overly long scenes into two or more.

6. Replace talky scenes with scenes that SHOW what's taking place.

7. Use your unique WRITING VOICE to stay true to the TONE and GENRE.

CHAPTER 6

The Dialogue

Y ou were probably wondering when I'd get to this. Well, I purposely saved dialogue for this late in the book because I didn't want you worrying about every little line when you're simply trying to get your script finished.

Plus, so many new writers hang their script on their dialogue instead of allowing good lines to come naturally out of the action. Good thing you made choices about story and character first. Now that you've met those intentions, you can finally indulge in talk, allowing your characters to connect with a great monologue, a killer line, or one perfectly chosen word.

Verbal Agenda

When people converse — on-screen or off — they rarely just talk for talking's sake. Instead, they use dialogue to help them meet a goal or serve a particular *agenda*. Approaching dialogue with character agenda in mind can make your scenes more interesting right off the bat. Even the smallest "Hi, how are you?" becomes intriguing when served up with a big side order of *want*.

Think about a first date. In real life, the agenda might be simply to get to know someone and see if the other person is compatible. But, when you're watching a movie, you want more. After all, how much can you watch people exchange backstory, question the other person about what they do for a living, and see if they like the same music? It's painful enough when we have to do it in real life!

Giving the characters different agendas on the date will kick that dating scene up a notch.

Imagine that two characters are on a date, but …

He wants a promotion.
She wants a corporate secret.

He wants answers.
She wants publicity.

He wants to steal her diamond.
She wants to sleep with the waiter.

And so on.

TAKE TEN:
CHARACTER AGENDA IN DIALOGUE-DRIVEN SCENES

Go through your dialogue-driven scenes and define or revise the agenda of your characters. Try to focus on as many scenes as possible in your ten minutes of time.

SCENE _____

CHARACTER 1 WANTS _____

CHARACTER 2 WANTS _____

WHAT YOU'VE ACCOMPLISHED
A potentially humdrum scene has become more exciting as the dialogue drives toward a goal.

Verbal Strategy

So, now that we know what a character wants from a dialogue-driven scene, how do they achieve that goal without just asking for it? It would be "on the nose" and, frankly, pretty tacky for our guy to ask, "May I have your diamond, please?" And her reply to be, "After I sleep with the waiter."

So, instead of asking outright, characters use *verbal strategies* to help them meet their goal. And we do this in real life, too. Whether it's a bank loan or just a laugh, we verbally manipulate people to get what we want from them.

We…

JOKE
COMPLIMENT
SEDUCE

LIE
ARGUE
INTERROGATE
FLIRT
INSTRUCT
CONFESS
TELL THE TRUTH
USE SILENCE

And so much more.

So now imagine our daters are using verbal strategies to meet their competing agendas. For couple number one, we've already established that:

He wants a promotion.

She wants a corporate secret.

Now imagine that he *jokes* to get his promotion, and she *flirts* in an attempt to get her corporate secret. Or, he *confesses* to get his promotion and she *lies* to get her corporate secret. Now we not only have two competing agendas that make the date more interesting; we also have two competing verbal strategies.

End of the bad-date blues ... at least for the reader.

In the movie *Magnolia*, Gwenovier, a reporter, tries to get information from Frank, a dating guru. Frank's strategy constantly changes as he avoids the truth. Hers changes as well as she tries to get an answer to a pressing question:

Her strategy = inclusion

> GWENOVIER
> Let's talk more about your background --

His strategy = distraction

> FRANK
> Muffy -- coffee?

> GWENOVIER
> I'm confused about your past is the
> thing.

His strategy = interruption

>   FRANK
> Is that still lingering?
>
>   GWENOVIER
> -- just to clarify --
>
>   FRANK
> So boring, so useless --
>
>   GWENOVIER
> I would just want to clear some things
> up.

His strategy = instruction

>   FRANK
>   (Muffy delivers coffee)
> Thank you, Muffy. Funny thing is: This
> is an important element of "Seduce
> and Destroy" — "Facing the past is an
> important way in not making progress."
> That's something I tell my men over and
> over.
>
>   GWENOVIER
> This isn't meant --
>
>   FRANK
> -- and I try and teach the students to
> ask: What is it in aid of?
>
>   GWENOVIER
> Are you asking me that?
>
>   FRANK
> Yes.

Her strategy = play student

>   GWENOVIER
> Well, just trying to figure out who you
> are, and how you might have become --
>
>   FRANK
> In aid of what?
>
>   GWENOVIER
> I'm saying, Frank, in trying to figure
> out who you are --

His strategy = seducing

```
                    FRANK
     -- there's a lot more important things
     I'd like to put myself into --

                    GWENOVIER
     It's all important --

                    FRANK
     Not really.
```

From Magnolia, written by Paul Thomas Anderson, 1998.

⑩ TAKE TEN:
VERBAL STRATEGY

Go through your dialogue-driven scenes and define or revise the verbal strategy of your characters. Try to focus on as many scenes as possible in your ten minutes of time.

SCENE _____

CHARACTER 1 WANTS _____

VERBAL STRATEGY _____

CHARACTER 2 WANTS _____

VERBAL STRATEGY _____

WHAT YOU'VE ACCOMPLISHED
By using "verbal strategies," you've avoided boring "Q&A dialogue" in which characters simply ask questions and deliver information.

The Happy Lie. The Awful Truth.

Readers or audience members will often criticize a piece of dialogue as not feeling "real." In response, a writer might try to make the scene more "honest" by throwing in a piece of backstory, or worse, having a character actually saying out loud what he thinks or feels.

And all the while, he should be doing the opposite.

What's the best way to keep your dialogue honest? Let your characters lie.

We all deliver "happy lies" just to get through our day.

"Great to see you!"

"It's been too long!"

"You look great!"

"So do you!"

Imagine if these characters actually told the truth?

"God, you again!"

"I thought I'd finally gotten rid of you."

"You look like hell."

"Better than you."

Now, which is the way that people *really* talk to each other?

The act of telling the truth is so weird, in fact, that we refer to articulated expressions of feeling or truth as "on the nose."

Imagine if, after signing divorce papers, a character proclaims:

"I feel a mixture of relief and regret!"

Or what if a character approaches another at a party and says.

"You are very attractive. I'd like to have an affair with you!"

See? Weird.

But the great thing about all of this lying we have to do is that it makes for much more interesting movie dialogue. The more a character talks *around* the truth, the more fun it is for an audience to figure it out.

Ultimately, even the phrase "I love you" is so powerful and so uncomfortably honest that it takes an entire romantic comedy's two hours to get to it. And, even then, the other person may or may not feel the same way.

Here's a scene in which a smitten character's *agenda* is to express love and the not-so-smitten character's agenda is to deflect love. Smitten's *strategy* might be to tell the truth. But, Not-so-smitten can't do that without hurting Smitten's feelings.

So, Not-so-smitten tries ...

COMPLIMENTING

Smitten: I love you.

Not-so-smitten: I love that tie!

ARGUING

Smitten: I love you.

Not-so-smitten: No, you don't.

INTERROGATING

Smitten: I love you.

Not-so-smitten: What do you mean by that?

LYING

Smitten: I love you.

Not-so-smitten: I love you, too.

What scenes in your script would benefit from the happy lie? Is some of the movie magic missing because you're being too honest? Remember that characters don't always lie to be duplicitous. Sometimes they lie to …

Hide a secret.

Save someone's feelings.

Save themselves from negative consequences.

Protect someone from harm.

Attempt a surprise.

TAKE TEN:
LIE A LITTLE

Write or rewrite dialogue-driven scenes to show characters hiding the truth.

SCENE INVOLVING A LIE _____

WHAT THEY'RE LYING ABOUT _____

REASON FOR LYING _____

WHAT YOU'VE ACCOMPLISHED

Subtext, subtext, subtext! By forcing the reader or audience to discover the truth between the lines, you're holding their attention.

Dialogue As A Game

A movie scene is often a power game. And, when characters talk to each other, they're often using dialogue as a way to win. Even getting the last word implies a winner.

Often, great movie dialogue is literally written as a game. And that game makes the scene.

Through game-playing, a proposal becomes a tongue twister:

                    MOZART
        Iram em! Iram em!

                    CONSTANZE
        No, I'm not playing this game.

> MOZART
> No, this is serious. Say it backward.

> CONSTANZE
> No!

> MOZART
> Just say it — you'll see. It's very serious. Iram em! Iram em!

> CONSTANZE
> Iram — marry. Em — marry me!

From Amadeus, *written by Peter Schaffer, from his play, 1984.*

A playful conversation between mother and son — a "welcome home" game — reveals a painful subtext:

> LYNN
> Well, you know what I did today? I won the Pennsylvania Lottery in the morning. I quit my jobs. Ate a big picnic in the park with lots of chocolate mousse pie and then swam in the fountain all afternoon … What did you do?

> COLE
> I was picked first for kickball teams at recess. I hit a grand slam to win the game and everyone lifted me up on their shoulders and carried me around cheering.

From The Sixth Sense, *written by M. Night Shyamalan, 1999.*

A conversation between a terrorist and a cop is turned into a game show:

> HANS
> Ah, how nice of you to call. I assume you are our mysterious party crasher. You are most troublesome for a … security guard?

> MCCLANE
> BZZZ! Sorry, Hans, wrong guess. Would you like to go for Double Jeopardy, where the stakes are double and the scores really change?

From Die Hard, *written by Jeb Stuart with revisions by Steven E. de Souza, 1987, based on the novel* Nothing Lasts Forever *by Roderick Thorp.*

Here's a "before and after" example of a dialogue-driven scene written by writer Jessica St. James. The first version gives the information in a direct way.

Version 1

INT. GARREN'S APARTMENT - LATER

Garren's on the computer looking up Marilyn Monroe sites...

                      GARREN
So there's four main theories: 1.
The Mafia killed her for revenge
against the Kennedy's for their
crackdown on organized crime. 2.
Robert Kennedy, aided by Secret
Service and CIA agents killed her
because of her affair with JFK and
his chances of re-election. 3.
Her shrink did it because he was in
love with her. 4. Marilyn killed
herself, suicide.

                      TED
Internet equals fact, bro.

                      GARREN
No, these are generally accepted
theories-- maybe Krista relates to
Marilyn in one of these ways...

The second version uses a "game."

Version 2

INT. GARREN AND TED'S APARTMENT

Garren's on the computer, beside him a pot of coffee. He's
on a mission, hasn't even slept.

>   GARREN
>   Question: what are the four
>   generally accepted conspiracy
>   theories about the death of Marilyn
>   Monroe?

Ted punches at the air...

>   TED
>   Answer: Don't care, she wasn't
>   that hot.

>   GARREN
>   JFK thought she was hot...

>   TED
>   He was all up in her biznaz behind
>   the wife's back, right?

>   GARREN
>   Theory #1: Robert Kennedy, aided by
>   Secret Service and CIA agents
>   killed her because of her affair
>   with JFK and his chances of re-
>   election.

>   TED
>   Bros before hoes...

>   GARREN
>   Literally. The other theories?

                    TED
          Marilyn's still alive, living as a
          transvestite in Canada.

                    GARREN
          Generally accepted theories. Give
          you a hint: "In Sicily, women are
          more dangerous than shotguns."

                    TED
          Her godfather killed her?

                    GARREN
          Try again, Tony Soprano.

                    TED
          The mob.

                    GARREN
          Theory #2: The mob killed her for
          revenge against the Kennedy's for
          their tough crackdown on organized
          crime. Next?

                    TED
          What about like a jealous actress
          friend-- chicks are total piranhas.

                    GARREN
          Think male. Think secret keeper.

                    TED
          Her tax attorney?

                    GARREN
          Close. Theory #3: Her shrink.

                    TED
          A screwed up shrink.

                    GARREN
          Screwed up and in love with her.

Ted punches the air harder...

                    TED
          This-- whole thing-- is what's
          screwed up--

                    GARREN
          We're still missing the last
          theory...

                    TED
               (sarcastic)
          Oh my god, I just found my list of
          stuff I don't give a crap about--
          and it's so weird but that's #1.

Ted chucks the controller into the wall... Collapses onto
the floor...

                    TED (CONT'D)
          Theory #4: She killed herself.
          Suicide.

Garren nods, impressed.

                    TED (CONT'D)
          Why do you even care?!

                    GARREN
          What if Krista Boswell relates to
          Marilyn in one of those four ways?

From Project Monarch, *written by Jessica St. James, 2009.*

The first scene gets the information across effectively enough, but we've seen the "lecture and listen" approach to this kind of scene many times. The second scene educates *and* entertains. Like Ted, we find ourselves drawn into Garren's game. No matter how much Ted resists, he ultimately plays along, and he even makes the "winning" guess. And through this game, Garren makes his point, the audience gets the information, and we move forward with the story.

Whether it's literal or just a power play, a great way to bring new life to your dialogue-driven scenes is to find the game in your scene. Ask …

What's the Name of the Game?

It could be "Tell Me You Love Me Too." Or, "Give Me the Information." "Confess to the Crime," or "Remember Who I Am." For you, titling the game will help you remember the overall agenda of the game player — and what the scene is about.

Whose Game is It?

The character that starts this process of game-playing usually does so because he thinks he has the power. Interesting to see if he still has it by the end of the game.

How Do You Play?

Is the game played by making someone guess, by comparing stories, or by role-playing? Verbal strategy plays a big role here.

Who Wins the Game and How?

The person who starts the game doesn't always stay in control. Where does the power shift and why? Think of the winning character's winning move. Was it an unexpected piece of information? Perhaps it was a killer line that cut to the quick. Once it was uttered, well, "game over."

TAKE TEN:
CREATE A VERBAL GAME

WHAT'S THE NAME OF THE GAME? _____

WHO'S GAME IS IT? _____

HOW DO YOU PLAY? _____

WHO WINS THE GAME AND HOW? _____

WHAT YOU'VE ACCOMPLISHED

By writing a conversation as a game, you've added an engaging element that keeps the reader and audience guessing. You've also brought new depth to your relationships by exploiting the power dynamic.

Finding Character Voice

One of the most common mistakes for new writers is making all of the characters sound the same. It doesn't matter how clever the game is; if the reader/audience can't hear a difference in character voice, they'll eventually get bored.

So, here's a trick that may put your script through instant dialogue rehab: Cast your script.

I know, I know. You've heard other people tell you not to do this. But, hey, if you're writing a spec script for a current TV show, you have the voices of existing characters to work with, don't you? Why not give yourself that advantage with all of your projects?

Don't actually write the casting on the page, just cast it in your head with your dream cast. How would Robert DeNiro say the line? Glenn Close? Jack Black? Ellen Page? Hearing the voice of your dream cast will help you find the different cadence to their speech, the different pace, the different rhythms. And, surprisingly, it may even help you find the correct language for a character.

When imagining the low, gravelly voice of Clint Eastwood, for example, the line, "Don't pick up that gun," easily becomes "Go ahead, make my day."

Take ten minutes to be your own casting director and you may start to "hear" your characters in a way you didn't before.

TAKE TEN:
FIND CHARACTER VOICE THROUGH CASTING

Make a casting choice for each character. (Keep it in your head. Don't write it in your scene direction!):

MAIN CHARACTER PLAYED BY _____

SUPPORTING CHARACTER PLAYED BY _____

ANTAGONIST PLAYED BY _____

WHAT YOU'VE ACCOMPLISHED
By writing with an actor in mind, you write with a specific language, dialect and rhythm. When all of the characters are cast, your pages feel new.

Verbal Rules

In *Juno,* the main character had a tendency to joke and elaborate in fairly graphic terms. Yet her boyfriend, Bleeker, was a one-sentence answerer. Vanessa, the woman she planned to give her baby to, was a bit of a teacher and explainer, while Vanessa's husband, Mark, shared Juno's language of music. Each of them had verbal rules for how they talked and what they referenced. Finding your characters' own verbal rules will instantly help your script.

Does your main character always joke around? Does his friend always swear? Does his love interest constantly reference movies or music? Does his boss quote statistics? A strong *verbal rule* can be the thing that makes a character stand out for an audience and makes for "actor bait" when casting.

TAKE TEN:
CREATE VERBAL RULES

MAIN CHARACTER VERBAL RULE _____

SUPPORTING CHARACTER VERBAL RULE _____

ANTAGONIST VERBAL RULE _____

WHAT YOU'VE ACCOMPLISHED
You've strengthened your characters by being specific about their verbal rhythms and language.

■ TEN-MINUTE CHAPTER REVIEW:
THE DIALOGUE

1. Determine the AGENDA of each character in your dialogue-driven scenes. What do they want from the conversation?

2. Create a verbal STRATEGY for meeting that agenda.

3. In order to prevent being too "on the nose," allow your characters to LIE.

4. Rev up your dialogue-driven scenes by turning them into GAMES.

5. Discover character VOICE through pretend CASTING.

6. Invent VERBAL RULES for your characters.

CHAPTER 7

The Rewrite

You've heard it from others, and you're going to hear it from me too: The secret to writing is rewriting. And just the idea of it gives most people a massive headache.

I'm with you. I wrote the first draft of this book years ago, made excuses forever, then finally found the one pass I needed to finish the darn thing. With two children, a consulting business, and teaching commitments, I found that those rewrite moments only happened in stolen chunks of time. Yet, once I made a choice about *which* rewrite pass I needed, those chunks were sufficient for getting the work done.

So here are a few tools and exercises to help you face the rewrite. The goal here is to find the one thing that will turn your script around; the one rewrite *pass* that will make it work. When you find it, spend as many ten-minute chunks as needed rewriting your script with that fix in mind. One hour — six ten-minute chunks — could make a huge difference.

We're going to cover a number of potential rewrite "passes" on your script. We'll start large scale, looking at the big-picture issues, then move in closer and closer until we're dealing with the minutia of the script. Don't feel you have to do every rewrite pass in every way. This chapter merely gives you the tools you need to test elements of your script and make them better if needed.

The Concept Pass

Let's pull back and really look at your script, starting from your main idea. When writing the first draft, you first figured out your big idea — your concept — and built your story off of that. Remember what a great idea that was? Well, is it still there?

If a reader implies that he didn't "get" your script, or understand why it's movie-worthy, it may be because your script just isn't honoring its own concept. You put a great idea out there ... and then backed off from it.

Your premise, for example, might be that a man can fly. If you don't have some major flying moments, however, or show how flying impacts his life, you're wasting your high concept.

Even something that doesn't have a high concept is best when it does justice to its main idea. *Slumdog Millionaire* explored many issues, covered several years, and took its main character on a series of adventures. But it always came back to its central premise: "What if the experiences of a slum kid's life help him to answer questions on a million-dollar game show?"

Frost/Nixon is a small movie about a tiny event: a post-Watergate interview between Nixon and David Frost. Yet we always get a sense of the importance of the event because the entire movie is built around the question, "What if the reputations of a TV journalist and an ex-President could be made or broken with one televised interview?"

The movie never backs off from its concept, and, as a result, the stakes are always out there and the tension remains high.

Here are a few ways to keep the idea front and center:

Tease the Concept

You may be saving the big idea for the end of act one, but those early pages could at least prep the audience for it. Perhaps a tonal teaser? Perhaps something mystical or supernatural if the big idea is going to go that way? It could even be that we see something in a character's behavior that suggests he needs to learn a lesson. Think about movies like *Liar Liar* and *Groundhog Day*. Those characters were so flawed in such specific ways that we were prepped for the big, high-concept lesson that followed.

Set the Concept by the Act Break

Maybe people aren't "getting" your idea, because you're not defining it at the end of Act 1. It's OK to be direct every once in a while. Clearly articulating what happens to a character and what he needs to do about it is not the same as being "on the nose."

Write Concept-specific Set Pieces

Let's go back to that guy who can fly. His world is the sky. What cool, visual sky-specific thing happens up there? If your concept has thrown your MC into a new arena, by all means take advantage of that and give us a set piece we've never seen before!

Use the Concept to Spark a Midpoint Event

If the guy who can fly rarely keeps his feet on the ground, his home life might suffer, and this could result in an emotional midpoint event. If the guy who can fly is spotted in the air by his nemesis and his secret is revealed to the world, the consequences could result in an even bigger midpoint event. If the guy who can fly slams into a tree and breaks his leg, there's yet another midpoint event to deal with. Bottom line: Your big idea is the catalyst for the midpoint event. If the complication in the middle of your movie has nothing to do with your central premise, that could be the problem.

Test the Concept in Act 3

Actually, a test of the concept could and should happen at other times in your script, but the big test may come at script's end. Does the antagonist have a fly-off with our MC? Does the MC have to prove to his loved one that flying is something they can both live with for the rest of their lives? Don't just drop your big idea at the end of the movie, use it as your final hurdle!

Make Peace With Your Concept at Script's End

The big idea fed your movie story. It was experimented with, exploited, and tested. At script's end, make sure that we see a way that the concept has been fully realized. Everything doesn't have to end happily ever after, but if there's a hanging thread, the reader may pass and audiences will grumble. *Eternal Sunshine of the Spotless Mind* was a high-concept movie that put its "erasing memories" concept through its paces. It was fully tried and tested by the end of the script, and its concept was fully realized. But it didn't feel wrapped with a bow.

In the exercise below, you'll put your script through a "concept test," making sure that your big idea is hit at key points in your screenplay. Where your script fails to pass the test, review. And, if needed, revise!

⑩ TAKE TEN:
CONCEPT TEST

I tease the concept in the opening pages in this way _____ .

I articulate the concept at the end of Act 1 in this way _____ .

In Act 2, I use set pieces to show the concept at work in this way _____ .

I use the concept to spark a midpoint event in this way _____ .

I test the concept in Act 3 in this way _____ .

At script's end, the concept is fully realized in this way _____ .

WHAT YOU'VE ACCOMPLISHED
By returning to the idea that inspired you to write in the first place, you've focused your script and emphasized its uniqueness.

The Structure Pass

Every writer dreads hearing that they may need a structural pass, because they think it means a page-one rewrite. Not necessarily. Go back to the tools you used to develop your first draft. They'll help you "see" your big picture. Use them to check your structure, or to remap the story.

Rewriting the Structure Sheet

Remember that the structure sheet is only four columns separating your script into four act segments, with a big "reveal" for each segment and key events that build up to those twists. Look at the structure sheet now and compare it with your existing draft. Are you hitting your act breaks where you said you would? Are you including the events you expected to? It's expected that your script will be better than your original structure sheet. But, if the original structure sheet looks tighter or more exciting than your screenplay, *that's* the rewrite you need to make!

The structure sheet also allows you the opportunity to test out some structural rewrites, without getting overwhelmed by an unexpected *ripple effect*.

Let's say we were writing a story about Rosa Parks. We all know what event we'd have to include to tell her story correctly: Rosa refusing to give up her bus seat to a white man. Let's call this the *defiant event*. The decision about where we put this event, however, completely alters the structure.

Let's say we've written the moment of defiance to come at the end of the movie in Act 3. Then, the script might be structured like a classic biopic, where we witness events in Rosa's childhood, the relationships she forms in adulthood, her dissatisfaction as racism affects her life, and finally, her proud moment of defiance.

childhood	adulthood	race obstacles	defiance
ACT 1	ACT 2A	ACT 2B	ACT 3

But what if we finished our script and the biopic structure made the story feel too slow? What if we wanted a faster pace?

Just use the structure sheet to move the event back a bit, and see what happens.

childhood	adulthood / race obstacles	defiance	_____?_____
ACT 1	ACT 2A	ACT 2B	ACT 3

Moving this event back shows us that we have to combine the events in Act 2A and 2B into one segment. In order to do this, we'll go into the script, pluck out those moments — emotional or physical — that might be repeating themselves, then compress the rest into one segment.

Using the structure sheet to move the event has also shown us where there will be a potential story gap: Act 3.

This is an opportunity, not a problem, as it allows us room for more story. Springing off of the defiant event, we can now show the personal and political consequences for Rosa Parks. Doing so may make the story bigger and richer. Instead of spending an entire story dramatizing a life leading up to an event, we've shown the before and after in one movie. And all of this was done by moving some words on a four-column sheet. Our new movie:

childhood	adulthood / race obstacles	defiance	consequences
ACT 1	ACT 2A	ACT 2B	ACT 3

TAKE TEN:
RESTRUCTURE PART 1

Take ten minutes to change your structure sheet in order to test new structural choices for your screenplay.

1. Tighten or broaden your script by moving a key event on your structure sheet.

2. Once the event is moved, note where you'll need to compress story beats.

3. Once the event is moved, note where you'll also need to add story.

TAKE TEN:
RESTRUCTURE PART 2

Using your structure sheet as a guide, take ten minutes per scene or sequence to make the story choices you need to create your new structure.

1. Go into your script and compress events by weeding out emotional or physical moments that repeat themselves.

2. Fill the story holes created by your new structure by adding setup that may now be missing or consequences that may not be there.

WHAT YOU'VE ACCOMPLISHED

A structural rewrite is a large rewrite, but your structure sheet has helped you focus on just what needs to be compressed and what needs to be expanded. Taking the time to fix your structure — if that's the pass it needs — can be the best thing you do for your script.

The Story Pass

Is this draft telling the story you want to tell? Are readers leaving it confused and thinking it's about something it's not? Sometimes, no matter how perfectly formatted, well-structured or nicely worded a script is, there are times when the story just doesn't do it for the reader. It should! The idea is there. The characters are well-realized. The scene direction is expertly crafted, etc. But the story itself ... well, it's just not coming together.

Sometimes, the writing of the script can actually cause you to meander in your storytelling or bury key pieces of information. So, this would be a good place to do a *beat check* to clarify your story and see where and when it slipped through the cracks.

We're going to start by examining the cause, effect, emotion, and need of every sequence.

 ### TEN-MINUTE LECTURE:

CAUSE AND EFFECT STORYTELLING

The event and consequences of a sequence create a CAUSE and EFFECT story. And every cause and effect story results in a new EMOTION experienced by the MC. And every new emotion creates a NEED to move on to the next sequence.

Bottom line: Event leads *to* consequences, *which create* emotion, *inciting* need.

END OF LECTURE

By testing cause and effect per sequence we're making sure that there's a clear and effective story line.

Rather than read the entire script and over analyze in the process, we're going to use our old *beat sheet* as a guide. If, in the writing of your script, your sequences have changed radically, go back into the beat sheet to revise or mark the beginning and end of the actual beats in your current script.

 ## TAKE TEN:
BEAT CHECK

Moving through your beat sheet, clarify the "cause and effect" within the sequence. Make sure that each beat focuses on an event, the physical consequences of that event, the emotion that follows, and the need that it incites.

BEAT 1: Cause _____
event that ignites a problem

Effect _____
physical consequences

Emotion _____
new feelings

Need _____
motivation to move to next sequence

BEAT 2: Cause _____
event that ignites a problem

Effect _____
physical consequences

Emotion _____
new feelings

Need _____
motivation to move to next sequence

BEAT 3: Cause _____
event that ignites a problem

Effect _____
physical consequences

Emotion _____
new feelings

Need _____
motivation to move to next sequence

BEAT 4: Cause _____
event that ignites a problem

Effect _____
physical consequences

Emotion _____
new feelings

Need _____
motivation to move to next sequence

BEAT 5: Cause _____
event that ignites a problem

Effect _____
physical consequences

Emotion _____
new feelings

Need _____
motivation to move to next sequence

BEAT 6: Cause _____
event that ignites a problem

Effect _____
physical consequences

Emotion _____
new feelings

Need _____
motivation to move to next sequence

BEAT 7: Cause _____
event that ignites a problem

Effect _____
physical consequences

Emotion _____
new feelings

Need _____
motivation to move to next sequence

BEAT 8: Cause _____
event that ignites a problem

Effect _____
physical consequences

Emotion _____
new feelings

Need _____
motivation to move to next sequence

WHAT YOU'VE ACCOMPLISHED
You've homed in on the areas of story that are weak. And you've done so without tearing your entire script apart.

Tighten Story by Moving Backward

You may have found that this linear way of writing or checking story causes you to get stuck in the same places every time. I hear you. Straightforward storytelling can be boring sometimes and doesn't work for everyone. So, why not test your story by moving backward instead?

First, here's a quick refresher of a suggested eight-sequence structure (moving forward):

1. CHARACTER FLAW triggers CONFLICT
2. CONFLICT triggers PROBLEM
3. PROBLEM triggers STRATEGY
4. STRATEGY triggers EMOTIONAL EVENT
5. EMOTIONAL EVENT triggers MAJOR ACTION
6. MAJOR ACTION triggers MISSTEP
7. MISSTEP triggers BATTLE
8. BATTLE triggers FINAL CHALLENGE

Using this structure, we can actually work backward to test your story and see if it's as tight and interesting as you intended.

TAKE TEN:
BACKWARD BEAT CHECK

Work backward through each beat to test for cause and effect storytelling, asking the following questions:

8. What's the final emotional or physical challenge from an antagonistic force?

7. What victorious battle incited this final challenge?

6. What misstep occurred that created a need for that battle?

5. What major action, taken by the main character, resulted in the misstep?

4. What emotional event led the main character to take a major action?

3. What attempt at strategy triggered an emotional event for the main character?

2. What problem occurred that created the need for the strategy?

1. What flaw-driven conflict created the problem?

WHAT YOU'VE ACCOMPLISHED

By telling your story back to front, you've strengthened and clarified the cause and effect connections.

I applied a backward beat check to *Slumdog Millionaire*, and it held up quite well. In doing so, I was also surprised to discover how much the relationship between the brothers drives the movie:

EXAMPLE: BACKWARD BEAT CHECK FOR SLUMDOG MILLIONAIRE

8. What's the final emotional or physical challenge from an antagonistic force?

He must get the answer to the Three Musketeers question and, in doing so, get the money and the girl.

7. What victorious battle incited this final challenge?

He guessed all but one of the questions correctly on "Who Wants to Be A Millionaire."

6. What misstep occurred that created a need for that battle?

He lost the girl to the bad guys and hoped getting on the show would get her attention.

5. What major action, taken by the main character, resulted in the misstep?

He joined with his brother, who was really involved with the bad guys and wanted his girl.

4. What emotional event led the main character to take a major action?
The brothers bonded as they escaped slavers and poverty together.

3. What attempt at strategy triggered an emotional event for the main character?
They attempted to survive by running away, conning, stealing, lying.

2. What problem occurred that created the need for the strategy?
Orphaned and set loose in the world with nothing, he must join with his brother.

1. What flaw-driven conflict created the problem?
He follows his brother, though the brother humiliates him in front of his pop star idol.

Subplots, Choices and Revelations
Below, you'll find some other general story passes that can take your script to the next level. Focusing on just one of these passes will change your story, so choose well!

TAKE TEN:
THE SUBPLOT REWRITE

In your scene list, build or expand on a subplot by adding one or two key scenes per sequence.

WHAT YOU'VE ACCOMPLISHED
You've fleshed-out your story and potentially given it the extra layer of story that it needed.

TAKE TEN:
THE CHOICE REWRITE

Convey a character's emotional turning point by showing a choice being made. Do your pages show one action being taken over another?

WHAT YOU'VE ACCOMPLISHED
A movie is simply a set of choices. By showing the moments where those choices are being made, you've let the audience in on key turning points.

TAKE TEN:
THE REVELATION REWRITE

If your turning point hinges on a revelation, *how* does the character get there? Does she simply remember? If so, try to replace that moment with activity; something *happens* that triggers the memory. Is she told the information? If so, replace with discovery. Use clues, skills, etc.

WHAT YOU'VE ACCOMPLISHED
You're showing, not telling. And you're building the story by leading us to the big reveal, step-by-step.

TAKE TEN:
THE PAYOFF REWRITE

Remember those running actions, themes and jokes. Don't forget those payoffs! Go through your script. Wherever you are setting up new information about the character, find the "matching" scene in which you pay it off. If there is no matching scene, write one, or cut the information entirely.

WHAT YOU'VE ACCOMPLISHED
You're rebuilding story by mining the goodies in your own script. You don't have to make anything up, because it's all there!

The Scene Rewrite

So now we're getting to the nitty-gritty: The rewrite that tackles the scenes head-on. Writers tend to finesse the smaller moments in a scene first, but sometimes it's the big-picture questions that need to be asked initially. That's why we're going to start with the *story* the scenes are telling, then move on to better ways to tell that story.

Scenes tell stories. On their own, they tell one story. Side-by-side, they tell another. Reversed in order, yet another. This following checklist asks you questions that help you decide whether to keep, lose or spiff up a scene.

TAKE TEN:
SCENE STORY TEST
(a.k.a. "Keep, Lose, or Spiff Up")

Be honest with yourself as you move through this list. Keep scenes that you feel cover one or more of these areas. Spiff up scenes that need to prove their worth. Lose scenes that don't add to the story in one of these ways:

1. Is the scene giving new information?

2. Is the scene covering a new emotion?

3. Is the scene holding a sequence together?

4. Does the scene contain a memorable set piece that also drives story?

5. Does the scene give the audience new insight?

6. Is the scene in the right place?

7. Does the scene work around its main intentions?

8. Does the scene tell its own story?

WHAT YOU'VE ACCOMPLISHED
You've done the hard job of evaluating a scene's worth in your script. Even if you love a scene, it may be weighing down your script or misleading the reader. The story may benefit if that scene is fixed or deleted.

Scenes Tell Their Own Story

When consulting with writers, I often find myself asking them this question about their scenes: "What story do you want to tell here?"

The scene itself may highlight a cool character rule, or show off a killer set piece, but if the reader or audience doesn't pick up on the *story* of the scene, it can still leave them flat.

So, I put it to you: If a scene is being misread, or the main point isn't being understood, or someone got a completely different understanding of the scene than you intended, ask yourself that question and edit or rewrite accordingly. If you need a reminder of your original intentions for the scene, review your scene list or speed draft.

The Fresh Take

Though it's extremely simple, finding the "fresh take" of your scene is, in my opinion, one the best rewrites that you can make. Often the genre of a script forces us to write a stock scene. After all, we can't have a courtroom thriller without a trial, a romantic comedy without a kiss, or a sports movie without a championship game. But that doesn't mean that your trial, kiss and game have to look, sound, or act like everyone else's trial, kiss and game.

Let's take an interrogation scene as our example. We tend to always see the same things in these kinds of scenes: A cold room, a dangling lightbulb, a two-way mirror. Realizing this, we could simply change the *setting* to find our fresh take. Maybe the interrogation could happen in a bathroom or on a bus or in an amusement park?

In an interrogation scene, we also tend to meet the same *characters*: cop and suspect. But what if we make this a scene between kids and parents? Cab driver and little old lady? Waitress and customer? Another fresh take!

Finally, we can pretty much predict the course of the *dialogue* in stock interrogation scenes. The cop accuses. The suspect denies. But what if the suspect questioned the cop? What if the cop confessed to a crime? What if the cop spoke in riddles? What if the suspect broke into song?

In the movie *Fargo*, an interrogation scene gets a fresh character take in that Marge, the cop, is extremely pregnant and Jerry, her inept suspect, runs a car dealership. The setting is different as the interrogation happens in Jerry's office, and the dialogue gets our attention because of its hilarious politeness. When Jerry gets flustered he says "darn" and "heck!" When Marge chastises him, it's to remind him that "you have no call to get snippy with me."

In the movie *Brick*, the dialogue is purposely written with a touch of crime-drama cliché, but the fresh take here is that our hard-boiled interrogation takes place in a principal's office:

PRINCIPAL: You've helped this office out before.
BRENDAN: No. I gave you Jerr to see him eaten,
not to see you fed.
PRINCIPAL: Fine, and well put.
BRENDAN: Accelerated English. Mrs. Kasprzyk.

From Brick, *written by Rian Johnson, 2005.*

Whether we look at this as a fresh take on the character and settings of a traditionally stock interrogation scene, or a fresh take on the dialogue of a stock principal/ student scene, the point is the same. We pay attention to it because it's doing something different.

TAKE TEN:
FIND A FRESH TAKE

Rewrite a stock scene by finding a fresh take. Try one of the different approaches below.

STOCK SCENE _____

FRESH TAKE ON SETTING _____

FRESH TAKE ON CHARACTER _____

FRESH TAKE ON DIALOGUE _____

WHAT YOU'VE ACCOMPLISHED
You've spun your potentially stock scene in a new way. Though it covers a necessary genre beat, no one will read your script and say, "I've seen that before."

The Character Rewrite

Sometimes, no matter how much work you've put into your story, what you really need is a new approach to character. Since your main character drives your story, it's worth a hard look to see if this is the rewrite pass you need.

Below, you'll find several ways to change your characters or give them a boost. I want to give you as many options as possible, so you may find that some of the approaches contradict each other. Pick the one that works best for *your* character and project.

Character Focus

Maybe your MC is just fine, but she's getting lost in her own movie. She doesn't have to be overly pushy or grab attention to get noticed. You simply have to point the camera at her by putting her more in focus.

(10) TAKE TEN:
PUT FOCUS ON YOUR MC

Find those scenes where your MC needs more attention and try the following:

1. CHARACTER REACTS: Even if she isn't involved in the central activity of the scene, show her reaction to it through her facial expressions. The camera will always come back to her that way.

2. CHARACTER ENDS SCENE: Button scenes with an MC activity or emotion.

3. CHARACTER LEADS: In a movie where your MC is surrounded by an ensemble, rework scenes in the second half of your movie so that she appears to take the lead. Let her make a discovery, come up with a new idea, etc.

4. CHARACTER SOLVES PROBLEM: Your MC doesn't have to save the day in every way at script's end. That's why she's amassed a bunch of helpers and supporting characters. But do give her at least one key move.

WHAT YOU'VE ACCOMPLISHED

You've brought your MC to the front and center and, in the process, given her the boost she may have needed.

Character Empathy — Dial Him Down

Trying hard to get the reader on the side of your main character? Doing everything you can to show him holding babies and saving cats? Well, here's some news that may give you some relief. Your job is not to make your main character likeable. Your job is to make him empathetic. There's a big difference.

The best tip I can give you is to stop trying. You know that guy at the party who wants to make everyone like him? He cracks jokes, asserts himself into conversations, and generally makes himself the center of attention. We *hate* him, right? So, don't make your character that guy. He doesn't have to get the punch line in your scene. He doesn't have to be the guy who always makes the big move, either.

Think about the traditional leading man. In the old days he was played by quiet square-jawed guys like Gary Cooper. Currently he's played by quiet, square-jawed guys like George Clooney. This leading man is the calm force in the middle of a storm; the straight man while everyone around him plays class clown.

Keep focus on your main character. But let other characters be drawn to him. He doesn't have to beg for attention.

TAKE TEN:
DIAL DOWN YOUR MC

Find those scenes where your MC needs to be more of an "everyman" and try one of the following suggestions:

1. Take away any lecturing or speechmaking on his part and replace with a wise comment.

2. Pump up the craziness around him, whether it's an extreme event or eccentric characters.

3. Focus on his clear, calm reaction to these moments. Is he amused? Befuddled?

4. Ground your character by limiting his actions. Have him make one strong choice in the scene rather than engage in small pieces of "business."

WHAT YOU'VE ACCOMPLISHED
"Less is more" has extended to your MC as well. By pulling back on your MC rather than forcing us to like him, you've created a mystery that makes him the most charismatic person in the room.

Character Definition — Make Him Worse

If this is a high-concept movie, you've probably put your character into an impossible situation. Good! He's instantly sympathetic. After all, how could you not sympathize with someone who's put in an extreme situation, with little help, against all odds!

But, if you now put a likeable person in an extreme situation, he's going to come across as a victim. It's not funny; it's just sad. The solution? Make him bad! Pump up his flaw. Give him a reason to have to go through hell in the first place! Larry David in *Curb Your Enthusiasm* is selfish, cheap, and socially awkward, but the writer/improvisers commit to his awfulness, and, as a result, the show is always entertaining.

Remember that some of the greatest main characters are utter jerks. Scrooge, the weatherman in *Groundhog Day*, the coach from *The Bad News Bears,* and even Elle Woods from *Legally Blonde* were all extremely flawed characters initially. But, when they are haunted by ghosts, forced to repeat the same day over and over again, given a losing little league team, or getting dumped by a boyfriend, we couldn't help but feel a little sorry for them.

Don't worry; if this is a movie, we'll eventually like your main character even if he is super-flawed. After all, he's going to have to change his ways if he wants to actually get out of his situation. Scrooge appreciates Christmas, the weatherman connects with others, the coach learns about teamwork, and Elle realizes she has a brain.

So go ahead: Make your main character rotten if that's what your script needs. If you do, the road ahead may be more entertaining.

TAKE TEN:
MAKE YOUR MAIN CHARACTER BAD

Find those scenes where your MC needs to be more flawed and try one of the following suggestions:

1. In Act 1, write in an amusingly selfish choice. Think of something you would never do (but wish you could).

2. In Act 2A, pump up an annoying character rule, something that can't be ignored.

3. In Act 2B, show the fun in the MC's terribleness by making his rotten qualities useful or entertaining to someone else.

4. In Act 3, clearly break the MC's annoying character rule to show a real change.

WHAT YOU'VE ACCOMPLISHED

You've created a memorable MC by committing to the trait that makes him most interesting. You've also strengthened your story by making it difficult for the MC to learn. The more unlikely he is to change, the more surprised we'll be at script's end when he actually does.

Character Specificity — Gender and Ethnicity

The film business is an industry about imagination, but when it comes to putting new faces in lead roles, it doesn't have any. So don't wait for change; write your lead as a woman. Or give your main character a specific ethnicity we haven't seen enough of on-screen. And don't be coy about it either. There's that first instinct to make a character as generic as possible. But, experiences define your characters and make them more interesting. If a character has experienced racism in his life, for example, he'll bring that into the scene with him.

In the movie *Philadelphia,* attorney Joe Miller overcomes his fears and reaches out to help when he sees HIV-positive Andrew Beckett being discriminated against in a library. Without having to say anything about it, we know that Joe, an African-American, has an understanding of Andrew's situation.

And, while one doesn't want to overly emphasize every traditionally female trait, ignoring the fact that your lead is a woman is also depriving your script of another layer. *The Silence of the Lambs* was a thriller first and foremost, but it also used the fact that it was female-driven to create unique obstacles. Clarice has to put up with a jail warden's advances before she can get to Hannibal Lecter. Lecter tries to seduce her by guessing her perfume, and her boss purposely alienates her in front of a group of men in order to get more information out of a local sheriff.

Gender-specific rules also create a fresh take on a fight scene in *Kill Bill.* Here "The Bride" fights off one of her female former colleagues in a kitchen. Their tools: kitchen knives and frying pans. When the fight reaches the living room, it's an all-out war until … a school bus pulls up.

TAKE TEN:
APPLY ETHNICITY AND GENDER

Use your MC's experiences with being a person of color, an ethnic minority or a woman to bring something new to a scene.

1. Show different rules of behavior for the MC when she's a face in the crowd vs. when she sticks out as the "other."

2. Commit to a point of view from the people around her. In which environment is she accepted? In which environment is she rejected?

3. Add emotional and physical obstacles that would naturally be part of that person's experience. Racism, sexism, etc.

4. Take the opposite tack and show the MC's ease in society or unwillingness to define herself by ethnicity or gender.

WHAT YOU'VE ACCOMPLISHED
Rather than making a character intentionally generic, you've made her more interesting by mining her experiences.

Character Stereotype — Working With It

So, as you can see, I'm of the "use it, don't lose it" school of thought when it comes to the experiential differences in characters. Working with those differences deepens the character and gives the script something unique.

And then there are the *perceived* differences when it comes to race, ethnicity and gender, assumptions about who someone is just because of how she looks or her ethnic background. Rather than fight these natural biases in the reader and audience, often the smart way to go is simply to play with perceptions by turning those stereotypes into skills.

In a class I teach called "Beyond The Chick Flick," I ask the students to shout out all of the negative things that are said about women. The list lengthens frighteningly quickly. They shout out: "Timid, bitchy, emotional, gossipy!" And more.

Well, you could ignore stereotype completely by creating a female character that was none of the above, *or* you could turn each of these *perceived* flaws into skills.

timid = cautious

bitchy = emotionally strong

emotional = empathetic

gossipy = communicator

In *The Closer*, Brenda's Southern, genteel nature is exactly the tool she uses to get a criminal's defenses down before reducing them to an emotional puddle. In *Erin Brockovich*, Erin's willingness to use her physical assets helps her obtain useful files. In *Clueless*, Cher Horowitz's busybody personality makes her a natural matchmaker. In *Aliens*, Ripley's "maternal instincts" cut the fat of having to set up exactly *why* she would fight so hard to protect a little girl.

TAKE TEN:
BEAT STEREOTYPE BY USING IT

List the stereotypes that might be attributed to a character. Then turn each stereotype into a skill.

CHARACTER _____
main character, supporting, other

STEREOTYPE _____
judgment made by others

SKILL _____
positive spin on the stereotype

SCENE _____
rewritten, using new skill

WHAT YOU'VE ACCOMPLISHED
You've made lemonade out of lemons by using stereotype to the character's advantage.

Character Stereotype — Writing Against It

And then there are the characters that completely surprise us by doing the opposite of what we'd think they'd do.

In *Juno,* the writer chooses to spin every single character. We see the characters, we naturally judge the characters, and then the writer goes a *completely different way* with them:

Character: Pregnant teenager
Stereotype: Uneducated. Sense of shame about her condition.
Script reality: Super-articulate. Sense of wonder about her condition.

Character: Cheerleader best friend.
Stereotype: Unsupportive. Embarrassed by friend.
Script reality: Emotionally supportive, helpful.

Character: Boyfriend
Stereotype: Womanizer. Uncaring.
Script reality: Seduced by Juno. Friendly and supportive.

Character: Parents
Stereotype: Angry and ashamed.
Script reality: Resigned and amused.

Maybe your character isn't working because you've fallen into the trap of stereotype yourself. This would be your opportunity to turn that around.

TAKE TEN:
BEAT STEREOTYPE BY PLAYING AGAINST IT

List the stereotypes that might be attributed to a character. Then, create a fresh "script reality."

CHARACTER: _____

STEREOTYPE: _____

SCRIPT REALITY: _____

SCENE REWRITE: _____

WHAT YOU'VE ACCOMPLISHED
You've created a fresh take on a character ... or, potentially, an entire cast of characters. This could be the hook that sells the movie!

Character Agenda and Strategy

You may have just put your characters through the ringer in terms of who they are, but what they're doing in a scene is equally important. Onscreen, we "get" characters through their actions and the choices they make. A great way to strengthen those actions and to show your characters making clear choices is to remember their *agenda* (what they want) and *strategy* (their way of getting it).

Sometimes, we forget that even the most minor character in a scene wants something. The waitress in a diner scene, for example, might want a large tip or she might want to just get through her day.

Though there are a number of characters in the movie *Crash*, the writers are extremely clear about what each character wants in a scene and how he or she intends to get it. In one scene, characters are pushed to a breaking point when a cop unfairly pulls over an African American couple and then proceeds to harass them.

Tensions rise and the action escalates as those competing agendas and strategies clash:

COP'S AGENDA: He wants to feel powerful.
COP'S STRATEGY: He uses police procedure as a way to sexually harass the wife.

WIFE'S AGENDA: She wants to go home.
WIFE'S STRATEGY: She verbally attacks and physically resists the cop.

HUSBAND'S AGENDA: He wants to protect his wife.
HUSBAND'S STRATEGY: He acquiesces and apologizes to the cop.

ROOKIE PARTNER'S AGENDA: He wants to get through it all quickly.
ROOKIE PARTNER'S STRATEGY: He stands by and does nothing to stop the cop.

It's a short scene, but it's powerful, and each character leaves it changed by the experience. Our couple — happy when they're first pulled over — has been torn apart by the scene's end.

Competing agendas and strategies also make for great comedy, as well. Think about *The Office.* Each character commits to his or her self-centered agenda per scene. One may want a promotion. One may want a date. One may want to make the office laugh. And those competing agendas and strategies result in hilarious moments of over-the-top conflict every week.

TAKE TEN:
CHARACTER AGENDA AND STRATEGY

Fill in these blanks for *every* character in a scene (no matter how minor):

Character wants _____ .
                                    agenda

Intends to get it by _____ .
                                    strategy

WHAT YOU'VE ACCOMPLISHED
By going through your script and simply making better use of a character's agenda and strategy, you've revived flat scenes and brought out strong personal moments.

The Dialogue Pass

At the time that I'm writing this, the H1N1 virus is sweeping the country. Last week, I received a letter from my kids' elementary school telling me that "now is the time to panic." So I did. I mean, I read a lot of end-of-the-world scripts, and if my school is telling me that now's the time to panic, I'm listening! It wasn't until the next day that they corrected the letter with *another* letter saying that they meant to write "now is the time NOT to panic."

All this to say that one word alone can change *everything*.

When rewriting the dialogue of your script, you'll find that it's sometimes the smallest change — a deleted word or an additional line — that completely changes a scene. Here we'll explore a number of ways to finesse the dialogue in your scenes and make what's said — or not said — a compelling read.

Avoiding Unnecessary Exposition

Exposition gets a bad rap. It's unavoidable in a script, since the job of the writer is to deliver information to the audience. The problem is that writers can go overboard in telling things that *should be shown*, *were just shown*, or are *about to be shown*. The result is dialogue that sounds false.

A great way to minimize this kind of "on the nose" exposition is to come from a place of knowledge in your scenes. Two sisters who just experienced the death of their mother aren't going to tell each other that the mother just died. They know. So, how do they tell *us*, the audience, without talking about it in a way that doesn't ring true?

In class, I asked my students to write a dialogue between two such sisters in which they spoke from a place of knowledge about the event. They were to convey to the reader/audience that the sisters' mom had died. But, they were *forbidden* to use the words "death," or "mom."

One student, Jocelyn Seagrave, wrote the following:

Annie: How long was it? The breath.
Bess: What breath?
Annie: Her last.
Bess: I don't remember.
Annie: Think.
Bess: Why?
Annie: I need to … see it.
Bess: Then you should have come.
Annie: Christ almighty.
Bess: OK! It was sort of long.
Annie: Oh, no —
Bess: Not long, but sort of, like this: (sighs)
Annie: Sad, then.
Bess: No. I can't describe it. Maybe I said too much. It wasn't sad.

Annie: Like pain?

Bess: I don't think so.

Annie: But she was in pain.

Bess: Yes.

Annie: You see!

Bess: But it was more like … the other part of pain.

Annie: What?

Bess: Like … relief.

Another student, Chad Diez, wrote this:

SISTER 1: What am I supposed to feel right now? What are the steps?

SISTER 2: I don't know. But I'm pissed.

SISTER 1: Me too.

SISTER 2: I think that's step five.

TAKE TEN:
EDIT EXPOSITION

Working with a problem scene, rewrite the dialogue so that the characters come from a place of knowledge about the event. Prevent "on the nose" dialogue by making a rule *not* to use certain key words in the scene.

Scene is about _____

Audience has to learn _____

Characters already know _____

Forbidden words _____

WHAT YOU'VE ACCOMPLISHED

By alluding to something, rather than talking about a subject directly, you've avoided the trap of exposition. You're now thinking of your scenes as more than an information dumping ground.

Editing and the "Perfect Line"

Dialogue editing is one of the easiest and most important passes to make. We love our words, though, so it's often the most painful. Sad to see your "angry wife" rant go? Devastated at the thought of losing your "declaration of love" monologue? Think of it this way: You're not losing a speech, you're gaining the *perfect line*!

It's often great lines of dialogue that we take away from a movie.

Great lines are often *metaphorical*:

"Fasten your seat belts, it's going to be a bumpy night."
— *All About Eve*

Great lines lead you to one conclusion, then *shift gears*.

"You're not too smart, are you? I like that in a man."
— *Body Heat*

Sometimes, they're loaded with *subtext*.

"We all go a little mad sometimes."
— *Psycho*

Often they reveal character personality in a *shocking* way.

"I love the smell of Napalm in the morning."
— *Apocalypse Now*

Every once in a while, a great line just cuts through the bull and *speaks the truth*.

"Mrs. Robinson, you're trying to seduce me."
— *The Graduate*

Sometimes, an extra *"tag"* is added for a big laugh.

"Mrs. Robinson, you're trying to seduce me ... aren't you?"
— *The Graduate*

So, how do we arrive at the perfect line?

Here's a trick. And it's a great ten-minute way of editing out unnecessary rambling. We simply dig into an overwritten passage, speech, or monologue and find the *one line* that says it all.

In the movie *Jaws*, Chief Brody sees the great white shark for the first time, and it's huge!

He could have said:

"Oh God! This gigantic fish almost leapt up on the deck! It's enormous and I don't know how in the world we're going to kill it. I mean, you're gonna need a bigger boat and better equipment. Maybe get a crew of Marines, or something like that. Without more resources, we're all gonna die!"

But all he said was:

"You're gonna need a bigger boat."

Simple. So understated that it's almost chilling. The *perfect line*.

What this all means is that somewhere in your overwritten passages, your pages of speeches, and your third-act cathartic monologues, there's a perfect line buried in there. Free it up! And, in the process, you'll also lighten your script and make it a better read.

TAKE TEN:
FIND THE PERFECT LINE #1

Edit overwritten passages in two steps:

1. Locate all of the overwritten passages in your script.

2. Circle the line in them that really brings out the point.

That's the perfect line.

WHAT YOU'VE ACCOMPLISHED
Bet you didn't know what a good writer you are. That perfect line was buried in your monologue the entire time. By spending ten minutes going into all of your monologues and circling the "perfect line," you've prevented your screenplay from feeling preachy, corny, or overwritten.

Stuck on what to say at all? Use the same exercise to find your words.

TAKE TEN:
FIND THE PERFECT LINE #2

When you're stuck on the next line, overcome the block in two steps:

1. *Write* the monologue your character might say if he were allowed to verbally "rant" in that moment. Feel free to be indulgent. Squeeze every thought and feeling out of your character.

2. Do not leave it that way! Instead, find one line within the monologue and circle it.

That's the perfect line.

WHAT YOU'VE ACCOMPLISHED
By taking ten minutes to write a monologue around a "stuck" line, then finding the key line within that "rant," you've created killer dialogue and pushed through writer's block.

The Format Pass

Word placement and word choice make all of the difference in a script. Sometimes a format pass is *the* pass a writer has to make. Below, you'll see some suggestions for creating more air in your pages and rewriting toward a cleaner read. In the past, I've told you to pick and choose what works for you. In this case, I'm urging you to do all of these format passes. They're quick, easy, and they could be the difference between a producer putting your script down at page ten or giving it the chance that it deserves.

Paragraphs and White Space

"You need more white space" is a common note from producers. It's also an extremely strange thing to say. White space? Huh?

It actually means that you have big clumps of scene direction that make your script look too dense and make it no fun to read.

Think about what you do when you see big paragraphs of instructions — or even worse, all that fine print on a contract. You skim, right? And, inevitably, you miss something important. That's why you missed a bolt on your kid's bike and why you didn't quite notice that your office lease doesn't include air-conditioner repair.

Keep the reader of your script from doing the same thing by breaking up big paragraphs into smaller paragraphs that move the eye down the page.

Imagine if this page of action had looked like this:

```
A BODYGUARD to the side DISAPPEARS with a scream,
and a SECOND BAT-SHADOW appears. The Chechen looks
taken aback. Three more BAT-SHADOWS appear … even
the dogs stop growling. BOOM! A hole appears in
the SUV next to the Chechen. The first bat-shadow
steps into the light carrying a SHOTGUN. CHAOS as
men scatter and the rooftop erupts in GUNFIRE.
The Chechen TURNS as he hears one of his men
SCREAM.
```

Fortunately, it looked like this:

```
A BODYGUARD to the side DISAPPEARS with a scream,
and a SECOND BAT-SHADOW appears.
```

The Chechen looks taken aback. Three more BAT-SHADOWS appear ... even the dogs stop growling.

BOOM! A hole appears in the SUV next to the Chechen. The first bat-shadow steps into the light carrying a SHOTGUN.

CHAOS as men scatter and the rooftop erupts in GUNFIRE. The Chechen TURNS as he hears one of his men SCREAM.

From The Dark Knight *by Christopher Nolan and David S. Goyer, 2008. Batman created by Bob Kane.*

In the example above, a shootout has become poetry. White space allows for a breath in the action. And, in a way, that white space is actually a line itself.

A line of silence.

Cool, huh?

Try it.

TAKE TEN:
PARAGRAPH YOUR SCENE DIRECTION

Work a page at a time to break your long scene direction passages into paragraphs.

1. Create a new paragraph when you feel that the shot is changing.

2. Create a new paragraph when you feel that the point of view is changing.

3. Allow for one-line paragraphs.

4. Create separate paragraphs for every new piece of choreography in a fight scene or chase scene.

WHAT YOU'VE ACCOMPLISHED

By breaking up heavy scene direction, you've allowed moments of silence to come through, implied different emotional beats and camera shots, and made your script more readable.

Eliminate Camera Direction

Screenplay format has become much less camera-direction heavy over the years. Some writers fear this is limiting as it prevents them from describing an important shot or angle. In reality, it frees the writer up to be more visual.

For example …

```
Close-up on Lucy.
```

… simply does not tell us as much as …

```
Lucy's face fills with anger.
```

Making objects *active* is the key to eliminating unnecessary camera shots.

Instead of:

```
Close-up on a candle.
```

Try:

```
C̶l̶o̶s̶e̶ ̶u̶p̶ A candle flickers.
```

A director, noting that flickering flame in the script, will automatically want to go close-up. In this way, you help guide the shots without being so specific as to tell the director her job.

Another scene direction misstep is the overuse of the word "we." *We're* not actually in the movie, so referring to "us" can be jarring. And just because we see it doesn't mean we know what it's doing. Again, this problem can easily be taken care of by making the object or person "we're seeing" active.

Instead of:

```
We see the knife.
```

Try:

```
W̶e̶ ̶s̶e̶e̶ The knife glints.
```

TAKE TEN:
REPLACE CAMERA DIRECTION

1. Replace camera direction by making the subject you're focusing on active.

2. Do the same with any description starting with "we."

3. Repeat until finished!

WHAT YOU'VE ACCOMPLISHED
You've brought your script into the 21st century and kept us embedded in the story. Camera direction isn't suddenly going to pull us out of the script.

Work Your Scene Headings

Moving or modifying scene headings changes the rhythm and flow of your story. But scene headings are not all created equal. *Primary scene headings* make a bold point by completely resetting a scene. *Secondary scene headings* maintain movement. A balance of the two helps overly constructed, heading-heavy scenes to read like poetry.

TEN-MINUTE LECTURE:

SCENE HEADINGS

PRIMARY SCENE HEADINGS, also referred to as sluglines, *tell us whether we're inside or outside, location, and time of day:*

INT. HIGH SCHOOL — DAY

SECONDARY SCENE HEADINGS, also referred to as minor sluglines, move the reader's eye to new locations in the same scene without indicating, once again, whether or not we're inside or out and what time of day it is. This is particularly helpful if characters are suddenly being chased by a killer into a …

CLASSROOM

And out of the classroom, into the …

HALLWAY

And through the hallway, sliding into the …

LUNCHROOM

And so on.

END OF LECTURE

Modern-day scripts use secondary scene headings to great advantage. The joke of this next scene would have been interrupted if the writer had used only primary scene headings:

INT. BASEMENT HALLWAY — DAY

Ben walks down the stairs, steering clear of the bathroom. He opens the door to his

WORKSHOP

He peeks in the small space and stares at the barren shelves and pegboards. It's cleaned out.

A tear rolls down his cheek.

From Weekend Warrior, *written by Bill Birch, 2007.*

And this next excerpt uses minor scene headings to make us feel that we too are moving under and above water.

EXT. RICKY'S HOUSE - DAY

The sun beats down. Ricky, passed out, sunburned, slowly slides off the chair into the pool. As he splashes into the water, he jerks awake.

UNDERWATER

Ricky stares at the bottom of the pool. Something glints in the sunlight; a diamond wedding ring.

ABOVE WATER

He shoots up, gasping for air.

From The Strikeout King, *written by Geoff Alexander, 2006.*

TAKE TEN:
CREATE SECONDARY SCENE HEADINGS

Create more flow with secondary scene headings. Focus on those big sequences that need to stay fluid such as chase sequences, parties, and moving from room to room.

WHAT YOU'VE ACCOMPLISHED

Not only have you helped the pace of your scenes, you've updated your script's look. The reader's eye now moves quickly down the page, pressing him to move on in the script.

The Element Pass

One change = an entire rewrite. In my rewrite class, I like to begin by showing a few scenes from the movie *Groundhog Day*. The premise of *Groundhog Day* is that a bitter man is condemned to repeat a day over and over again until he gets it right. Therefore, his movie is just a handful of scenes being written over and over again.

I usually show a scene where an insurance salesmen, Ned, recognizes the main character, Phil, and talks too closely to him, fills him in on everything he's been doing with his life (even though Phil doesn't care), and tries to sell him insurance. It's filled with entertaining exposition, reveals a lot about why Phil doesn't like this town and people in general, and sets up Ned as being a fairly obnoxious person.

But, of course, Phil is forced to replay this day over and over again, constantly having to deal with this guy. This is where the rewrites come in.

Rewrite 1: Ned approaches. Phil knows the information, so he "guesses" instead of being told.

Rewrite 2: Ned approaches. Phil physically pushes him away, but Ned only moves closer.

Rewrite 3: Ned approaches. Phil calmly punches him in the face, smiles, and walks away.

Rewrite 4: Ned approaches. Phil holds him close … too close. Ned backs away.

Rewrite 5: Phil buys insurance from Ned.

In watching the scenes, you can see how the simple act of guessing, pushing, hitting, hugging or buying completely changes the scene and the story.

So, while I've given you big rewrite passes to consider, also look to the small stuff. In this book, you've already focused on some major elements of a screenplay. A rewrite pass that focuses on only one of these elements could be the pass your script needs. So consider rewriting with a focus on one of the following:

Activity
Character Flaw
Complication
Emotion
Entertainment
Game-playing
Goals
Payoff
Point of View
Power Play

Set Piece

Triggers

The Holistic Pass

Connection, balance, and focus. Sounds like terms more suited for a yoga class. But they're also words that describe the magic of an edgy, nonlinear movie like *Pulp Fiction* to a tee.

When trying to articulate what works or doesn't work about a screen-play, I find myself using these phrases again and again. And trust me, I have *never* made it all the way through a yoga class. Regardless, here are some general passes for your script; approaches that "align" your movie, so to speak.

Connection

Whether it's witnessed in a heated moment between characters or realized when fingerprints match a murder weapon, we seek out con-nections in our movies. We match images to images. We connect emotion to event. We string locations and time together. Your job as a writer is to guide those connections. So, in your last pass at your script, try doing just that.

TAKE TEN:
CONNECT THE DOTS

Smooth out your script by making connections.

1. Connect random characters in terms of their relatives, friends,or world.

2. Connect characters to an event, allowing them to come together around one common goal.

3. Connect objects to people. Objects that bring luck, objects that symbolize love, objects that can be used as weapons, etc.

4. Connect locations so that we get a better sense of world.

5. Connect time so that we get a sense of the order of events or a ticking clock.

WHAT YOU'VE ACCOMPLISHED

By making these connections, and allowing the reader to discover them in your script, you've created extra surprises and made the read more engaging.

Balance

When a script feels unbalanced, everything suffers. If it's too top-heavy with setup, we feel let down at the end when everything suddenly rushes to its conclusion. If the midpoint event suddenly tips the movie in a completely new story direction, you lose the reader and audience. If the last act of a romantic comedy is suddenly weighted down by action and chase sequences, the script is in danger of falling right off the scale.

So take a moment to balance out the good and the bad, the light and the dark, and see if that's the pass that will work for your script.

TAKE TEN:
FIND BALANCE

Try out one of the following suggestions in order to find balance in your script.

1. Scatter genre moments throughout your script.

2. Place key set pieces in different sections of your movie, not just one.

3. Move between action and talk. Don't let either one dominate.

4. Spread out or bookend your narrative devices like voice over and flashback.

5. Combine characters so that you're not randomly dropping in new people throughout the movie or abandoning those you've established. Allow characters we meet in the first half to travel through or pay off in the second.

6. By Act 3, answer a question posed in Act 1.

WHAT YOU'VE ACCOMPLISHED
You've created a fully fleshed-out story that doesn't feel like two movies and is a more rewarding read overall.

Focus

By focus, I mean commitment: commitment to a story idea, commitment to a way of exploring that idea, commitment to a scene. I've read many scripts where ideas compete with each other. Where narrative devices clash. Where the writer keeps throwing in new characters because she doesn't know what to do with the old ones. Where new rules about the world are constantly being made up and then broken by its own creator.

I'm about as good with psychoanalysis as I am with a "salute to the sun" pose, but when I come across unfocused projects such as this, I can't help but think that the writer doesn't trust herself. Worried that it's not enough, she digresses or throws a new element into the pot. So, "focus" is the magic word for scripts like this. Take ten minutes to see if that's what your script needs.

TAKE TEN:
FOCUS YOUR SCRIPT

Focus your script in one of the following ways:

1. Edit the beginnings and endings of your scenes so that they return to working around the main scene intentions.

2. Eliminate any objects, pieces of information or character rules that do not pay off later.

3. Take a hard look at supporting or minor characters and see if they're flip-flopping. Your script may not have enough time to bring out every side of a character.

4. Eliminate one of your narrative devices. Your flashback story may be competing with your fantasy sequences.

5. Smooth out the choreography of your final showdown and commit to one bold, clever move.

WHAT YOU'VE ACCOMPLISHED
You've made the read easier, but also added emotional punch. We won't be distracted from the story by the fussier details.

Focusing the Rewrite

You've spent many ten-minute chunks analyzing your script and testing out different rewrite possibilities. Now you can focus on the rewrite that works best for you and use your ten-minute calendar of eating, coffee slurping, kid sleeping, office work procrastination, etc., to consistently apply the lessons you've learned.

■ TEN-MINUTE CHAPTER REVIEW:
THE REWRITE

1. Rewrite with a CONCEPT PASS by running your script through a CONCEPT TEST to see where you're being true to your big idea.

2. Rewrite with a STRUCTURE PASS by moving a KEY EVENT and seeing how that affects the pace and focus of the story.

3. Rewrite with a STORY PASS by running through a BEAT CHECK, strengthening CAUSE and EFFECT, and working backward to clarify the triggers.

4. Rewrite with a SCENE PASS by running your scene list through a SCENE STORY TEST and finding the FRESH TAKE on stock scenes.

5. Rewrite with a CHARACTER PASS, making your MC the FOCUS of the scenes, determining character AGENDA and STRATEGY, and using the character's gender and ethnicity to add depth.

6. Rewrite with a DIALOGUE PASS by mining your overwritten passages for the PERFECT LINE and eliminating exposition by editing out FORBIDDEN WORDS.

7. Rewrite with a FORMAT PASS by ELIMINATING CAMERA DIRECTION, creating more WHITE SPACE, and creating SECONDARY HEADINGS.

8. Use a HOLISTIC PASS to create CONNECTION, BALANCE and FOCUS in your screenplay.

CHAPTER 8

The Craft

In this section, we'll fine-tune and polish your script.

By tweaking lines, editing scenes, and streamlining format, you will meet your own page intentions and make the script that much more entertaining and readable.

Further toying with format and word choice also means more emphasis on mood and emotion. And the more compelling the read, the more likely your script will be to move up through the ranks of a production company or studio.

We're going to cover as many of the smaller artistic details of the page as possible. Notice the emphasis on emotional writing. Yes, your job is to tell us what we *see*, but it's also to guide us toward what those images actually *mean*. I've said it before, and I'll say it again: Emotion + Action = Story.

The Placement of Action Lines

In scripts, the story is written between the lines. The characters say one thing, but the action lines tell you the real story. Therefore, it's extremely important that those lines of action are clear and descriptive. They need to be placed on the page in a way that forces the eye to look at them, and written in a way that tells your story.

Do readers skim? Only if you make it easy for them. Action lines that move across a page imply a continuous shot or idea and tell a reader that he's simply reading more of the same.

So fool him by …

drawing

the eye

down

the page.

This writer, Ryan Boyd, created just the right amount of tension when he wrote:

```
She stops.
Three minions stand there.
She taps at the window.
One of them looks up at her.
Three shots and they crumble.
```

From The Sleeper Agent, *written by Ryan Boyd, 2009.*

This passage would be far less effective if these lines were all crowded into the same paragraph. The weight of each moment is lost when it reads like this:

```
She stops. Three minions stand there. She taps at
the window. One of them looks up at her. Three
shots and they crumble.
```

In fact, a busy reader's eye may be drawn only to the first sentence: "She stops." And the last: "Three shots and they crumble." He'd still pick up on the intention of the scene. But the fun of the moment would be lost.

TAKE TEN:
WORK DOWN THE PAGE

1. Find the moments in your script that need additional suspense or that build to a surprise.

2. Then, break your scene direction up into beats and work down the page.

WHAT YOU'VE ACCOMPLISHED
You've made your script skim-proof, and you've kept the reader focused on each beat of activity, suspense, fear, or delight.

Choreography In Action Lines

Did you break your action scene into paragraphs or one-liners, only to see that it was now taking up two pages where it was once one?

That means that you over-choreographed. And I see this error in scene direction over and over again.

Imagine that the previous example looked like this:

```
She stops.
Looks around.
Three minions stand there.
They scratch their heads.
She taps at the window.
The minions look around, confused.
One of them looks up at her.
He nudges the other one.
He sees her too.
They glare.
She raises her gun.
She aims.
She pulls the trigger.
Shoots one.
Bang
Shoots the other.
Bang.
They clutch their hearts.
They crumble.
```

Too much, right? First, we've probably increased the page count. Second, all of the slickness is gone. Third, the reader is going to be onto us and simply develop a new way to skim.

Sometimes it's synopsizing, rather than a line edit, which is the correct fix for an over-choreographed scene.

Scene direction that reads …

```
The phone rings. She reacts. Who could it be?
She drops what's she's doing. Stands up. Walks
across the room. Reaches for the phone. Hugs the
receiver to her ear. Answers.
```

… could simply read:

```
She answers the phone.
```

TAKE TEN:
EDITING OVER-CHOREOGRAPHED SCENE DIRECTION

Find the over-choreographed moments in your scene direction and do one of the following:

1. Take out extra lines of action that slow down the action or make it feel fussy.

2. Synopsize activities that don't require a step-by-step breakdown.

WHAT YOU'VE ACCOMPLISHED
You've significantly cleaned up the read, emphasizing those active moments that need extra attention and de-emphasizing those moments that don't.

Fight Scenes

Over-choreography is a big issue when it comes to fight scenes. The thing to remember is that these kinds of scenes tell stories; the story of characters confronting each other and attempting to take power. The "winner" then has the power going into the next scene.

In order to tell that story and still get a sense of how the fight looks or feels, think about building or editing your scene around the following elements.

Emotion before fight.
Tone of the fight.
Method or weaponry.
Fight move #1.
Fight move #2.
Upper hand.
Winning moment.
Emotion after fight.

Let's try it:

Emotion before fight.	Eyes blazing, Dave attacks and they
Tone of the fight.	fight like gladiators in the ring,
Method or weaponry.	fists and teeth bared.
Fight move #1.	A punch to the gut and Dave goes down.
Fight move #2.	But he hurls himself forward and
Upper hand.	knocks Tom backward.

Winning moment.	Tom rises to his feet. A punch to the jaw
Emotion after fight.	and Dave is knocked unconscious. Tom grins and stares down the crowd, daring anyone else to take him on.

Or:

Emotion before fight.	Fed up, Dave pushes him, and they
Tone of the fight.	fight like little girls,
Method or weaponry.	kicking and slapping.
Fight move #1.	A poke in the eye, and Dave goes down.
Fight move #2.	But he hurls himself forward and
Upper hand.	grabs Tom by the hair.
Winning moment.	Tom kicks him in the shins,
Emotion after fight.	and Dave falls to the ground. Tom grins and does a happy dance, daring anyone else to take him on.

(10) TAKE TEN:
WRITE A FIGHT SCENE

Write or rewrite a fight scene around the elements below:

EMOTION BEFORE FIGHT _____

TONE OF FIGHT _____

METHOD OR WEAPONRY _____

FIGHT MOVE #1 _____

FIGHT MOVE #2 _____

UPPER HAND _____

WINNING MOMENT _____

EMOTION AFTER FIGHT _____

WHAT YOU'VE ACCOMPLISHED
You've told the story of a power play, and you've contained your fight so that it doesn't get tedious with excess choreography. Try out this formula on car chases as well!

Emotional Action Lines

If you're going to tell your movie story between the lines, you also have to guide the reader as to what's emotionally going on in your script. Some writers are afraid to put anything in scene direction that isn't straightforward. I'm here to tell you that your script needs more. *Strong action lines integrate emotion.*

Imagine that an action line reads:

```
She leaves the room.
```

Fine. That tells us what she does.

But see what happens when we put an *emotion* up front that shows us the motivation behind her wanting to leave in the first place:

```
Frustrated, she leaves the room.

Worried, she leaves the room.

Afraid, she leaves the room.

Delighted, she leaves the room.
```

These words completely change the emotion of the action, helping the reader understand the subtext as well as the choreography.

While emotional words can add a lot to an action line, the actual verb itself could also be changed. Look at our example: "She *leaves*."

With a new verb, our action line might now read:

```
She storms out of the room.

She flees the room.

She backs out of the room.

She skips out of the room.
```

It's up to you to determine when to add emotion and when to replace the verb. Frankly, I'm fine if you do both:

```
She storms out of the room in frustration.
```

When I tell writers this, they start to worry. They've heard from others that emotion is frowned on! Nope, writing what is solely internal — what can't possibly be shown — is frowned on. The *bad* version of this example might look like this:

```
She storms out of the room in frustration,
thinking back to the time when she was a little
girl and her brother was allowed to go out, but
she wasn't. Ah, her brother. Where was he now?
Would he ever call again? And her parents; had
they forgiven her yet for not appearing at her
sister's wedding? Perhaps she should call, or
write. But, what was her sister's address again …
```

I'd like to say that I've never read a script like this, but I'd be lying.

Bottom line, as you hit the next "Take Ten," remember that emotion is necessary in scene direction, but a little goes a long way.

(10) TAKE TEN:
CREATE EMOTIONAL ACTION LINES

1. Look at the major action beats in your screenplay — the action you feel moves the story forward.

   ACTION LINE _____

2. Add descriptive words in front of the action lines so that we understand what's really going on in the moment.

   EMOTION + ACTION LINE _____

3. Or replace the verb in the action line. Match the verb to the emotion of the moment.

   ACTION LINE WITH NEW VERB _____

4. If it's an extremely important moment, try both:

   ACTION LINE WITH NEW VERB PLUS EMOTION _____

WHAT YOU'VE ACCOMPLISHED

Your use of descriptive words has helped guide the reader. Rather than just know what characters are doing, we now know why they are doing it. In addition, you've worked emotion into scenes that might otherwise read as dull.

Well-chosen verbs also make us feel that we're experiencing the action along with the character. The more the reader feels that she's inside of the movie, the more she'll want to see it on the screen.

The "Tell" of the Scene

Because a screenplay is a "show it, don't say it" medium, *how* some-one says something is sometimes more important than *what* they are saying. Audiences automatically look for visual cues from the characters. Are they saying that line in an angry or happy way? Do they smile? Do they snicker? Do they clench a fist or throw a glass?

These physical moments are what I like to refer to as the *"tell"* of the scene. As in the game of poker, the "tell" is that emotional moment in which a character accidentally shows their cards to the audience and lets us know what the scene is really about.

Focusing on the "tell" of the scene — that "between the lines" moment that gives it all away — can make the difference between an emotionally effective scene and a merely serviceable scene.

Let's imagine a scene in which one character gets in a car accident with another.

```
EXT. PARKING LOT - DAY

Lucy surveys the nearly totaled car and hands
Mike her license and registration.

                    LUCY
        My information.
```

To find the "tell" of the scene, it sometimes helps to ask, "What does that character wish she could say?"

Maybe she wishes she could say, *"This is all your fault, idiot!"*

Assuming she can't say that, we're going to add a "tell" to show it:

```
EXT. PARKING LOT - DAY

Eyes blazing, Lucy surveys the nearly totaled car
and throws her license and registration at Mike's
head.

                    LUCY
        My information!
```

If you change the intention of the character, the inner voice changes … and so does the "tell."

So now her eyes blaze, and she throws her license at Mike. She may be saying the right thing and doing what she's supposed to, but her feelings are coming through loud and clear.

What if we went the other way, and Lucy wishes she could say, *"Crashing into you is my way of getting your attention."*

We'd then rewrite the scene with a different "tell":

```
EXT. PARKING LOT - DAY

Drawing close to Mike, Lucy hands over her
license and registration. Her fingertips graze
his.

                    LUCY
          My information.
```

"Drawing close," "fingertips graze." These small moments allow the reader and audience special insight. And the great thing about a movie or TV show is that the camera can go as close as it wants, capturing even the tiniest detail to help us tell the story.

 TAKE TEN:
CREATE SCENE DIRECTION "TELLS"

Add to a straightforward scene with a "between the lines" story.

SCENE _____

DIALOGUE _____

CHARACTER WISHES HE/SHE COULD SAY _____

"TELL" OF THE SCENE _____

WHAT YOU'VE ACCOMPLISHED
By adding "between the lines" moments, you've visually brought out the subtext. You've also avoided "on the nose" dialogue by using action instead of words.

The Button

When does a script become a "page turner?" When you've ended each scene in a way that makes us want to know more. A simple and effective way to bring emotion to your screenplay, and to keep us wanting more, is to "button" your scenes with a great line or piece of action.

Scene buttons often leave us with a key question or hint at problems or issues to come. They are sometimes called "the blow" of a scene, or the scene "out."

Comedies end scenes on strong verbal or physical punchlines. (Think rim shot.) Character-driven dramas end scenes with a spoken or silent question. Thrillers end scenes with verbal or physical clues.

We could add more to our parking lot scene, for example, by giving Mike a clever response that *buttons* the scene:

EXT. PARKING LOT - DAY

Drawing close to Mike, Lucy hands over her
license and registration. Her fingertips graze
his.

              LUCY
   My information.

Mike hands over his own information: license,
registration, and … a family photo.

              MIKE
   My wife.

This line brings the scene to an end in a way that shows Mike's devotion to his wife and seems to close the case.

But what if we wanted to indicate that Lucy isn't going to go away easily? An additional verbal button moves the story in a different direction.

EXT. PARKING LOT - DAY

Drawing close to Mike, Lucy hands over her license
and registration. Her fingertips graze his.

              LUCY
   My information.

Mike hands over his own information: license,
registration, and … a family photo.

              MIKE
   My wife.

Lucy takes the photo and coolly studies it.

              LUCY
   For now.

This verbal button makes us realize that Lucy has more up her sleeve. Add a *physical button,* and even more is added to the scene:

```
Mike offers a weak smile.
```

Adding Mike's weak smile shows a chink in his armor and suggests to the reader/audience that Lucy may succeed in seducing him.

A new, emotional action line buttons the scene in a very different way:

```
                    LUCY
          For now.

Mike snatches the photo from her hand. Lucy's
face fills with anger.
```

Notice that the different buttons create entirely different tones. The first button, with Mike smiling weakly, would work for a romantic comedy. The second button indicates possibilities for a thriller. And with that one facial "tell" — "Lucy's face fills with anger" — we wonder what Lucy might do next!

(10) TAKE TEN:
CREATING SMART SCENE "BUTTONS"

Add verbal or physical buttons where they will benefit the script's tone or help further the story.

SCENE _____

VERBAL BUTTON _____

PHYSICAL BUTTON _____

TEST IT OUT:

BUTTON MOVES STORY IN THIS WAY _____

BUTTON LEAVES READER WITH THIS EMOTION _____

WHAT YOU'VE ACCOMPLISHED
By spicing up your scene endings, you've added to the comedy or drama and helped push your story forward.

Scene Transitions

In a screenplay, each scene is informed and affected by the scene that comes before it. For that reason, an easy way to keep your story moving is to begin a new scene by building off of the button that preceded it.

Let's imagine that we just ended our Lucy/Mike scene. Building off that last scene button, we could pick up with a new scene that deals with the recent information that Lucy might be, well … psycho:

```
INT. OFFICE — DAY

Mike's coworker, RICHARD, can barely contain his
smirk.

                    RICHARD
          I told you she was nuts. But you just
          had to help her out. Always the good guy.

                    MIKE
          I think she might do something to Tina.

                    RICHARD
          You're overreacting.

                    MIKE
          And you're not helping.

Fed up, Mike starts to leave.

                    RICHARD
          Here.

Richard retrieves a gun from the drawer and hands
it to him.

                    RICHARD
          Am I helping now?

Mike weighs the gun in his hand, deciding.
```

Because we ended the preceding scene with Lucy's ominous moment, we understand which "nut" Mike and Richard are referring to.

We also didn't have to go into exposition about what happened because we already saw it. Instead, we came into the scene mid-discussion.

Notice that the button in this scene furthers the story and builds tension. Mike is deciding something. Will he kill her?

The gun button then transitions us to the next scene:

```
INT. BEDROOM — NIGHT

Mike's wife, TINA, stares incredulously at the
gun.

                    TINA
          I'm not taking it.

                    MIKE
          It's just for safety.

                    TINA
          Since when do I need to be this safe?
```

We began by mirroring the visual button of the gun in Mike's hand. Can you see the director make the "match cut"?

We could continue with our buttons and transitions, but then we'd have an entire screenplay that's not yours. So, take the next ten minutes to do some transition work.

TAKE TEN:
SCENE TRANSITIONS

In order to create better scene flow, try out one of the following scene transitions:

1. Mirror the last image.

2. Pick up from a last moment of dialogue.

3. Answer the question from the previous scene.

4. Twist the setup of the last scene with an unexpected revelation.

WHAT YOU'VE ACCOMPLISHED
Smarter transitions help you string the scenes together in a way that makes sense and helps the reader track the story.

Narrative Devices

Voice over, flashback, breaking the fourth wall … these devices have been exploited so badly that some writers now think that they should *never* be used.

This is my feeling on this issue or any "rule" of screenwriting: Never say never. Voice over intrudes … until it works. Flashbacks feel corny … until they don't. In other words, the rules are there for a reason, but they were also meant to be broken.

Still confused?

Here are a few guidelines.

Voice over

Voice over works when it says something that cannot be conveyed in the action or dialogue. The character of Red in *The Shawshank Redemption* voices feelings that the strong, silent main characters cannot.

Voice over works when it benefits the tone of the script. In *The Lovely Bones,* the story is narrated by a dead girl named Susie. Every time Susie speaks, it's a reminder of her fate; her voice over adds a chill to the scene.

Voice over also works well when it's the punchline of a scene, delivering the funny one-liners that the characters wish they could say, but can't. The movie *Election* focuses on a bossy girl running for student president and the disempowered teacher who wants to see her fail. These two hate each other, but because of their teacher/student relationship, only the voice over betrays their real feelings.

Sometimes voice over also adds to the joke when it contrasts with the visuals:

```
INT. REAL VALU HARDWARE - DAY

Wearing the red vest and "ask me" button of a
Real Valu foot soldier, Dave stands above a case
of SPRAY PAINT. He is stamping prices on every
cap.

                    TRACY (V.O.)
          I wonder what he's doing now. Maybe he
          finally finished his novel.
```

From Election, *written by Alexander Payne & Jim Taylor, 1997, from the novel by Tom Perrotta, 1997.*

Sometimes voice over breaks conventional rules with a higher purpose. In the movie *The Informant!,* the audience is privy to the voiced-over thoughts of a wannabe whistleblower. The voice over rarely connects with the reality of the situation, but that's actually the point. By story's end, we realize that the "informant" has actually been living in his head; in a fantasy world in which he's dragged along everyone he's known … including us!

Flashbacks

Flashbacks go wrong when they show too much of the past and don't allow that information to come out naturally and organically through the present-day narrative.

But flashbacks work when the images tell a story or solve a mystery.

In *A Few Good Men,* we see different flashbacks of the same event, as told through the point of view of different characters on the witness stand. Eventually all of the stories converge, illustrating "the truth." Movies like *Citizen Kane* (my personal favorite) do the same thing, but they leave the audience with the clear idea that *none* of the characters ever know the full picture … only the audience.

A constant flash of images also work well when it creates an evidence trail in one-hour procedurals, like *CSI*. It would be dull to just hear the characters talk in "forensic-speak." *Seeing* the evidence as they describe it makes the episodes more visually interesting and helps build the story.

Narrative Device = Storytelling Rules

Looking at the examples above, one thing is clear: When they're effectively dealt with, narrative devices like voice over and flashback work because they help tell the story. In order to tell that story with clarity, however, you must decide what rule you're going to follow with these devices. Do your flashbacks follow one character only or tell the story from many different points of view? Does your voice over address the audience only or is it delivered to a person in the script? Once you've decided on these rules for your narrative devices, commit to them. The reader and audience will appreciate the focus.

TAKE TEN:
FOCUSING YOUR NARRATIVE DEVICE

Focus your flashbacks or voice overs by creating a storytelling rule. Pick from this list or create your own.

FLASHBACK:

Tells one story from several points of view.

Flashes to shocking images, creating an evidence chain.

Shows separate sections of one event, eventually leading up to the "big picture."

Shows a memory.

Reveals a truth when a character in the present is lying.

Takes place at key structural moments (the teaser, act break, ending, etc.).

Only shows up when MC is experiencing heightened emotion.

VOICE OVER:

Is delivered by an all-knowing narrator whom we never meet.

Is delivered by a character in the story.

Is delivered by several characters in the story, shifting point of view.

Is delivered to the audience.

Is delivered to another character in the story.

Is written in the past tense, as though events have passed.

Is written in the present tense, as events take place.

Speaks a character's thoughts out loud.

Delivers the punchline of scenes.

Glues years and events together.

Quotes from one source (a poem, the Bible, a rock song, a list of rules, etc.).

Comes in at key structural moments (the teaser, act break, ending, etc.).

Only shows up when MC is experiencing heightened emotion.

Only "bookends" the script, speaking to us at the beginning and at the end.

WHAT YOU'VE ACCOMPLISHED

You've focused your narrative device to better help you tell your story. By doing this, you've brought clarity to your script and prevented confusion on the part of the reader or audience.

Remember that you can create these "story rules" for any device: Fantasy sequences, dream sequences, etc. Determining how these devices help you to tell your story will make all the difference in the read.

Narrative Device = Tonal Variation

Anywhere But Here and *Tumbleweeds* both came out in 1999 and had similar concepts, similar relationships, and even a similar opening sequence of mother and daughter in a car, fleeing a domestic situation to find happiness elsewhere.

In sequence one of *Anywhere But Here*, however, the action is peppered with narration and flashbacks that fill us in on backstory and feelings. The devices intentionally soften the sequence. Though there was conflict in the mother's life, we experience it as a flashback told to us from a safer place. And though the daughter is unhappy, the fact that she survived to tell the tale suggests that everything eventually comes out OK.

In contrast, sequence one of *Tumbleweeds* slams us into the present with an unsettling scene of the mother fighting with the boyfriend. We experience the conflict right along with the characters. Then, the daughter and mother flee in the middle of the night, and their scene in the car relies on loaded lines and emotional tells to convey backstory and feelings.

Both movies serve their genre and satisfy the audience. Both movies tell a similar story. But there are clear tonal differences that make them very, very different.

This is all to say that the tone of a script can be completely changed by the use of a narrative device. Add fantasy to a comedy, and it's a new kind of script. Bring dream sequences into a drama and the mood changes.

It's up to you to decide whether or not to use a device to add to or make changes to your tone. Will your flashback sequences soften the moment or make the script feel more visual and immediate? Only you know the answer to this question. But it's definitely worth ten minutes of your time to make the evaluation.

TAKE TEN:
NARRATIVE DEVICE TEST

Ask the following questions to see if a narrative device is working for or against script tone. Once you've made a decision, hone your narrative device or delete it.

1. Does it make the story events feel more immediate?

2. Does it create distance?

3. Does it make your story feel fanciful?

4. Does it make your script feel more hard-hitting?

5. Does it add a different perspective that's necessary to tell the story?

6. Does it create a new subplot that needs to be shown?

7. Does it answer a pressing question or solve a mystery?

8. Would we understand the story if it wasn't there?

9. Would it have the same emotional impact if it wasn't there?

10. Are there more effective ways to tell the story without it?

WHAT YOU'VE ACCOMPLISHED
By making a choice to use or lose a narrative device, you've strengthened your tone.

Character And Setting Descriptions

The "less is more" rule applies to all aspects of screenwriting — even character description. Writers tend to be so anxious for you to "see" the character that they overwrite by describing every single detail. Unfortunately, this actually limits the reader's vision and closes off casting choices.

Imagine that we meet …

VANESSA (25), blonde, tall, and wearing a cocktail dress.

Well, this description tells us only so much. And, in a way, it's limiting. Will this description allow us to cast an actress who's younger or older? A brunette? An African American? Every detail in this tells us "no." Worse, we don't actually get a sense of her character. What's her personality? When the camera's on her, what story is told?

For all of these reasons, capturing the *essence* of a character in a one-line description can actually be more effective. Instead of "blonde, tall, and wearing a cocktail dress," we could meet:

`VANESSA, vampish and beguiling.`

Now, we get a sense of how this character could potentially affect the story. Plus, we can cast anyone from Jessica Biel to Halle Berry.

Characters catch our eye when even the description of them tells a small story. The trick is to give us just enough to make us "see" the character, and not so much that it feels you're writing in prose.

Rather than describe a character as overweight, the description could read:

`He never met a jelly doughnut he didn't like.`

After introducing:

`TRACY, small and mousy.`

You can bring color to the description by adding:

`Blink, and you'll miss her.`

Each of these statements suggests age and physical characteristics, without going into excessive detail.

Rooms and settings can also be described this way.

Instead of writing:

`Paul Harmer's corner office. A large desk. A big leather chair. Plaques and commendations on the wall.`

You could write:

`Paul Harmer's corner office screams "CEO."`

Set-decorating a scene does little. Giving the room a personality does much.

TAKE TEN:
CREATE "ESSENCE STATEMENTS"

Polish your character and setting descriptions by replacing them with personality-filled one-liners.

MAIN CHARACTER ESSENCE STATEMENT _____

SUPPORTING CHARACTER ESSENCE STATEMENT _____

ANTAGONIST ESSENCE STATEMENT _____

WHAT YOU'VE ACCOMPLISHED
With your "essence statements," your characters make an immediate impact on the reader. We get a sense of who they are, not just how they look.

Essence Plus Action

As mentioned earlier, bringing your characters into the script with a defining action tells us more about the character than do pages and pages of setup. Add an essence statement, and we'll immediately connect.

GEMMA BALE (25), tough by necessity, furiously packs the crabs into straw boxes.

From Little White Lies, *written by Heather Ragsdale, 2008.*

In the front row, WILLIAM, a tightly-wound dandy, stares blankly at the stage. He winces in disapproval as the orchestra hits a wrong note.

Next to him sits his wife, NOREEN, a peaceful woman who could find beauty in a dirty puddle. She sways to the aria onstage.

Written by Brendan O'Neill, 2009.

CHET, a good-looking jock who reached his pinnacle in high school, plops down at the table holding a crumpled Starbucks apron.

From Gilfs, *written by Chip James, 2008.*

SUZIE, a mousy cubicle worker, sits at her desk and stares at a thin slice of sky through a distant window.

From That Other Me, *written by Leslie Lawson, 2007.*

TAKE TEN:
ESSENCE + ACTION

Add an action to your essence-statement character introduction.

MAIN CHARACTER ESSENCE STATEMENT + ACTION

_____

SUPPORTING CHARACTER ESSENCE STATEMENT + ACTION

_____

ANTAGONIST ESSENCE STATEMENT + ACTION

_____

WHAT YOU'VE ACCOMPLISHED
By getting a sense of who they are and seeing what they're doing, we
"get" your character from the moment they're introduced.

Tonal Writing

Word choice is everything when it comes to creating tone and mood
on the page. Below, you'll find the opening passages of three different
screenplays. They're all comedies, but they all "feel" different. You get
a sense of their particular take on the genre from the very first words.

```
JOEY CASANOVA (27), more charming than handsome,
struts down the busy streets of Manhattan like
he's John Travolta on a hot Saturday night.

A pre-teen GIRLIE says a flirtatious hello, an
OLD LADY gives him a nod and wink, and a SMALL
DOG wags her tail as Joey passes by. Yep, Joey's
got a way with the ladies.
```

From Double or Nothing, _written by Karen Nation, 2002._

The writer starts off with an essence statement — "more charming
than handsome" — then adds a memorable first action: He "struts."

In addition, the reactions of minor characters suggest he's a ladies'
man. The writer's small aside to us, "Yep, Joey's got a way with the
ladies," also establishes a wry, mischievous tone that carries through the
screenplay.

Note: The industry is split as to whether or not these kinds of asides
help or hinder the page. My personal feeling is that the occasional
clever comment can work, provided it doesn't suddenly jolt us out of

the script. Personal asides to the reader like, "It's a car chase — you've see one, you've seen 'em all" feel flippant and lazy.

Here's another comedy example:

```
EXT. BULE FIELD - DAY

Laughter swirls in the twilight over a stone
relic of a football stadium as a gaggle of
wheezing MEN in need of golf carts stumble
through a pick-up game of football.

ALAN "SALLY" SIZEMORE is a white walrus in
polyester shorts. An unlit stogie juts from
Sally's yap. He grabs his back, rises from his
quarterback position, and launches the football
toward the press box.
```

Written by Paul Pender, 2002.

In this script, we don't just hear laughter; laughter "swirls." The scene direction doesn't just mention a bunch of guys; it focuses on "a gaggle of wheezing men." And Alan Sizemore isn't just a big man, he's a "white walrus."

Another example:

```
INT. A BEDROOM - NIGHT

It's really, really, really late.

NOAH RILEY (32) sleeps as if she's never shared a
bed. Arms flung, blanket mussed, pillows strewn.
In the background, CNN is on. It always is.
```

Written by Karin Gist, 2002.

Unlike the other descriptions, this passage gets right to it. Like the main character, the words are frank and no-nonsense, written the way one girlfriend might talk to another.

We also get a sense right away, from the description "sleeps as if she's never shared a bed," that this is a woman who's been single for a long time … and may be just fine with that.

You may argue that the audience can't see the words on the page, but I'd argue back that they certainly can. The director and production people bring words to life, casting, set decorating, and moving the actors per a writer's subtle "instructions."

TAKE TEN:
TONAL WRITING

Choose a word that describes the tone of your work. Pick from this list or find a word that works for you:

COMEDY: Whimsical
    Dry
    Silly
    Sarcastic
    Cutting-edge
    Crass
    Smart

DRAMA: Suspenseful
    Deep
    Intense
    Gritty
    Sexy
    Mournful
    Wistful

Use your ten-minute breaks to go through the script and apply new words and phrases to the scene direction that meet your tonal intention.

WHAT YOU'VE ACCOMPLISHED
By paying close attention to tone and mood, you've graduated from screenwriter to artist.

■ TEN-MINUTE CHAPTER REVIEW:
THE CRAFT

1. Emphasize dramatic and comedic moments by writing DOWN THE PAGE.

2. EDIT scenes that have excessive CHOREOGRAPHY.

3. Focus FIGHT SCENES around KEY ELEMENTS.

4. Bring EMOTION into your ACTION LINES.

5. Show SUBTEXT with the "TELL" of a scene.

6. Move story and punch up the tone with a physical or verbal BUTTON.

7. Create STORY RULES for your NARRATIVE DEVICES.

8. USE OR LOSE a narrative device to aid TONE.

9. Edit and open up casting by using ESSENCE STATEMENTS to describe characters and places.

10. Emphasize TONAL WRITING with word choice that speaks to the mood.

CHAPTER 9

The Final Edit

Polishing your script means fine-tuning. And fine-tuning means editing.

By tweaking lines, editing scenes, and streamlining format, you meet your own page intentions and make the script that much more entertaining and readable.

Remember that your script isn't just a blueprint for a television show or movie. It also showcases you as a writer. It's your industry calling card. And, ultimately, a well-written script could be the thing that turns you from a "coffee break screenwriter" into a full-time, working screenwriter.

With that in mind, it's worth one more rewrite. Keep stealing those ten-minute moments to chisel away. That masterpiece will reveal itself.

Story Intention Edit

Editing. You've simply got to do it. To show you why, here's a "before" and "after" example of a screenplay scene:

EXT. LANCE'S BUNGALOW - DAY

Two men in VERY nice suits exit from the back of a black
Lincoln Towncar and look at each other and shrug. As they
walk up the round stone path that leads to a small bungalow
with bars on the windows they look at an aging Chevy Camaro
Berlinetta sitting in the driveway.

They step onto a small concrete porch and the taller of the
two reaches out and pushes the doorbell button on the
doorframe of a battered and barred door. The button, a cheap
RF transmitter that people buy when they can't afford an
electrician, pops off the doorjamb and hits the ground,
popping into several pieces. The men look at each other again
and search for a safe place to knock on the door. One of them
reaches through the bars to try and knock on the screen,
which promptly rips. They look at each other again. The
silence between them speaks volumes - the futility of the
attempt but the need to continue on their quest. One of the
men bends down and picks up the pieces of the transmitter and
tries to figure out how to put it back together again. The
other snatches the pieces after half a minute and slaps them
together and presses the button.

A crashing noise from the side of the house draws the men's
attention and they run around the side of the house to see a
man in bright green shorts and a faded concert T-shirt that
has seen better days laying in the driveway nursing a swollen
and scraped knee. Next to him lies a window screen that has
fallen from the window he recently crawled out of. The two
men look at each other and stand over the man.

                    SUIT #1
          Lance Cocksure?

The man looks up from where he is seated on the ground. He
leans back, his hands resting on the driveway. He puffs out
his chest and across it reads "Lance Cocksure - Blow Me Away
Tour '84"

                    LANCE
          What do you want?

The writers' intentions with this scene are interesting, but the page is filled with choreography and dense, novelistic paragraphs, so the story and the joke of the scene isn't coming through.

To approach an edit like this, we first have to ask …

What's the Story of the Scene?

Once that's determined, the writers can edit around those story intentions. In this case, it appears that the story of the scene is that two guys visit another guy at his bungalow, only to witness him attempt an escape.

This is a dark comedy, though, and the tone just isn't coming through, so the next thing to ask is …

What's the Joke or The Dramatic Moment?

In this scene, the writers want to make two jokes: One is the fact that the bungalow is so rundown that these guys can't even ring a doorbell without destroying the place. The second is the fact that their target falls while trying to sneak out the window.

What Has To Be Shown?

There are certain objects and characters that can't be eliminated in our rewrite. We have to see ..

The bungalow and car.

The men, dressed in suits, arriving at the house.

The bungled doorbell.

The escape through the window.

Editing around what has to be shown and keeping in mind the story and the joke, the writers pulled off a strong rewrite:

EXT. LANCE'S BUNGALOW - DAY

A run down bungalow with barred windows that aches for
demolition. The driveway hosts a beat up bronze
Camaro...foam explodes from the ripped vinyl seats.

BRAKES SQUEAL. Two Armani suits exit a black Lincoln Town
car. Suit #1 presses the doorbell.

DING DONG...DIZZZZZ.

The DOORBELL

POPS OFF and

SMASHES on the ground.

Suit #2 puts a meaty hand to the screen and it RIPS.

Suit #1 scrabbles in the dust and plays Legos with the broken
doorbell. Nothing fits.

Suit #2 grabs the bits of plastic from Suit #1 with a growl,

                    SUIT #2
          Here!

Suit #2 puts it back together,

SLAPS it on the wall and

ABUSES the button twice.

DING DONG! DING DONG! It's slumland Fort Knox.

A window screen TEARS AND FALLS onto the concrete path. The
suits RACE around the side of the house. On top of it sprawls
LANCE COCKSURE, aged rock-star, in a faded concert T-shirt.

                    LANCE
          What do you want?

From Jukebox Zero, *written by Keith Armonaitis and Lynne Christensen, 2009.*

Let's look at what they did to make the improvements.

First of all, they got the setting out of the way in two sentences: "A rundown bungalow with barred windows that aches for demolition. The driveway hosts a beat-up bronze Camaro ... foam explodes from the ripped vinyl seats." It's edited way down, but the description is vivid because they've made objects active: "driveway *hosts*," "foam *explodes*."

Then they moved on to the SUITS. Notice that they no longer describe what the men are wearing. What they've named the characters says it all.

Instead of micromanaging the journey to the door and the search for the doorbell, the writers compressed it into the simple phrase, "Two Armani SUITS exit a black Lincoln Towncar. Suit #1 presses the doorbell."

No more looking at each other or feeling around for stuff. Those moments don't matter because they don't add to the joke.

Instead, they put the focus back on the real joke of the scene: the doorbell set piece. In order to get the funny action across, the writers use simple words that we can see and feel — "DING-DONG, POPS OFF, SMASHES" — and work them down the page.

An over-choreographed moment — "One of the men bends down and picks up the pieces of the transmitter and tries to figure out how to put it back together again" — was replaced with this terrific metaphor: "Suit #1 scrambles in the dust and plays Legos with the broken doorbell. Nothing fits."

Here's that word choice again:

"ONE OF THE MEN" replaced by "SUIT #1"

"BENDS DOWN AND PICKS UP" replaced by "SCRAMBLES IN THE DUST"

"TRIES TO FIGURE OUT HOW TO PUT IT BACK TOGETHER AGAIN" replaced by "PLAYS LEGOS WITH."

Beautiful!

Moving on. With the introduction of Lance, the writers originally gave us lots of wardrobe information: "A man in bright green shorts and a faded concert T-shirt that has seen better days." The rewrite, however, describes him as: an "aged rock star." Now we get a real sense of who he is, not just what he's wearing.

TAKE TEN:
EDIT TO THE STORY

Focus your editing by asking the following questions:

WHAT'S THE STORY OF THE SCENE? _____

WHAT'S THE JOKE OR DRAMATIC MOMENT? _____

WHAT HAS TO BE SHOWN? _____

WHAT YOU'VE ACCOMPLISHED

You've focused your editing by working around the major beats. Since you know what you want from the scene, you won't be in danger of editing out too much.

Genre Intention Edit

Here's another scene to take a look at. As you read it, ask yourself what genre you think the writer's going for.

A large brown cricket jumps off her shoulder onto the bed.

>   MARTY
>   Where'd you come from?

She holds out her finger. It climbs on and stares back at her.

>   MARTY
>   You can stay here if you want.

She grabs a jar with holes poked in its lid and discards the old dead contents.

>   MARTY
>   I guess I have to call you something.

She drops it into the jar. A handful of black soot falls from her sleeve onto the cricket and flashes with light.

>   MARTY
>   Did you do that?

As she lids the jar, another lump of soot falls down on the cricket. Bright light flashes again.

```
The cricket shakes the stuff off in an irritated
almost human way and stares at her, tapping its
foot.
```

> MARTY
> OK. I'm sorry. I won't do it again.

So, when thinking of a genre for this scene, did you say "horror movie?" No? Perhaps that's because it feels more like an animated princess movie. The sympathetic protagonist, a cricket who taps his foot — we've seen this in lighter, softer movies to great success. But is it creepy? Not one bit.

Once the writer figured out that she wasn't meeting her tonal intentions, her editing approach became very clear. Her rewrite reads like this:

```
She picks up a sealed jar, covered in years of
dust, and looks at the big dead spidery thing
inside.
```

> MARTY
> You're an ugly beast aren't you?

```
She taps on the jar. It looks back at her, bares
its fangs and angrily throws itself against the
glass.
```

> MARTY
> Aaaa …

```
She falls back and drops it on the floor. The
glass breaks.
```

```
The creepy thing scurries into a dark corner and
disappears.
```

Written by Leslie Lawson, 2009.

No more sympathetic little girl. Marty calls the cricket an "ugly beast." And the cricket itself is now a "big dead spidery thing." It doesn't tap its foot; it "bares its fangs." And, when it "scurries into a dark corner," we wonder if and when it will come back, and what it might do next! Creepy.

⑩ TAKE TEN:
EDIT TO THE GENRE

Edit to the genre by trying one of the possibilities below:

1. TRY OUT A NEW EMOTION
   EX: Horror instead of pleasure.

2. HEIGHTEN WORDS
   EX: "She slithers away" instead of "She leaves the room."

3. DELETE PASSAGES AND LINES
   EX: A thriller may have less conversation. A comedy may have less action lines.

WHAT YOU'VE ACCOMPLISHED
You've turned your scenes into something genre-worthy!

Line Cut Edit

Here's an opening scene that makes its point but is cluttered up by too many words.

INT. WALDORF ASTORIA, RECEPTION ROOM - EVENING

A hundred tables with guests in glittering evening wear fill
a large reception room. There is a loud cacophony of clicking
cutlery, well-bred murmuring, and the quiet whoosh of service
doors.

The sound system hums and TAYLOR BERGMAN (55, tall, craggily
handsome and white-tie suited) comes to stand at the
microphone at the podium. Behind him a banner reads
"Celebrate Live Coral" in large letters, surrounded with
oceanic motifs. One after another, the guests stop their
activities and focus on Taylor.

> TAYLOR
> Hello again. I wanted to have the
> chance to say good night to you,
> after this splendid dinner and
> uplifting speeches.

The crowd applauds. Some people start to stand up. Taylor
manages to look bashful, for a moment, and waves them to sit.

> TAYLOR (CONT'D)
> Please, everyone, have a seat.

There is a rustle as people settle back to their seats.

> TAYLOR (CONT'D)
> Thank you again for your kind
> messages. I know that it's you,
> every one of you, who should be
> applauded. As we all know, this has
> not been a good year for the
> economy, my friends. And so I thank
> you all the more for being here
> tonight. I am truly grateful that
> you show your generosity so freely.
> Together, we will change the world.
> We will make a better life for our
> children and our grandchildren.

From Dark Pools, *written by Carole Ryavec, 2009.*

Let's keep the scene beats, but cut out lines:

INT. WALDORF ASTORIA, RECEPTION ROOM - EVENING

A hundred tables with guests in glittering evening wear fill
a large reception room. ~~There is a loud cacophony of clicking~~
~~cutlery, well bred murmuring, and the quiet whoosh of service~~
~~doors.~~

The sound system hums and TAYLOR BERGMAN ~~(55, tall,~~ craggily
handsome and white-tie suited) comes to stand ~~at the~~
~~microphon~~e at the podium. ~~Behind him a banner reads~~
~~"Celebrate Live Coral" in large letters, surrounded with~~
~~oceanic motifs. One after another, the guests stop their~~
~~activities and focus on Taylor.~~

> ~~TAYLOR~~
> ~~Hello again. I wanted to have the~~
> ~~chance to say good night to you,~~
> ~~after this splendid dinner and~~
> ~~uplifting speeches.~~

The crowd applauds. Some people start to stand up. Taylor
manages to look bashful, for a moment, and waves them to sit.

> TAYLOR (CONT'D)
> Please, everyone, have a seat.

~~There is a rustle as~~ people settle back to their seats.

> TAYLOR (CONT'D)
> ~~Thank you again for your kind~~
> ~~messages. I know that~~ it's you,
> every one of you, who should be
> applauded. ~~As we all know, this has~~
> ~~not been a good year for the~~
> ~~economy, my friends. And so I thank~~
> ~~you all the more for being here~~
> ~~tonight.~~ I am truly grateful that
> you show your generosity so freely.
> Together, we will change the world.
> ~~We will make a better life for our~~
> ~~children and our grandchildren.~~

The edited scene now looks like this:

INT. WALDORF ASTORIA, RECEPTION ROOM - EVENING

A hundred tables with guests in glittering evening wear fill
a large reception room.

The sound system hums and TAYLOR BERGMAN, craggily handsome
and white-tie suited, comes to stand at the podium.

The crowd applauds. Some people start to stand up. Taylor
manages to look bashful, for a moment, and waves them to sit.

                    TAYLOR
          Please, everyone, have a seat.

People settle back to their seats.

                    TAYLOR (CONT'D)
          It's you, every one of you, who
          should be applauded. I am truly
          grateful that you show your
          generosity so freely. Together, we
          will change the world.

You'll see that the intentions of the page stay the same. We've just weeded out a lot of miscellaneous details in the scene direction. And nothing's lost by eliminating the "cacophony of cutlery," or the banner.

We also deleted and cut into the speeches. This is because the story of the scene has more to do with the character's position in life and what he's doing at the event, than about what he's saying. So we've skipped the niceties and focused on one paragraph that highlights generosity and change; the reasons the guests are attending that night.

 TAKE TEN:
LINE EDIT

Go into your scenes and scratch out lines that aren't working for your scene. Use this list as a guide:

1. Delete lines that repeat set decoration.

2. Delete lines that repeat emotion.

3. Delete lines that show intricate steps of a simple action.

4. Delete lines of dialogue until you have a great dramatic or comedic one-liner.

5. Delete polite exchanges when people meet.

6. Delete speeches that repeat information.

WHAT YOU'VE ACCOMPLISHED
You've cleaned up your script. It's not only a great story; it's a great read.

Scene Trim Edit

Enter late. Leave early. It's the best advice on editing *ever*. Unfortunately, I didn't come up with it. William Goldman did. Just check out some of his movies to see how good he is at this.

Cutting the tops or bottoms (or both) of scenes is sometimes the quickest and smartest editing pass you can make on your script. Come in to a scene as conflict is brewing. Get out just as you've raised a question or upped the stakes. Go before more talk and description robs the scene of the suspense and romance. I mean it. Leave!

TAKE TEN: ENTER LATE, LEAVE EARLY

Where it's needed, cut the beginning of scenes or chop off the ending. Use this suggested list for places to make this change:

1. Open on people in conversation. Cut introductions.

2. Open on a character on a phone call. Cut the ring and "hello?"

3. Open mid-party.

4. Open mid-dinner.

5. Open mid-love scene.

OR

6. Cut scene just after the first moment of seduction.

7. Cut the end of the phone call. Leave on a reaction instead.

8. Cut the delivery of bad news.

OR

9. Cut the reaction to bad news.

WHAT YOU'VE ACCOMPLISHED

You've succeeded in tightening your own material and, in the process, given your script a quicker pace.

The General Edit

In a final polish, *do* sweat the small stuff. Here's a bunch of small, but important, items that are worth taking ten more minutes to change or delete.

Who Deserves a Name?

Every time you name a character in a script, it implies that he is an important enough character for the reader to track. Prevent confusion by naming people by their profession if that's their only role in the script. Example: WAITRESS, SECURITY GUARD, FLIGHT ATTENDANT, etc.

Note, because that is the "name" you're giving them, it's still capitalized when first introduced into the script.

Film Means Never Having to Say "Hello"

Because a play is often limited to one or two fixed sets, characters are forced to "enter" and "exit." But the beauty of film is that you don't have to slow down your scenes with people arriving, greeting, getting situated, etc. Nor do you have to exchange the kinds of pleasantries leaving a scene that you might have to in real life. Forget "I'll see you later" as the character walks out. Just cut out of the scene!

I Kill Receptionists

As someone who's read thousands of scripts, "I Kill Receptionists" could easily be the title of my autobiography. Why? Because, in script after script, I strike my red pen through the scene where the receptionist helps the main character make an appointment. Or the one where she says, "You can't go in there!"

There's also a special graveyard for all of the waiters who've taken valuable screen time (and minutes of my own life) writing down dinner orders in scenes. Cut!

And don't get me started on nurses who exist simply to bring the doctor to the patient. "Dr. So-and-so will see you now." Red pen!

So kill your own receptionist. You'll be glad you did.

And That Reminds Me

"By the way." "Speaking of." "That reminds me..."

Do you see a lot of those kinds of phrases in your script? Consider those to be red flags that you are going on too long in your dialogue. Cut whatever was said *after* those phrases and bring up the subject you were going to address in a new scene.

Yeah, So, and Well

"Well, the first thing to do is find Dr. Mars."

"Yeah. He'll know where the formula is."

"So, how do we get to him?"

Can you hear how awful that sounds? Unless you're writing the sequel to *Scooby Doo*, edit these words out!

Say My Name!

Actually, don't. When characters constantly address other characters by name, it starts to sound artificial.

"Michael, I've been meaning to tell you something."

"Susan, what is it?"

"I've been seeing someone else, Michael."

Run through your dialogue and see if you're guilty of this. Sometimes, it's a natural habit to fall into when you're trying to put emphasis on a line. It's also one of the easiest edits to make.

Good News, Bad News

When it comes to bad news, our own imagination is the best writer. Rather than have a character react to news of a tragedy, cut the scene before that character can say anything. Our imagination will fill in the rest.

Cut the Score

I'm very, very sorry to have to say this. But "scoring" your movie distracts and takes us out of the read. Think about it this way. If something really great or really awful happened in your own life, wouldn't you be annoyed if music suddenly started to play from nowhere? That's how the reader feels when a song "plays over" a scene.

The good news is that you can be specific about music when it comes from a source. If a character singing "I Will Survive" at a karaoke club actually moves the story, then fine, write it in. Though prepare for that song to possibly be replaced with another if the producers can't get the rights to it. ("Hit Me With Your Best Shot" maybe?)

(10) TAKE TEN:
EDIT THE SMALL STUFF

Take ten minutes and edit in one or more of the following ways:

1. Rename minor characters using their professions.

2. Cut character entrances and exits.

3. Edit out minor characters who steal scene time: Receptionists, waiters, nurses, etc.

4. Look for awkward segue phrases like "that reminds me" and "speaking of." Then cut the dialogue that follows.

5. Wherever possible, cut "Yeah," "So," and "Well" from your dialogue.

6. Edit dialogue that overuses names for emphasis.

7. Let our imagination run wild by cutting verbal reactions to bad news.

8. Lose the music unless it comes from a source.

WHAT YOU'VE ACCOMPLISHED
You've made your script "reader-proof."

■ TEN-MINUTE CHAPTER REVIEW:
THE FINAL EDIT

1. Edit scenes, working around the STORY, the JOKE, and WHAT HAS TO BE SHOWN.

2. Replace words in order to be truer to your GENRE.

3. LINE EDIT for a cleaner read.

4. Edit tops and bottoms of scenes to COME IN LATE and LEAVE EARLY.

5. Edit the small stuff like overuse of NAMES, PHRASES and MINOR CHARACTERS, unnecessary VERBAL REACTIONS, and MUSIC that doesn't come from a source.

CHAPTER 10

The Presentation

You thought you only had ten minutes. But in those stolen ten-minute chunks of time, you actually finished your screenplay. You started with an idea. You built it into an outline. You roughed it out, wrote the first draft and then rewrote it! The story is well thought out. The characters have depth. The scenes move the story along. The pages have emotion. The read is clean.

Until an executive or producer actually pays you to do another rewrite, you're finished screenwriting. Congratulations! Celebrate by taking ten minutes to do something human for a change — like clip your nails or hug your spouse.

Print and Bind

Done clipping and hugging? Good. Back to work.

After all, you have this screenplay that you must now show to the world. Pretty it up!

TAKE TEN:
MAKE YOUR SCRIPT PRESENTABLE

1. Your script should be written in 12-point Courier font. If it is not, change it now.

2. Write a title page with the title in the middle, your name underneath it, and contact information on the bottom right side. Resist all temptation to add cute fonts or illustrations.

3. Put a plain card stock cover on your screenplay. Add two brads with fasteners, preferably Acco #5 brads (one at the top and one at the bottom, no brad in the middle hole).

WHAT YOU'VE ACCOMPLISHED

The script looks real. You can parade it around. You can get your picture taken with it. You can even sell it for $250,000 against $1,000,000.

Protect Your Material

All of your stolen ten minutes of work time might be for nothing if someone actually uses *his* ten to steal your script.

So, take an additional ten minutes to register and copyright. And definitely do both. Registering with the Writers Guild is a must, but it only provides a paper trail of evidence, whereas copyright legally protects your words.

TAKE TEN:
REGISTER YOUR SCRIPT

Go to www.wga.org and register online, or by downloading the forms.

TAKE TEN:
COPYRIGHT YOUR SCRIPT

Go to www.copyright.gov and download the forms.

WHAT YOU'VE ACCOMPLISHED
Peace of mind.

Pitch Your Script

I'm glad you took those ten minutes to celebrate, because you're really going to have to do some work now. Any working screenwriter will tell you that writing the script is just the beginning. Now you have to convince others to read it. And that often starts with a short pitch.

You thought that ten minutes was a short amount of time to write your script. Try pitching it in *one*. Why one minute? Because that's all the time the producer has at that moment. He's riding in an elevator with you. She's on her way to lunch. He's got an agent to meet. She's about to go into a development meeting. You've got one minute, and one minute only, to get their attention and convince them to read your material.

So, you need to create a *minute pitch* for your screenplay: a short, telephone-friendly, verbal synopsis of your story and its selling points.

To help you, I've created a *minute pitch template* — and, though we're going to go through it element-by-element, it's really only going to take ten minutes to fill out. The template will also get you back on track with the big-picture issues, reminding you of the main concept of your script and recommitting you to your story.

I've broken the template you're going to use into the separate elements. Let's take ten more minutes to look at them:

● *PREMISE*

LOG LINE _____ .

Concept

Remember that log line from the early pages? Well, now that you really know what your script is like, hone it until it feels just right to you.

You can "what if" if you want. Or just lead with "my script is about." However you present your logline, remember that it's *the most important part of the pitch*. The listener may cut you off, saying "I'll buy it" or "I hate it," based on that one sentence alone.

No pressure or anything.

● *TITLE AND GENRE*

_____ is a _____

Title of script   specific genre

The branding process begins with your *title*. Putting a title into a producer's head is one of the first steps in painting the picture. *I Was a Teenage Werewolf* tells you a lot about a movie. And *Blood Diamond* suggests a specific tone.

Being specific about the *genre* adds color to that painting. Your script isn't just a thriller; it's a psychological thriller or, perhaps, a courtroom thriller.

● *TONE*

... in the vein of _____ .

similar film

Comparing your script to another project helps bring out genre and tone. Producers often want to get an immediate sense of the kind of project you're pitching. You don't have to compare your project to one that's similar in premise, just in its mood, scope, or look.

Some examples:

The Sixth Sense is in the vein of *Rosemary's Baby.*

Old School is in the vein of *Animal House.*

Garden State is in the vein of *The Graduate.*

The Bourne Identity is in the vein of *Three Days of the Condor.*

● *CHARACTER*

It focuses on _____ and _____

                   main character   supporting character

Why two characters? To give the main character someone to relate with and to suggest subplots and B-stories that you might not otherwise have time to pitch.

If you describe a *hard-nosed cop* and *a hooker with a heart of gold*, for example, that pairing alone will suggest career conflict and romantic problems.

In your pitch, don't just name the characters; describe them:

Method 1: Flaw plus occupation.

Thelma and Louise become ...

A feisty waitress and a put-upon housewife.

Method 2: All flaw.

Harry and Sally become ...

A chauvinistic loudmouth and a prissy know-it-all.

Method 3: Use their issues.

Cole and Malcolm become ...

A boy who communicates with spirits and a disheartened psychologist.

Method 4: Bring in backstory.

Cole and Malcolm become ...

A psychologist shot by a patient, and a boy haunted by ghosts.

In the case of an ensemble of characters, treat them as one character in a situation:

A group of college friends, now hardened by life.
(*The Big Chill*)

An aging group of outlaws.
(*The Wild Bunch*)

● *ACTIVITY*

... as they _____ .

                       second act activity

As you know from writing, characters in movies and TV don't just think and feel, they plot and act. The second act of the movie *is* your movie, and the producers you're pitching to are aware of that. They're listening for the verbs. What are your characters actually *doing* in the movie and *how* are they doing it?

In *Die Hard*, John McClane doesn't just rescue hostages, he **launches a one-man war.**

In *Sideways*, Miles and Jack don't travel wine country, they **turn a California wine tour into a bachelor-party weekend.**

Ocean's Eleven doesn't just show eleven guys robbing a casino. It follows **a slick con-man and ten talented accomplices as they rob three Las Vegas casinos at one time.**

Erin Brockovich follows the journey of an unappreciated single mother as she **investigates a suspicious real-estate case and discovers that it's a cover-up to buy land contaminated by a deadly, toxic waste.**

Words like "investigate" and "discover" make the second act feel truly active while leaving out unnecessary setup details.

● *COMPLICATION*
Problems occur when _____ !

complication

Now that you've nailed the second-act activity and drawn the listener into the story, you need to shake it up a bit. You risk boring people, even in this short time, unless you imply that a new complication comes around.

Depending on what pitches better, this could be the complication that comes at the midpoint of your script or at the end of your second act.

How to find your complication? As we discussed earlier, the big complication of the movie is usually *antagonist-driven*:

Problems occur when **a dark arts teacher attempts to destroy Harry by using his knowledge of Harry's past against him.** (*Harry Potter and the Sorcerer's Stone*)

But complication can also be caused by an *event, a group of events,* or *the flaw of the main character.*

● *STRATEGY AND STAKES*

Now they must _____ !

third-act strategy

Describing the third-act strategy gives a sense of new urgency at the end of your pitch.

You're describing something our main character *has* to do that reminds us of the stakes. It also leaves us wanting answers that can only be found if we request the script!

Now they must **visit the ghosts at the scene of their deaths to determine what they want from Cole.** (*The Sixth Sense*)

Now they must **murder their son's murderer or feel tortured by his freedom for the rest of their lives.** (*In The Bedroom*)

Now he must **stop her from marrying the wrong man before it's too late.** (*The Graduate, Four Weddings and A Funeral, Shrek*)

● *TALKING POINTS*

The remaining elements in your minute-pitch template are talking points that will help you stress the commercial possibilities of your project once you're done pitching the story. Use them to answer questions from the producer, or to keep selling your project if she seems to want more.

● *ORIGINALITY AND MESSAGE*

This movie is unlike any in its genre because of _____.

unique approach

At this point, just in case there are *any* doubts as to the project's appeal, you bring home what's truly unique about the project. Your approach is your unique stamp; *how* you'll be telling this story in a different way.

It could be a *cinematic technique.*

This movie is unlike any in its genre because of **the mixture of live action and CGI.** (*Avatar*)

This movie is unlike any in its genre because of **the way characters experience an emotional breakthrough by morphing from black-and-white to color.** (*Pleasantville*)

It could be that you're breaking the rules of *structure* in an interesting way:

This movie is unlike any in its genre because **it's told backward, from final reveal to initial motivation**. (*Memento*)

● *THEME*

Audiences will respond to _____ .

theme

This is your opportunity to tell the listener that your script is about bigger things — that it delivers a message as well as a big concept:

Audiences will respond to **the way that education helps a pregnant teenager overcome adversity**. (*Precious*)

Audiences will respond to **one man's courage to risk it all and challenge corporate America by telling the truth**. (*The Insider*)

● *SCENES*

And they'll love scenes such as _____ .

trailer moment

The final element of your pitch is one that's going to leave the listener with a picture in his head. And it's going to be an image or idea that's so compelling that he'll have to ask for the script or forever be haunted by the memory of your incredible scene!

Focus on a unique set piece or describe one image that tells a great story.

The mother's legs buckle as a service man tells her that three of her sons have been killed in the war. (*Saving Private Ryan*)

Two hitmen casually talk about France and foot massages before busting down the door of a group of unsuspecting victims. (*Pulp Fiction*)

A secret agent rappels silently downward in midair so as not to activate the alarm system. Then his knife falls. (*Mission: Impossible*)

A rowdy frat guy pretends he's a human zit and then maniacally starts a food fight. (*Animal House*)

While you don't want to get overly detailed with the other elements, when it comes to these trailer moments, the smaller details matter. For example: Audiences won't just love the battle scene; they'll love the battle scene using cream pies.

As you can see, the elements in a short pitch are the same elements necessary to make a script great. Next time you write a script, you can even use this template *before you write* in order to make decisions about your story, writing approach, and special scenes.

⑩ TAKE TEN:
THE MINUTE PITCH

What if _____ ?
                                    premise

_____ is a _____
        Title of script   *specific genre*

in the vein of _____ .
                                    similar film

It focuses on _____ and _____
                    main char.   *supporting char.*

as they _____ .
                                second-act activity

Problems occur when _____ .
                                    complication

Now they must _____ !
                                    third-act strategy

This movie is unlike any in its genre because of _____ .
                                                            unique approach

Audiences will respond to _____ .
                                                theme

And they'll love scenes such as _____ .
                                                    trailer moment

WHAT YOU'VE ACCOMPLISHED
Prepare to hear: "Send me the script immediately!"

This is a pitch that's perfect to use the next time you've cornered your dream producer at a cocktail party, finally gotten that agent's assistant on the phone, or been brought in for that studio meeting and they ask, "What else have you got?"

So write it down, take ten minutes to memorize it, practice it for another ten, and be prepared to pitch it whenever and wherever there's opportunity.

In Your Own Words

Though I've given you a template to follow, it's important that you use your own words and find your own voice. You've used the template to make decisions about the major elements within your pitch, so don't worry about loosening up the language, combining elements, or moving them around. One of my favorite writers, Nick Johnson, filled out the minute-pitch template for his script, *Nothin' But A Party*. It read:

What if a group of teens really did have to fight for their right to party?

Nothin' But A Party is a teen sex romp in the vein *of Superbad* meets *Sixteen Candles* meets *Rock 'n' Roll High School.*

It follows Ryan and his gang of trouble-seeking pals as they attempt to throw the perfect houseparty in order to help Ryan get his would-be girlfriend, Lisa, back in the mood for love.

Problems occur when Lisa decides to go to the party with someone else and local authorities declare all-out war on good times.

Now Ryan must prove his love and win Lisa back before the cops bust in and put an end to the most glorious bash the town has ever seen.

This movie is unlike any in its genre because it harkens back to the teen party comedies of the '80s with its hilarious and affectionate portrayal of teen life and love.

Audiences will respond to the over-the-top humor and colorful characters as well as Ryan and Lisa's awkward teen romance.

And they'll love scenes such as the climactic sequence in which an LSD-crazed police officer breaks up the house party by using tear gas and non-lethal rounds on the rebellious revelers.

As you can see, all of the elements are here. But the pitch was missing the energy of the actual party. So, I encouraged him to reorder some of the statements. The result was this:

Nothin' But A Party:

When you really do have to "fight for your right."

Sixteen-year old Ryan almost gets to third base with his girlfriend, Lisa, when … the cops are called and the party they're at is broken up! Now, he must recreate the perfect house party in order to get her back in the mood for love.

The job seems easy enough: Get the music, the venue, the booze, and the crowd. But when Ryan's only musical choice is emo, his house is a real-estate model home, and his alcohol connection is experiencing acid flashbacks, the task gets a little bit complicated.

Ultimately, Ryan must prove his love and win Lisa back before the cops bust in and put an end to the most glorious bash the town has ever seen.

Edgy and affectionate, *Nothin' But A Party* is a hilarious look at teen life and love that harkens back to the teen party comedies of the eighties. Think *Sixteen Candles* and *Rock 'n' Roll High School* with a touch of *Superbad*.

TAKE TEN:
PITCH IN YOUR OWN WORDS

Reword your pitch template by following one of the suggestions below, or mixing and matching the elements as best suits you:

1. Lead with the stakes.

2. Tease with the commercial appeal.

3. Build up to the log line (but DO get there).

4. Start with character.

5. End with title.

WHAT YOU'VE ACCOMPLISHED
You've made your pitch a bit less scripted and a whole lot more "you."

The Personal Pitch

Almost more important than being able to pitch your movie idea is being able to pitch yourself. When a producer buys a script, they're investing in a relationship that could go on for years. So, it's important for them to feel at ease when they meet you. When they leave the meeting, they need to believe that you're someone who's got a great script *and* is easy and interesting to work with.

Icebreaker

Your intuitive nature as a writer — your ability to observe surroundings and empathize with characters — will serve you well when meeting someone for the first time. Throughout this book, I've asked you to consider story from another character's point of view. In a meeting with a new person, you can do the same thing. What's the manager or agent's "movie?" What "scene" is he in the middle of? Does he look overwhelmed? Is she clearly busy or on the tail end of something big?

Try out an *empathetic statement*, then, to break the ice — something that suggests you "get" what's going on with your listener. I watched one writer earn a smile from a producer at a pitch fest when she joked that she was "writer number 356" then added "you must be exhausted!" Having opened with that "I get you" icebreaker, the writer helped the producer to relax for a minute and made her that much more open to hearing the pitch. Of course, not every listener is the same, and you'll need to keep your eyes and ears open for that opening line that will best draw her in. But having a brief conversational moment, even one line to establish a human connection, is a very good start.

Find Your Personal Hook

"So, tell me about yourself." Great, the producer wants to know about you. Do you go back to childhood and tell him every fascinating detail? No, you do not. Instead, you log line. Not your story; you! You create a *log line of yourself*, focusing on the "hook" of you and the highs of your life. Here's one:

```
A script read for a friend catapults a slacker
sandwich girl into a job at a major studio and a
career teaching screenwriting.
```

That's me ... spun. But, yeah, I really was an over-educated and underemployed twenty-something, selling sandwiches out of a cart when a friend asked me to read a script for a production company. And a career as a studio reader, consultant, teacher, and lecturer eventually followed. That's my story, built around its hook and its high points. And creating a log line of myself helped me communicate that to you in one sentence.

Express Your Passion

Your job with a personal pitch is not only to get someone interested in you, it's to segue them into talking about your work. A great way to do both is to use the log line of your life to talk about the *inspiration* for your project. In this way, the listener gets more insight into you and gets interested in the project you're about to pitch. Let's say I wanted to segue from talking about myself into discussion of a script. I could say:

```
In fact, it was this radical change in my life
from service person to script analyst that made
me think about the ways our lives can change in
an instant, and ultimately led me to write my
script, Change of Heart.
```

Sneaky, huh? I expressed a passion for my work, but also got that title on the table! (I'm not actually writing this script; so, it's all yours.)

Deliver the Big Idea

You've drawn them in and opened up the floodgates, so now you can launch into the pitch of your project. Include the elements discussed in the minute pitch and proceed to wow them.

(10) TAKE TEN:
CREATE A PERSONAL PITCH

Craft a personal pitch that follows the following steps:

1. ICEBREAKER: Empathetic statement that creates a personal connection.

2. PERSONAL HOOK: Create a log line of yourself in order to briefly show off the "highs" of your life and the "hook" of you.

3. YOUR PASSION: Ease the listener into a discussion of your script by talking about how your own life inspired your current story.

4. THE BIG IDEA: Use the discussion of inspiration to segue you into the logline of your movie. Then proceed with the minute pitch.

WHAT YOU'VE ACCOMPLISHED
You've lowered the defenses of your listener, made a connection, and spiked an interest in you and your project.

Marketing Materials

If I had my druthers, all a writer would need to get her script noticed would be the words on the page. But there's a lot of competition out there, so it's not a bad idea to have an arsenal of other materials to help market and promote your work. Before I elaborate more, here's a rundown of some terms:

 TEN-MINUTE LECTURE:

PITCH, QUERY, ONE-SHEET ... AND MORE

A SHORT PITCH briefly describes your story and its appeal, whetting the appetite of the listener and encouraging them to read your script. A QUERY LETTER is a letter most often sent to AGENTS and MANAGERS that requests they consider you and your script for representation. A PITCH FEST brings producers, representation and writers together, allowing a writer to briefly pitch his material. A ONE-SHEET is a mini-poster of a movie that can serve as a visual aid during a short pitch. This is not to be confused with a ONE-PAGE SYNOPSIS, which is a page-long, beat-by-beat synopsis of your movie.

PLEASE NOTE: These are marketing materials only. Once a script is requested by a producer or representation, it should be submitted unaccompanied by any additional material.

END OF LECTURE

The Query Letter

Some agents and managers find new writers via query letters and some do not. Still, somewhere in your communication with an interested party, you're going to need to introduce yourself and your work in letter form. So it's good to take ten minutes to write one down.

The great part is that, if you were following along with the minute pitch and the personal pitch, you've already written one!

TAKE TEN:
WRITE A QUERY

Write a query letter that incorporates information about you and your project.

LEAD WITH THE PERSONAL PITCH:
Icebreaker
Personal hook
Your passion
The big idea

CONTINUE WITH THE MINUTE PITCH FOR PLOT POINTS:
Concept
Title
Genre
Comparison
Description of characters
Second-act activity
Complication
Third-act strategy

CONTINUE WITH THE MINUTE PITCH FOR SELLING POINTS:
Unique approach
Theme
Trailer moment

END WITH A SIGN-OFF AND PERSONAL INFORMATION:
Request for a script read
Your contact information
Thank you

WHAT YOU'VE ACCOMPLISHED
You've created a cover letter or query that sells both you and your script and convinces an agent, manager or producer to meet with you or request your material.

The One-Page Synopsis

Once you have her attention, an agent or manager may ask for a one-page synopsis of your screenplay. This is a way of finding out even more about your project without having to read the whole thing. It's also your opportunity to give her a few extra details that will help push the sale.

If you're overwhelmed with the idea of synopsizing your entire screenplay, just go back to the earlier tools in this book. The BRIEF SYNOPSIS, BEDTIME STORY TEMPLATE or BEAT SHEET are easily translated into a summary. Just glue the beats together with words that create a narrative flow.

 TAKE TEN:
ONE-PAGE SYNOPSIS TIPS

When writing a one-page synopsis, keep in mind the following points:

1. KEEP YOUR FIRST ACT SHORT
Don't dwell on setup. Jump into the main character's problem.

2. WEAVE CHARACTERS INTO THE STORY
Don't introduce them in one block. Instead, work them into the synopsis as they actually affect the story.

3. GUIDE THE READER EMOTIONALLY
Describe an emotion that triggers a major action. Sum up a plot-heavy paragraph by emphasizing the personal effect it has on the main character.

4. DON'T CHEAT THE ENDING
Describe at least one moment that triggers the reveal, or a clever move that helps solve the problem.

WHAT YOU'VE ACCOMPLISHED
You now have a beat-by-beat, one-page synopsis that can be pulled out whenever needed. You've saved your potential buyer precious reading time.

The One-sheet

The one-sheet is simply a mini-poster for your movie. It often includes a *tag line*, a one-sentence teaser for the theme or story.

Tag Line Examples:

"Man has made his match … now it's his problem."
— *Blade Runner*

"Somebody said get a life … so they did."
— *Thelma & Louise*

"Sometimes you have to go halfway around the world to come full circle."
— *Lost in Translation*

A one-sheet can also include the kind of *image* that you'd see on a poster itself. If you're going to include one, though, make it look clean and professional. You do your movie a disservice by cobbling together anything less.

Add to your one-sheet a *log line* or *brief synopsis*. And, whatever you do, make sure your *contact information* is on there as well. Put the elements together and your one-sheet is finished.

TAKE TEN: CREATE A ONE-SHEET

Create a one-sheet (mini-poster) by following the steps below. Note that you do not have to include an image if you don't want to.

1. HIGHLIGHT THE TITLE

2. ADD A TAG LINE

3. FEATURE AN IMAGE

4. INCLUDE A LOG LINE OR BRIEF SYNOPSIS

5. CONCLUDE WITH CONTACT INFORMATION

WHAT YOU'VE ACCOMPLISHED

You've created a one-page selling tool that's a perfect "leave behind" when attending pitch fests or conferences.

Create a Blog or Website

Though it's an investment and it certainly takes more than ten minutes to create, a website that showcases you and your script can be a terrific marketing tool. It should include your writing biography, log lines and one-sheets, and your contact information. You could also consider adding music and visuals that convey the world of your script.

I'm a little more hesitant about blogging, but a well-written blog certainly shows off your voice and point of view. If this is a journal of your adventures in writing, you could get a reader interested enough in your process to want to read your script. On the other hand, be careful about being overly snide about "the business." Don't bite the hand *before* it feeds you.

■ TEN-MINUTE CHAPTER REVIEW: THE PRESENTATION

1. PRINT and BIND your script using the correct font, cover, and fasteners.

2. Develop a SHORT PITCH for your project by working around the major elements of your script's STORY and APPEAL.

3. Develop a PERSONAL PITCH by creating a log line of yourself and expressing your INSPIRATION for the project.

4. Write a QUERY LETTER by combining the minute pitch with the personal pitch.

5. Write a ONE-PAGE SYNOPSIS by working with earlier storytelling tools such as the Brief Synopsis, Bedtime Story Template, or Beat Sheet.

6. Write a ONE-SHEET that incorporates a TAG LINE, log line, brief synopsis, image, and contact information.

7. Set up a WEBSITE that includes your one-sheet, log lines, and writing bio.

CHAPTER 11

The Opportunity

Atat one point, I was going to call this chapter "The Sale." "The Sale," however, is not and should not be the brass ring after you write a script. Yes, it would be wonderful if it sold outright for a lot of money, but it would also be wonderful if it turned out to be a terrific writing sample that launched your career rewriting or adapting existing material. And it would also be pretty terrific if your script earned you a staff-writer position on a television show. How great would it be if this was the script that got the attention of an independent producer or became the script you filmed yourself, showcasing your talents as both a writer *and* director? Or perhaps it's the script that you break up into webisodes that gets you noticed as a new-media writer.

Opportunity is what we're going to focus on in this chapter. You've got the script. Now you need the break.

There are so many different "players" in the industry, though. It'll help to know what their role is.

 TEN-MINUTE LECTURE:

AGENTS, MANAGERS, LAWYERS, and PRODUCERS

MANAGERS manage a writer's career, helping develop the writer's scripts and making relationships for the writer, including getting them the right agent. They take 15%. An AGENT negotiates the deal on a particular script and has a license to do so (a manager does not). She takes 10%. When an agent is not involved, however, an ENTERTAINMENT ATTORNEY can also handle the contract. He often takes 5%. Once an agent or manager is acting as representative, he'll try and get a writer's script into the hands of a PRODUCTION COMPANY,

which will then bring it to a STUDIO in order to get it made.
An INDEPENDENT PRODUCER could desire to make it without
a studio, which means that she'll arrange financing, get talent
attached, etc. In that case, that producer will usually OPTION
your script, paying you to let her hold onto the script for a
limited time while she tries to set it up. If she fails to do so before
the option runs out, it goes back into your hands.

END OF LECTURE

Networking

Your script doesn't exist in a bubble and, in the previous chapter, we focused on the materials you may need to help push it out into the world. Once you feel it's where you want it, you should do everything in your power to get it into the hands of an agent, manager, or producer.

How do you do that? I wish I had just the right answer to that question. But it wouldn't hurt to start making as many friends as possible, a.k.a. networking.

It's a small world, and everyone in Hollywood is connected in some way. Even you. Don't think so? Once you put pen to paper and remind yourself of who you know and who *they* know, you're going to feel like you could run a studio.

So write it down!

People You Know

Alumni, friends, the cousin who goes to the right parties, that agent's assistant who you always see at the coffee shop, that dentist who bragged that his son ran HBO. You've got more connections than you think.

I currently host a podcast where I interview successful writers in the industry. Every one of them has a "big break" story that's entirely unexpected. One writer met a producer at their kids' preschool. Another writer hired a commercial director at his ad agency and then packed up with him and went to Hollywood. Another writer started in the business by delivering ThighMasters while working as a production assistant for Suzanne Somers' talk show. Take it from a former sandwich girl

— opportunity is right around the corner. You just never know who you know.

People They Know

Your contact list may look weak on industry contacts, until you play the "two degrees" game. By writing down the acquaintances or relatives of the people that your friends know, you'll realize that you're only one beat away from making an important relationship.

Establish Contact

This is the part where you're going to have to do some legwork. Go to that alumni mixer and reacquaint yourself with your classmates. Get that teeth cleaning you've been putting off. Become your cousin's "friend" on Facebook. You've probably meant to do these things anyway. And while you're doing these things, make a genuine connection. There's only good in this. Even if all you get out of the experience is a shiny smile and a reconnection with family, you'll still be happier and ahead.

Ask for a Favor

Go ahead. Ask. But make sure it's one favor, and make sure it's the right one. Asking your dentist to read your script isn't going to help you in any way. But it's reasonable to ask if you could use his name when contacting his big-shot son. A name alone is a precious commodity. It could open the door.

Track the Result

After you've made a connection and/or asked a favor, keep track of the outcome. Who did you talk to and what did they say? You'll need these facts on hand so that you can make the proper follow-up call later if you need to remind someone to read the script or just want to say "thank you" to the assistant who connected you with her boss.

I encourage any writer who pitches at a pitch fest, for example, to create a database of who they talked to and what was said about their idea. That way, if a connection is made or a script is requested, the writer can remind their new contact that they "loved the energy and the surprise ending," or that they "responded to the lonely truck-driving main character." Keeping a database of outcome, even if it's a negative one, will also help if you ever feel your script has been taken or your words used without your permission.

TAKE TEN:
CREATE A CONTACT LIST

Discover and connect with your contacts by making the following list:

PERSON I KNOW	PERSON THEY KNOW	CONNECTION PLAN	FAVOR	RESULT

WHAT YOU'VE ACCOMPLISHED
Your checklist has helped you to realize just how connected you are and to make a plan for moving ahead in your career.

Conferences and Pitch Fests

There are a lot of conferences and pitch fests out there, and they all have different personalities. Pick yours by determining your agenda going in. Is it to pitch to a particular company? Is it to connect with a community of writers? Is it to learn more about the film business by taking classes?

Broad goals, like "sell my script," should be reconsidered. If producers and agents are at a conference, they're there to meet new faces, see if they spark to a new idea, and generate new submissions.

A more realistic goal might be to "make a relationship." Remember that one genuine relationship — that one person who "gets" you and is passionate about your work — can make all the difference.

TAKE TEN:
CONFERENCE AND PITCH FEST DATABASE

Make a list of events that interest you. Then use this list to track your goals going in and your achievements coming out.

CONFERENCE	GOAL	RELATIONSHIP MADE	COMPANY PITCHED TO	REACTION	FOLLOW-UP

WHAT YOU'VE ACCOMPLISHED
You set realistic goals at a networking event, and you met them. You're one step closer to a writing career.

Virtual Pitch Fests and Online Opportunities

Don't live in Los Angeles? Can't afford to fly to a pitch fest? As communication becomes more "virtual" via e-mail and texting, the playing field levels for the out-of-town writer. There are also a multitude of online resources to help you learn, track industry news, network, and pitch: imdbpro.com, virtualpitchfest.com, zoetrope.com, moviebytes.com, donedealpro.com, inktip.com, theartfulwriter.com and trackingb.com just for starters.

Social Networking

Social networking sites like Facebook and MySpace break down barriers and allow even the biggest hotshot to become your "friend." But *do* compartmentalize. Create separate accounts, wherever possible, that distinguish your everyday life from your writing life. Your new "friend" may be the head of NBC, but do you really want him to see your embarrassing photos from your last party?

Follow Up

It's a scary thing to do, but you have to do it. Haven't heard anything since that producer requested your script? If two weeks have passed, send her a quick e-mail acknowledging her busy schedule, but also reminding her that she has your script and you'd love to know her reaction.

Two weeks later, let her know about some of the other positive responses you've been getting and emphasize that you're excited to get her thoughts as well.

Two weeks later, chat up her assistant and ask her if she could send a gentle reminder the producer's way.

Only give up when you're told that you should. But also be careful that you don't bully or whine. When industry people tell you that they're busy, they mean it. At the same time, don't put your career on hold waiting for them. Keep casting your net!

New Media

There is no greater opportunity in the entertainment industry than can be found in the wide-open and somewhat untamed world of new media. Production companies, agencies and studios are developing new-media divisions at a rapid pace and regularly combing the Internet for undiscovered talent.

A talented client of mine, Mike Maden, had a terrific feature script but was having a hard time getting the attention of representation. One day, he told me that he had to go to Texas because he was going to shoot "something for the Internet." In less than two weeks, he and his producing partner had created ten episodes of a Web series Mike had written called *Pink: The Series*. They put it on YouTube, and it quickly earned over a million hits. The public interest got both of them signed with a major agency. That agency helped them get financing for the next ten episodes, arranged meetings all over town, and Mike's career as a writer was reborn with a blind TV script deal and new Web series production agreement with a major studio.

Webisodes

Webisodes are the perfect medium for "The Coffee Break Screenwriter" because they're short, focused stories told in three to ten minute chunks of time. Below, you'll find episode number two of Mike's webisode series. (NOTE: Camera direction and P.O.V. shots have been written in as this was meant for the director alone.)

FADE IN:

EXT. TEXAS RANCH - BACK OF THE HOUSE - DAY (FLASHBACK)

E.C.U. The mouth of a deer rifle barrel. A black hole.
Ominous. Devouring.

The camera tracks along the barrel like a slow caress,
starting at the front sight, then up the barrel, reaches the   *
front end of the scope, along the scope body, then finally
the rear sight of the scope.

Stops at the cornea of a blinking eye. A small one.

A pretty little tom boy, NATE (age 10). She lies prone in the
dirt, the rifle perched in her tiny hands. Baseball cap on
backwards. Overalls. Smacks hard on a massive wad of pink
chewing gum.

A smudge of pink lipstick on her little mouth.

She takes a deep breath. Stops chewing.

A tiny finger wraps around the trigger. Dirt caked beneath
the jagged fingernails.

The finger squeezes.

BOOM!

The 30-06 cracks like a bolt of thunder.

500 YARDS DOWN RANGE

A blood red apple, the size of a human heart...EXPLODES!

BACK IN THE DIRT

Young Nate blows a giant pink bubble. It bursts. She resumes
chewing furiously.

She turns. Looks up. Smiles. Shields her eyes from the
bright sun.

Her towering DADDY (30s, muscled) looms over her. His face
nothing but a shadow, the sun a blinding halo around his
head. He wears black military fatigues, combat boots. Pistol
on his hip. Dark sunglasses.

She beams with pride.

                    DADDY (O.S.)
          Not hard to shoot at something not
          shootin' back at ya.

Nate frowns, disappointed that she hasn't pleased her father.
Her face screws into a determined scowl. She rolls back over.
Sights up through the scope.

                    DADDY (O.S.)
          Ready?

                    NATE
          Yessir.

500 YARDS DOWN RANGE

A line of twelve apples hanging by their stems, suspended in
mid air from a long pipe attached to two smaller pipes, like
a soccer goal without a net. The frayed string from the first
apple that exploded still swings in the air.

BACK IN THE DIRT

P.O.V. Rifle scope. Apple #2 is sighted up in the cross
hairs.

SFX: Nate smacking gum.

                    DADDY (V.O.)
          Unleash hell.

END P.O.V.

Nate slaps the rifle bolt. It flips out the spent shell. She
rams the bolt back home, chambering a new round. She takes a
deep breath.

P.O.V. Daddy's eyes. He lifts his hand. A .45 semi auto
pistol pointed toward his prone daughter.

END P.O.V.

Nate's finger squeezes the trigger--

BAM! An explosion of dirt next to Nate's head.

Nate unfazed. She squeezes slowly--

P.O.V. Rifle scope. Apple #2 explodes.

END P.O.V.

>   DADDY (O.S.)
>   That the best you can do? Faster!

Nate slams the bolt again, loading another round as BAM! BAM!
BAM! .45 caliber slugs plow into the dirt between her legs,
on either side of her torso, near her head. She squeezes the
trigger--

500 YARDS DOWN RANGE

Off camera, we hear the crack of Nate's rifle ten more times
along with the ear splitting blast of her Daddy's .45 pistol
fifteen more times.

At the same time, we see ten apples explode in a row. Wet
shards of apple flesh sling through the air.

BACK IN THE DIRT

Nate standing up. Glowing with pride. Left hand shielding her
eyes from the sun. Gun slung in the crook of her right arm.

Over her Daddy's broad shoulders, we see her smiling face.

Daddy points at her mouth.

>   DADDY (V.O.)
>   What's that?

E.C.U. The smudge of pink lipstick on Nate's mouth.

Nate realizes she forgot to take off her lipstick this
morning. She quickly wipes it off with the back of her hand.

>   NATE
>   Sorry, Daddy.

She stares at the toes of her tennis shoes. Waits for Thor's
hammer to fall. This is really bad.

Finally--

>   DADDY (V.O.)
>   Go fetch 12 more.

All's forgiven?! Her face explodes with joy.

>   NATE
>   Yessir!

Over Daddy's shoulder we see her turn and run for the front porch.

> DADDY (V.O.)
> And hurry up! Don't wanna be late for church.

He chuckles to himself.

FRONT OF THE RANCH HOUSE - SAME

Nate turns the corner.

Stops dead in her tracks.

A dark sedan. Gov't plates.

A SCARY MAN in mirrored sunglasses and a cheap dark suit stands on the porch. A bucket of apples at his feet.

He takes a massive bite out of one, the apple flesh crunching in his yellowed teeth.

He chews.

Smiles at Nate.

<u>END WEBISODE</u>

Script excerpt of Pink: The Series *courtesy of Generate Context LLC. 2009*

The writer has done an excellent job of telling an exciting story that moves quickly and doesn't break the bank. He …

USES SMALL SCREEN IMAGES: The story is told in close-up images such as, "The mouth of a deer rifle barrel." "The cornea of a blinking eye." "A smudge of pink lipstick."

WORKS ON A BUDGET: Two actors. One set. Cans and guns.

TELLS A SMALL STORY: We watch a little girl at target practice with her dad, worried about being caught with lipstick, only to have a bigger problem on her hands when she comes face-to-face with a scary government man.

ADDS TO THE BIG PICTURE: The scary government man will, of course, come back in future episodes. And, seeing how Nate was brought up and obtained her shooting skills also pays off later in the series when it's revealed she's become an assassin-for-hire.

KEEPS IT SHORT: Each webisode in the first season runs an average of three to five minutes.

Keep in mind that this was episode number two. When the Web series got to play with real money, the shots grew wider, the episodes went longer and the production values got bigger.

The point, however, is that the writer partnered with friends to direct and distribute their work on their own *outside of the studio system*, and you can too. And, if you do it on the Web, there's a good chance it will be noticed. While the Internet is filling rapidly with new shows, it's still the only place you can distribute your material for free, 24/7, to a global audience that only continues to grow.

You don't have to create an entire series. You could simply tell a short story in five minutes and get people interested in your writing or directing.

You can work in any genre. The comedy distribution site *Funny or Die* features short, funny sketches and films.

You can use your technology. Many successful Web series incorporate computer technology into the story line, beginning with the main character either working at a computer or video blogging — "vlogging" — into their computer. Check out *CTRL* or *The Guild* as examples.

You can keep it small. Some Web series purposely contain the environment. *Life On The Inside* focuses on an agoraphobic jingle writer.

You can make the low-end production values part of the story. *Break A Leg* is all about the making of a sitcom with no budget.

The point is to write something that tells a quick, tight story with impact; a filmed piece, cheaply made, that's visual and sparks an emotional response. Then upload and showcase your talent around the world.

TAKE TEN:
WRITE A WEBISODE

Use several ten-minute chunks of writing time to outline and script an online story or webisode.

1. OUTLINE YOUR OVERALL SERIES

    What story do you want to tell?

    How many episodes do you think you'll need to tell that story?

2. OUTLINE THE STORY OF THE EPISODE

    What's the beginning, middle and end of your episode?

    What's the key emotional "tell?"

    What's the scene button that pushes the series or makes an audience want to see additional stories from you?

3. WRITE THE EPISODE

    Use your new writing skills to see how much you can write as quickly as possible.

    Remember to first write around main intentions and then expand to add more details and emotion.

WHAT YOU'VE ACCOMPLISHED

You've taken power into your own hands by committing to the writing and filming of your own work. You've also opened yourself up to new career possibilities through new media.

Video Games, Game Shows, Promos, and Reality TV

Opportunity, opportunity, opportunity, opportunity. So don't turn your nose up. There are countless storytelling and structural possibilities in video-game writing. Game shows that require colorful questions often hire writers with a comedy background. Television "promos" are written by writers who know how to entertain in one line. And reality television is never just filmed reality. It employs writers to create involving stories out of mundane footage. (I *know* you watch at least one of them!)

What If They Like Me?

I've seen writers work hard at their scripts, then actually blow it *after* they've made a sale or received terrific coverage. They simply weren't ready for what was next. So, here's a quick rundown of what might happen and what it all means:

 TEN-MINUTE LECTURE:

MEETINGS, STAFFING, ASSIGNMENTS, AND PITCHING

If you're writing a movie script that no one has hired or assigned you to write, you are writing a FEATURE SPEC. You may also be showing off your writing skills by writing a TELEVISION SPEC of an existing show. Or, you could be writing an ORIGINAL PILOT that you'd like to see made into a SERIES.

Your TV spec will most likely be submitted to a SHOW RUNNER in charge of a different television show with a similar tone. That show runner may then hire you on the writing STAFF of its next season. Once staffed, you'll be asked to pitch episodes, jokes and character arcs in a WRITERS' ROOM.

If your original pilot gets attention, you'll be paired with a show runner who will attach himself to your work as EXECUTIVE PRODUCER and help you create a show BIBLE that covers the story arcs of the characters and show for up to five years.

Once your feature spec is submitted to a PRODUCTION COMPANY, it will get COVERAGE, which is a written book report that covers the script's strengths and weaknesses. If the report reads CONSIDER or RECOMMEND, it will most likely go on WEEKEND READ, which means that all of the producers or CREATIVE EXECUTIVES in the company will read it. If they like it, they will submit it to a STUDIO. If the studio likes it, it could SELL. If that happens, your agent will work out a contract that usually involves you getting paid for at least one REWRITE on the script after you receive STUDIO NOTES as to how to make it better and meet its creative and commercial needs. If you rewrite the script to the studio's satisfaction, it may then get a GREEN LIGHT for production.

If your script gets good coverage, but the studio doesn't want to buy it, production companies all over town will still hear about you and call you in for MEETINGS. That meeting could be a MEET AND GREET, in which they get to know you and ask about your other material. In that case, be prepared to run through a SHORT PITCH of at least three different projects. Being charming won't hurt either.

The production company might also consider you for a REWRITE ASSIGNMENT or BOOK ADAPTATION. In that case, they'll ask you to pitch your TAKE on existing material. If you've sold a project, you might also have the opportunity to sell an original story on pitch alone. Your agent or manager will then set up a meeting for a LONG PITCH of the project, during which you colorfully describe your project's main plot points, central characters, and relationship arcs.

If the company likes the pitch, they might hire you to write the script and, after you've rewritten it to their satisfaction, they'll take it to the studio, where the process will happen all over again.

END OF LECTURE

The Long Pitch

As mentioned above, there might come a time when you're such a successful writer that you'll be called into a producer's office to pitch your latest idea or a new "take" on a current project.

I'm going to offer you two different guides for a long pitch. The first simply keeps you on track by reminding you of the key elements to hit within the pitch. The second is a scripted template.

You can take ten minutes to fill out as much as you know — or take each act ten minutes at a time.

TAKE TEN:
LONG-PITCH GUIDE

Run through your story casually and conversationally, making sure you move forward by hitting the points below.

1. PERSONAL INSPIRATION

Talk about what happened in your own life that inspired you to write this story.

2. LOG LINE

Make sure they know where your pitch is going to go by pitching the central idea right up front.

3. MAIN CHARACTER DESCRIPTION

Tell us who we're following and why we should care. Describe personality, flaw, occupation and — only if it's relevant — backstory.

4. CHARACTER GOAL

Let us in on the main goal of the MC when we meet her in the story.

5. ACT-ONE EVENT

Describe the central event that causes our MC to begin a new journey.

6. GOAL AND STRATEGY INTO ACT 2

Synopsize what the MC wants to do in the central part of the movie and how she intends to do it.

7. LOVE INTEREST / BUDDY

Describe the MC's friend or love interest.

8. ACT 2 ACTIVITY

Reveal the entertaining steps the MC takes toward accomplishing her mission.

9. ACT 2 SET PIECE

Incorporate at least one trailer-worthy moment that mines the big idea (concept) of the story.

10. ANTAGONIST ACTIVITY

Bring in the villain of the piece and show how he disrupts the mission of the MC.

11. MIDPOINT EVENT

Describe an event that heightens the act.

12. EMOTIONAL UPSET

Reveal what the MC is now feeling as a result of her journey thus far.

13. GOAL AND STRATEGY INTO ACT 3

Synopsize what the MC wants to do in the last part of the movie and how she intends to do it.

14. STAKES AND TICKING CLOCK

Remind the listener of what the MC has to lose at this point and how much time she has to accomplish her new mission.

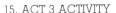

15. ACT 3 ACTIVITY
Using characters, tools and skills obtained on the journey, describe the ways that the MC attempts to accomplish her mission.

16. ACT 3 CLIMAX
Use emotion and detail to describe the clever, winning moment that saves the day.

17. STORY LESSON
End by giving us a sense of how the MC has changed or changed others.

WHAT YOU'VE ACCOMPLISHED

Long pitches scare even the most seasoned writer. But now with some guideposts, you'll be at ease in "the room."

TAKE TEN:
LONG-PITCH TEMPLATE

This template follows a conventional story structure, so use it as a guide; don't feel you have to bind yourself to it. Apply your own language and cadence. Even skip story beats where they don't work for you. A 10- to 20-minute pitch will actually feel like two hours when you're delivering it, so it's important that you feel comfortable and sound unscripted.

10 Minutes:
TEASER

Imagine that _____ !
scenario

What if _____ ?
high-concept strategy

LOG LINE INTRO

_____ is a _____
title of script   *adjective + genre*

in the vein of _____
similar film

about _____ .
log line

10 Minutes:
ACT 1

Meet _____ .
name of main character

He's _____ and _____ .
good quality   *good quality*

The only problem is that he's _____ .
flaw

He'd like to _____ .
original goal

But _____ always gets in his way!
problem

An opportunity arises, however, when he _____ .
new idea

Determined, he sets out to _____ .
first-act activity

This creates a huge problem, however, when _____ .
problem occurs / strategy backfires

Now, he must _____ or risk _____ .
rise to challenge   *stakes*

10 Minutes:
ACT 2A

He thinks he may have help when he meets _____ .
supporting character

She's _____ , but he soon discovers that she's also
good quality

_____ .
flaw

He wants to _____ , but she thinks it might be
strategy

better to _____ .
opposing strategy

When _____ occurs, it soon becomes clear to
antagonist-driven action

both of them that they'll have to _____ or risk
second-act activity

_____ .
new stakes / ticking clock

The two soon find themselves in over their heads as they

_____ .
activity

They try to solve the problem by _____ , but
trailer moment / set piece

_____ happens.
obstacle

To complicate matters even more, _____
main character

feels _____ .
emotional complication

Should he _____ ?
questioning of self and others

10 Minutes:
ACT 2B

An opportunity arises to _____ .
reward

The plan is to _____ .
new strategy

But to do so, he must _____ .
goal

With the help of _____ and _____,
character   *acquired skill*

he _____ .
small victory

As a result, he's finally able to _____ .
small reward

In fact, all seems fine until _____ .
antagonist-driven complication

Feeling _____, he _____.
negative emotion   *return of flaw*

This causes _____ .
estrangement or loss

He begins to believe he should just _____ .
temporary surrender

10 Minutes:
ACT 3

However, _____, and he _____.
telling event   *pivotal choice*

As a result _____ which reveals _____.
object or line payoff   *key answer*

He _____ and now understands _____.
action that pursues clue   *new insight*

Filled with _____, he decides to _____.
positive emotion   *new action*

This causes _____ to _____ .
                 supporting character   *reunion*

Together, using _____ , _____ , and
                      other characters   *skills*

_____ , they are able to
              tools from journey

_____ .
        climactic action, defeating antagonist

Unfortunately, _____ .
                         final hurdle

But this time, _____
                         new behavior

resulting in _____ .
              change in character's situation

10 Minutes:
SELLING POINTS

This movie is unlike any in its genre because of _____ .
                                           unique approach

Audiences will also respond to _____ .
                                      theme

And they'll love scenes such as _____ .
                                 trailer moment

WHAT YOU'VE ACCOMPLISHED

You've scripted out a movie story that will keep the listener awake and entertained.

■ TEN-MINUTE CHAPTER REVIEW:
THE OPPORTUNITY

1. Create a CONTACT list with people you know and ONE FAVOR to ask.

2. Draw up a DATABASE tracking goals and successes at PITCHFESTS and CONFERENCES.

3. Reach out from out-of-town via VIRTUAL PITCH FESTS and other ONLINE WRITERS' RESOURCES.

4. Use SOCIAL NETWORK sites like Facebook to help you connect with industry contacts.

5. Discover opportunity with NEW MEDIA by writing a WEBISODE.

6. In MEETINGS, stay on point while delivering LONG PITCHES by following the MAJOR ELEMENTS and structural beats of your story.

Fade Out

You've brainstormed, organized, written, rewritten, pitched, and potentially sold your screenplay. Take ten minutes to jump up and down and do the happiness dance. Seriously, you deserve it. You've worked hard and used every moment of stolen time to move forward in your script and your career.

Better yet, you might have discovered that your small ten-minute window has become a healthy hour, now that you're finally doing something that you love. And how great would it be if that hour could turn into a full day? A *paid* day!

Just imagine — instead of sneaking ten minutes of writing on your job, your job could actually *be* writing. That way, on your coffee break, you could … just drink coffee. Or, order your new Porsche.

I wish you luck. I wish you lots of writing time. I'd wish you even more good stuff, but I've got a script to read and kids to pick up from school.

And I only have ten minutes.

Writers' Thoughts on Taking Ten

Is this really possible? Can you make progress on your script with only ten minutes of spare time? I put this question to a handful of working writers.*

I asked them:

If you had ten minutes to do one thing to make a *scene* better, what would it be?

If you had ten minutes to do one thing to make a *sequence* better, what would it be?

If you had ten minutes to do one thing to make your *script* better, what would it be?

If you had ten minutes to do something for your *career*, what would it be?

And, if there's *anything extra* you'd like to add, please do.

Their answers follow.
And they're killer.

*The writers polled in this survey have all been guests at or students and clients of On The Page, Inc.®

Mark Fergus

co-writer of Children of Men, Iron Man, First Snow, Cowboys & Aliens

If you had ten minutes to do one thing to make a *scene* better, what would it be?

Find the scene's bottom line. People don't know much, but they ALWAYS know what they want. What do the players in the scene want? (with brutal honestly, as if there were no consequences to their wants). What's in the way of getting what they want? Sounds too simple, but it's anything but — and it always unlocks a scene.

If you had ten minutes to do one thing to make a *sequence* better, what would it be?

Find the weak link, which is often your favorite scene in the whole script. You may love it, but if it's not serving the almighty structure, it's got to go. Don't kill it. Recycle. It probably belongs in a different story.

If you had ten minutes to do one thing to make your *script* better, what would it be?

Scroll through it on your computer screen, take it all in, fast, like you were listening to a great pop song. Like the way actors do a 'speed-read' of a scene. Let the rhythm hit you, assault you, overwhelm you. If it sings, you might have a damn good script on your hands. If it bumps, trips, sputters, if you keep getting pulled out of it... there may still be work to do.

If you had ten minutes to do something for your *career*, what would it be?

Do one thing every day. Write a query letter. Enter a competition. Send a script to a contact. The little things add up. But, mainly... don't drive yourself nuts. Spend ten minutes a day thinking about your career, then get your nose back to the keyboard and write. And write and write.

Heather Ragsdale

Synesthesia, *optioned by Christmas in July Productions;* Tender Age, *optioned by Headlong Entertainment*

If I had ten minutes to make a *scene* better...

I'd make sure the scene served a PURPOSE. What information are we learning that is propelling the character (and the reader) along? It's hard

to be ruthless, but I try to get rid of scenes that indulge me as a writer rather than serve the story.

If I had ten minutes to make a *sequence* better…
I'd make sure the sequence has TENSION, i.e. answers a question. For example, in my current screenplay: Will Nick be able to pay off his debt before he ends up floating in the Hudson?

If I had ten minutes to make my *script* better…
I'd strengthen the act breaks.

If I had ten minutes for my *career*…
Admit that I am a writer.

Peter Vanderwall

A Year In Mooring, *Joule Films;* Reverse Angle, *Incendo Media;* Shadowheart, *Desert Moon Productions*

If you had ten minutes to do one thing to make a *scene* better, what would it be?
Make sure the scene starts at the latest possible moment and ends at the earliest possible moment and still progresses the story.

If you had ten minutes to do one thing to make a *sequence* better, what would it be?
Take that ten minutes a few days after you write the sequence for a fresh, objective view.

If you had ten minutes to do one thing to make your *script* better, what would it be?
Scan all pages and make sure none of the action paragraphs exceed 3 lines. Break the longer paragraphs into shorter paragraphs to make the script more reader-friendly. Important information is often missed by readers because it is buried in dense paragraphs that are skipped over in favor of reading the dialogue.

If you had ten minutes to do something for your *career*, what would it be?
Read a tracking board for the loglines of specs that are going wide and specs that are selling to get a sense of what the market is looking for. Then ask yourself two questions. Can you condense your story into a

similarly concise and interesting logline? Are you writing a story that you truly believe in or are you just chasing the market?

Jimmy Miller
winner of the Adult/Family category, 2007 Austin Film Festival; winner of the Drama category, 2007 Page International Screenwriting Awards

If you had ten minutes to do one thing to make a *scene* better, what would it be?

Read it out loud. If that feels weird, have your screenwriting software read it to you. Even the computerized voices can really help you figure out if dialogue and pace are working. It also really helps you find spelling and grammatical errors a lot faster. It's a twofer.

If you had ten minutes to do one thing to make a *sequence* better, what would it be?

Experiment with rearranging and splitting up scenes. It's a great way to create tension and momentum if you feel like your script needs it. And it lets you see some possibilities you might not have considered. If you do a rearrange well, you might find out that certain scenes interplay very well. At the very least, you can confirm that what you have is the best way to write a sequence.

If you had ten minutes to do one thing to make your *script* better, what would it be?

Do a title search on IMDb (IMDbPro if possible) and make sure there aren't any films being released or in development with your title. A great title is really important. It needs to be unique. If you find a film in development with your title, it might still be OK. Just have a good alternate ready.

If you had ten minutes to do something for your *career*, what would it be?

Convince yourself to never send out a query letter ever or again. Instead, invest that time and money in making your script better. Or, buy lottery tickets. Both have a better chance of paying off than query letters.

Andrew Robinson
writer on The Spectacular Spider-Man, *Disney XD; writer on* Transformers: Animated

If you had ten minutes to do one thing to make a *scene* better, what would it be?
READ IT OUT LOUD OR HAVE SOMEONE DO IT FOR YOU. Dialogue that sounds just fine in your head and on the page, sometimes reveals hidden weaknesses when vocalized. You may discover an odd turn of phrase, words that are hard to pronounce in sequence, or just plain awkward bits that don't produce the dramatic or comedic sparks you were anticipating, when you and your friends... or better yet, actual actors... play the parts.

If you had ten minutes to do one thing to make a *sequence* better, what would it be?
MAKE SURE THAT IT TRACKS LOGICALLY AND HAS A POINT OF VIEW. I once worked on a script with a producer who was seemingly obsessed with whether the characters were getting from point A to point M via points B, C, D, E, and so on, because — as he explained it — if HE couldn't understand it, he was pretty sure an audience wouldn't either. The POV element is that when you're on a roller coaster, either it's physical or emotional, the ride is more engaging and/or fun when you're (identifying) with someone.

If you had ten minutes to do one thing to make your *script* better, what would it be?
SPELL CHECK. And run through the script doing a HUMAN spell check. There are too many words that are spelled similarly to the one you want. Think about the difference between "any more" and "anymore." Or God help you, "threw," "through," "thorough" and "though." Spell check won't always catch them. It's up to *you* to make sure you don't look like an ignoramus to the producer or contest or agent who's reading your script. You can't blame Microsoft or Final Draft for that.

(Alternatively, call or email Pilar Alessandra and ask her to give you notes on your script.)

If you had ten minutes to do something for your *career*, what would it be?

See above, as regards calling Pilar. Then make more phone calls. Network your brains out, and don't let your contacts fall by the wayside. Call at least one person every day (it doesn't always have to be a new person, but it should not always be the SAME person) and you should be able to build up a good network of people - who, if they like you, may help your career.

Josh Stolberg

writer of Good Luck Chuck; *writer and director of* Kids in America

If you had ten minutes to do one thing to make a *scene* better, what would it be?

Sometimes, when I'm stuck on a scene, I save a copy of my script (to protect what I have), and then save a side-copy, which I very deliberately call "JUNK." It's incredibly freeing to know that what you are about to write has nothing to live up to. Then I go through the scene and DELETE my favorite couple of lines. One of my main problems as a writer is that I fall in love with a joke or a turn-of-phrase and then move mountains (and destroy the rest of the scene) to keep it in there. I'll realize that I've spent a half a page setting up a line just because I love it. By deleting my favorite stuff, it opens me up to come at the scene in a different way — it forces you to. Once you get the scene to work, you can try to insert the line back in. If it fits, great. If not, you've probably fooled yourself into finding a better way to tell the story.

If you had ten minutes to do one thing to make your *script* better, what would it be?

As soon as I'm feeling REALLY good about my script, I'll open up Final Draft, start up Speech Control and have the computer read my script out loud. It's a horrible experience. Imagine the very worst actor in the world performing your dialogue. It's a nice seven-minute break and will at least inspire you to keep working (because chances are at least one of the actors the studio hires will be that bad).

If you had ten minutes to do something for your *career*, what would it be?

Take the ten minutes after a meeting or phone call with a producer, executives, director, hell, ANYONE you've met that can help you... to take notes on THEM. Start a file with their name and write down all the personal stuff you can remember from your conversation, as well as all the little clues that might come back to help you later. Personally, I use a Mac so I do it all in the "notes" section of my address book. I'll start with their credits, so I have a quick reference in case they call my office. Then I write down everything that might help me connect with them on our next phone call (keep in mind they may be working for a different company and it may be ten years from now). Are they a sports fan? What team do they like? Did they mention a favorite movie (that I might "miraculously" say is MY favorite movie when we talk three years from now)? Husband, wife and kids' names? Birthday? If you meet them in person, DESCRIBE them. There's nothing worse than walking into a meeting and saying "nice to meet you" when you've met them five times already. This is a very simple, small, ten-minute step that can get you a job in the future.

Andy Maycock

writer of The Best Man's Privilege, *in development with Josh Stolberg*

If you had ten minutes to do one thing to make a *scene* better, what would it be?

Get rid of all parentheses and cut the action lines as much as possible. You should never have to say "sarcastically" to indicate the way an actor should read the line. Instead, find a way to suggest it in the dialogue itself.

"Yeah, because *that's* cool" evokes sarcasm without any signpost saying "sarcastically."

Similarly, don't direct the scene with too much action. Keep the focus on the motion of the scene, not the little details that are up to a director. I've read dozens of scenes where, after each line of dialogue, I'm told what happens in the scene. Sometimes it sounds really good:

"He blinks. Twice."

I like that, but is it worth the space? Nah.

If it's critical, or technical, like "she ratchets the pressure up to seven," then it's probably important. But even then, you've got to make it kinetic and visual: "she grinds the valve control as the gauges flash yellow." But if it's just to tell us that "she leans forward," or "she buttons her coat," or "she takes a reluctant bite of cake," if it provides no momentum, leave it out.

If you had ten minutes to do one thing to make your *script* better, what would it be?

David Mamet says there's no need for exposition. So here's an experiment. Imagine a scene that takes place before the action of your script. Pretend all the exposition is in there. Who are these people? Why are they here? What's the deal?

Then, go through your first couple of actual scenes and hack out all the exposition that you revealed in your (imaginary) opening scene. Does this new kickoff to the story (now without exposition and of course STILL without the imaginary scene) work? If so, keep it. If not, tell Mamet he's wrong.

If you had ten minutes to do something for your *career*, what would it be?

As ridiculous as it sounds, as I'm driving my very sporty minivan, I imagine I'm being interviewed by James Lipton, or Jay Leno, or Roger Ebert, or Pilar (yep!) on the podcast. And invariably, one of those people asks me what my script is about. And since they don't give me much time, I have to really boil it down. What is the theme? In other words, what does it say about life, or relationships, or men and women, or the Red Sox, or the Galactic Republic, or whatever? If I can't get to the very essence of the script, then I don't even know what it's about, and Jimmy or Jay or Rog or Pilar is going to send me home.

If you're worried that people will think you're talking to yourself, simply tap your steering wheel in rhythm. They'll think you're singing.

Tiffany Zehnal

writer, Veronica's Closet, That '80s Show, Dag, Lost at Home; *spec feature* Shotgun Wedding, *sold to DreamWorks*

Ten minutes to make a *scene* better:

If a scene seems too long to you, it's going to seem really too long to someone else. And that someone else does not have that kind of time. Be it your agent, manager, mom or mailman. People are busy. So, delete half of it. Either arbitrarily or at the beginning and end of the scene. This will be hard to do so save it as a new this-isn't-a-real-scene file. Knowing your original really too long scene is still intact in the script will give you the freedom to go nuts and trim the fat, the unnecessary and the not really working. And in the end, you'll have something new. Maybe better. Possibly sharper. Definitely shorter.

Find your least favorite line out of any scene and fix it. It deserves to be better. One way to do that is to take ten minutes and write ten new replacement lines. Nine of those lines will be bad. Embarrassing. Make you want to quit the business. But one of those lines won't. One of them will be better than what you had. One of them might very well be great. Maybe even awesome. I am so confident of this equation, I'd bet my baby on it. If I bet babies.

Ten minutes to help my *career:*
My favorite fortune cookie of all time: the biggest risk in life is not taking a risk at all. So, risk it! Do anything, email anyone, submit anywhere. People will say no but all you need is one person to say yes.

Ten minutes to make your *character* better:
Ask yourself what your character wants at the beginning of the script and what your character needs at the end. Your answers should be the exact opposite of each other. If they're not or too similar, you're missing an opportunity to tell the best story. Knock it off. Rethink your character's wants and needs so that they are in direct conflict with one another. Or else people will suffer. You, your reader and, most of all, your character.

Brian Turner
writer, with Garrett Frawley, of Santa Baby, Santa Baby 2, *and* Snowglobe

If you had ten minutes to do one thing to make a *scene* better, what would it be?
End it on a question compelling the next bit of action.

  Bob: "What are you going to do?"
  Tom: "I'm going to go over there."

  Lose Tom's last bit of dialogue and you've got a more compelling scene ending.

If you had ten minutes to do one thing to make a *sequence* better, what would it be?

Change a location. A couple arguing about an affair while driving isn't nearly as compelling as a couple arguing about an affair while at the gun range, or digging a shallow grave, or videotaping an alien invasion. OK, silly examples, but you get the idea.

If you had ten minutes to do one thing to make your *script* better, what would it be?

Increase white space. Flip through the pages without reading them. Where do you find blocks of text? Mark those pages as places you need to shed action direction. The less words, the faster the read. The faster the read, the better overall impression of the script.

If you had ten minutes to do something for your *career*, what would it be?

Google. In today's Internet age it's easier than ever to reach out to people in the industry. If you're writing romantic comedies, find out who wrote the one you just saw in the theater and send him/her an email. If it's an industry bigwig, you probably won't hear back, but if you reach out to someone with only 2-3 movies under their belt, you can probably strike up a conversation.

Don't try and shove your script on them. Ask them questions about how they got their ideas, how they got their agent, what sort of troubles they went through between script and screen. People like to talk about themselves, and there's a good chance you're going to learn something you didn't know.

Maybe it leads to something, maybe it doesn't. But it certainly doesn't hurt to start making contacts.

Elisa Wolfe

screenwriter and owner of "Reader Ready" Proofing and Editing Services for Screenwriters

If I had ten minutes to do one thing to make a *scene* better...

I would go through and focus on the physical activity of the characters. What can they be doing in the scene that doesn't directly pertain to what they're saying but reveals something about their character?

If I had ten minutes to make a *sequence* better...

I would go through the individual scenes and make sure they were all absolutely necessary and weren't just filler because I didn't have a better way to get from A to B when I initially wrote it. Sometimes, when you know where you're going and can't wait to get there, it's easy to "cheat" those in-between moments that carry you to the final scene.

If I had ten minutes to do one thing to make my *script* better...

I'd try to give a main character a distinctive trait, whether it's a physical attribute, an interesting style of speech, an accent, etc.

If I had ten minutes to do something for my *career*...

I'd learn how to manage time better so I had more than ten minutes to spare. :)

Marc Haimes

former Vice President of Development at DreamWorks; screenwriter with projects in development at Summit, Fox and Paramount

If you had ten minutes to do one thing to make a *script* better, what would it be?

Read a scene over. Say it out loud. Ask myself: is the rhythm of it working, the back and forth of the dialogue, the movement from shot to shot? If not, I'll put my subconscious to work. I'll write down any "questions" I might have in my notes. I'll say, "what is a better button?" or "what's a more arresting opening image?" I'll read over my notes before I go to bed. Then I'll forget about them and trust the rest to the dreamer. More often than not, I'll be looking back over my questions from the previous day and realize I now have the answer.

If you had ten minutes to do something for your *career*, what would it be?

Read the newspaper. Read a good book. Be with somebody smart. Engage myself in learning or discussing something that will allow me to continue feeding my mind and keep it active.

One other thing ...

If a scene is taking a long time for me to "crack," I find it's usually because of a bigger conceptual mistake that I am making about the sequence itself. That's usually a good time for me to go for a run and get a little distance.

One thing I should probably do more of ...

Keeping readily accessible lists. Partial ideas. Interesting professions. Character quirks. Funny moments. Anything and everything. I compare not keeping lists to not writing down your dreams. When you wake up, you think you will never ever forget... until you do. I should really make a point to keep more lists.

Bill Birch

writer of Shazam, *Warner Bros.*

If you had ten minutes to do one thing to make a *scene* better, what would it be?

Sometimes when I'm in the midst of a first draft I'll get to a scene where I haven't figured my plan of attack yet. What I do is write the heading, "What's the purpose of this scene?" on paper and then take ten minutes to try to answer the question. It may look something like this:

What's the purpose of this scene?
—Set up Bob's bar and that he's the owner
—Get out info he's about to lose bar to bank
—Introduce Carol
—Audience learns Carol is rich

Now I have a road map to write with and I've also proven to myself that the scene is full of purpose. If the only answer you can come up with is "it develops character," most likely you'll be cutting that scene out later. It's important to remember that every scene must advance the plot as well as develop character.

Lisa Dalesandro

writer of Gender Blender, *in development at Nickelodeon; writer of* Escape to Grizzly Mountain, *MGM*

If you had ten minutes to do one thing to make a *scene* better, what would it be?

I'd first make sure that the beginning of the scene is actually the beginning. Writers frequently begin a scene too early. Ask -- where does this scene really start? The same is true for the end of a scene. Could you cut out of this scene sooner? Tightening up a scene gives it better flow and ultimately makes it more powerful.

If you had ten minutes to do one thing to make a *sequence* better, what would it be?

In ten minutes, I would work on the flow of the whole sequence. Do the transitions between the scenes work well? Could they be better, smoother, more interesting, more symbolic, etc? Does this sequence as a whole build to the dramatic incident that I'm working toward? Does the tension/drama build?

If you had ten minutes to do one thing to make your *script* better, what would it be?

Pick a single character and start to follow only their dialogue through the script. Is the voice of this character always consistent and unique from any of the other characters? This will surely take more than ten minutes, but you'll get a good sense of the character if you only focus on their voice.

If you had ten minutes to do something for your *career*, what would it be?

I have contradictory advice. On one hand, I would say stop worrying about your career and get back to writing. As soon as you finish one project, start another with less concern for selling the first one and more concern for becoming a better writer.

On the other hand, if I had spent only ten minutes a day keeping up on the business side of the business instead of focusing solely on writing, I would probably have a much more lucrative career. Make that call. Follow up on that email. It is a business and artists need to cultivate that as well. (Now I have to go spend ten minutes calling my manager.)

And, if there's anything extra you'd like to add, please do.

This is advice that I stole from a writer who stole from a writer who stole from … you get the point. The best thing a writer can do is write a little, read a lot. It's the best advice ever.

Mike Maden

writer of Pink: The Series *on Hulu, The WB.com and KoldCast.tv*

If you had ten minutes to do one thing to make a *scene* better, what would it be?

Ask four questions: Is there conflict in this dramatic scene, and if so, how can I raise the stakes for the battling parties? (Of course, some kinds of non-dramatic scenes don't need conflict, but all dramatic scenes do.) Is the dialogue original and organic to the character — or clichéd and "on the nose?" How can I button (end) this scene in a surprising or unexpected way? Most importantly, can I toss this scene out and not affect my story? (If so, toss it!) Do I "start late" and "end early" enough?

If you had ten minutes to do one thing to make a *sequence* better, what would it be?

Attack the transitions — how do the scenes connect to each other? Is there an exciting/interesting flow? Is there a rising (or falling) momentum from beginning to end of the sequence?

If you had ten minutes to do one thing to make your *script* better, what would it be?

Do I know what my story is really about? Does every character, location, scene, symbol somehow express or reflect that theme? If not, why is it there?

If you had ten minutes to do something for your *career*, what would it be?

Read ten pages of the best new screenplay that fits the genre of the next project I'm going to write.

And, if there's anything extra you'd like to add, please do.

When rewriting, do specific passes; don't try to rewrite the whole script one page at a time. Do a dialogue pass--in fact, in Final Draft, you can generate Character Reports, and then pull up ONLY the dialogues for specific characters. (This works great in ten-minute chunks, btw). That way you can critically read all of a character's dialogue, see patterns, pull out repetitions (unless needed), etc. Do a Header pass (again, in FD, you can pull these out in reports). Do an Action/Description pass.

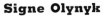

Signe Olynyk

director of The Great American Pitch Fest; writer and producer of Below Zero

If you had ten minutes to do one thing to make your *script* better, what would it be?

I would reverse the sexes of my characters.

I would put them in the most compromising situation.

I would ask if my "who, what, why, when, where, and how" choices are the best answers for the overall story. (e.g., 'where does this scene take place' — is the location I chose the best choice? Does it heighten the conflict or contribute toward character by having the scene take place in that particular location?)

I would identify a goal for each character in each scene.

I would give each of my characters opposite 'mini-goals' for each scene that they either reach or do not reach. Explore both outcomes to make sure you chose the best one.

I would pretend they could not talk, and see how they would still communicate what they need.

I would pretend my protagonist had a secret he/she could not reveal, and see how it changed their actions, dialogue, etc.

I would make sure my protagonist is backed into an impossible corner with real jeopardy and high stakes for them, and see what he or she does to get out.

I would look for exposition, and see if I can either lose it or make the "telling" of any factoids more interesting.

If you had ten minutes to do something for your *career*, what would it be?

Query three new people a day.

Touch base with an update for three people I've been in touch with before. (Always give them something relevant, short & new.)

Watch a trailer for a film I haven't seen yet and research the filmmakers involved.

Practice pitching my script verbally to someone new (e.g., not an industry person until the pitch is comfortable.)

Pick a "person of the day" I want to know more about (actor or actress, another writer, producer, director, studio exec, etc.) and Google them, read articles, blogs, etc.

Listen to a podcast such as *On The Page*. Keep one on while you're doing other things , e.g., making dinner, doing dishes, exercising, etc.

Write sincere, short 'fan letters' by email to anyone I admire, want to know, or appreciate. Do not ask for anything! Try to build a relationship if they respond.

Use Facebook and other social networking sources to reach out to people you want to know.

Go to film festivals, screenings, conferences, and meet new "up and comers." Get to know them. They are 'on their way' and it is always better to build relationships with people BEFORE you need them.

Find someone you'd like to work with, and reach out to them. See if they'd consider co-writing with you, or maybe mentoring you. You never know unless you ask.

To sell my script, I would:

See if I can 'sex up' my script in a way that hopefully enhances or improves the overall story.

Try to write an indie, low-budget version of my script, as well as one with somewhat more expensive scenes for a studio version.

Andy Raymer

former studio executive at DreamWorks; screenwriter for The Walt Disney Co.; adapted William Steig's The Zabajaba Jungle *for Vanguard Films*

If you had ten minutes to do one thing to make a *scene* better, what would it be?

Flip the scene — start with the last line and use it as the first. See if this opens up a new angle on the characters or what you're trying to accomplish.

If you had ten minutes to do one thing to make a *sequence* better, what would it be?

Put it on notecards. See which scenes are truly integral and cut or combine the rest.

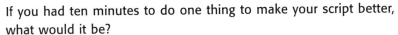

If you had ten minutes to do one thing to make your script better, what would it be?

Brainstorm a better title. You'd be amazed at how important a good title is, especially in comedy.

If you had ten minutes to do something for your *career*, what would it be?

Invent a time machine, travel back to college and become a doctor. Failing this, I'd pick up the phone, call one person whose work I admire and ask them out to lunch.

Matt Harris

writer of The Starling, *optioned by Palm Star Entertainment, John Lee Hancock attached to direct; 2002 Nicholl Fellow*

If you had ten minutes to do one thing to make a *scene* better, what would it be?

I would ask myself "who wants what?" in this scene and then try to make sure I've made that clear. Plus I'd see if there wasn't a better way to end the scene (e.g., shorten the ending or find a unique place to cut out that I may have overlooked).

If you had ten minutes to do one thing to make a *sequence* better, what would it be?

I would look at the sequence — the action, the dialogue, the settings — and think hard if it's something we've seen before. If so, I would ask how could I do it differently and just brainstorm ten quick ideas (with no idea being a bad idea) just to see if something cool doesn't come up.

If you had ten minutes to do one thing to make your *script* better, what would it be?

With only ten minutes to make my script better I would spend that time on the first page of the script and make sure I'm hooking the reader RIGHT OFF THE BAT... which means it better not be a page of block text.

If you had ten minutes to do something for your *career*, what would it be?

Write something to do with a script for ten minutes — whether it's an outline, a few lines of dialogue on a current script or reviewing the last thing I wrote. A lot can be done in ten minutes.

And, if there's anything extra you'd like to add, please do.

Here's my favorite thing about the ten minute rule: you can do just about anything for ten minutes, except maybe hold your breath or stand in fire. It's a pretty painless time period. So giving yourself ten minutes frees you up to be spontaneous and unrestricted, to silence that internal editor. And ninety-nine times out of one-hundred you're going to look up and see that you've just been working for an hour when all you had planned was ten minutes. It's an incredible boost to your confidence and ultimately, your accomplishments.

David Wright

writer, Malcolm in the Middle*,* Family Guy

If you had ten minutes to do one thing to make a *scene* better, what would it be?

Maybe you can add a visual device to help sell the tension/suspense in your scene. For example, in Alfred Hitchcock's *Notorious*, Cary Grant and Ingrid Bergman worry about Claude Rains discovering that the key to the wine cellar is missing during a party. As guests consume the wine, Cary and Ingrid nervously eye the bartender's quickly diminishing supply. The shot of the wine bottles serves as a visual "ticking clock," which is far more interesting than the characters constantly checking their watches. Also, whatever the most important thing in your scene is, make that your scene blow... in other words, end the scene there. Don't drag it out past the point of the scene's intention. And if you're writing a comedy, end the scene on the biggest joke.

If you had ten minutes to do one thing to make a *sequence* better, what would it be?

If it's a sequence meant to keep us on the edge of our seats, then make sure that from the start of the sequence, the tension/dramatic action builds all the way to the end. For inspiration, check out *The Graduate*. Ben races from Berkeley to Los Angeles, back to Berkeley, and then to Santa Barbara to stop Elaine from getting married. There are obstacles along the way: Mrs. Robinson, frat guys, figuring out the location of the church, running out of gas, etc. It's one of the best sequences in any film.

If you had ten minutes to do one thing to make your *script* better, what would it be?

Brevity. Read the first ten pages and trim the excess fat. If your scene descriptions are too long, then you're better off writing a book. Also, try to make something really cool/interesting/funny happen at the bottom of that first page. Maybe it's an explosion, or someone is killed, or just a hilarious joke. Whatever is organic to your story and genre, make it pop at the bottom of page one.

If you had ten minutes to do something for your *career*, what would it be?

It's always good to keep an eye on where the industry is headed, if not to conform to it, then to be different. Read the trades like *Variety* and *Hollywood Reporter* to see what types of scripts the studios are buying and producing. Also, take ten minutes to read screenwriting magazines and books to sharpen your skills and keep you energized and excited about what you're doing. Spend ten minutes searching for a writers group to join. Or send an email telling a friend that you're writing a script so it forces you to finish it - the only thing worse than not finishing your screenplay, is knowing that others know you're not finishing your screenplay.

William Flannigan

writer of Johnson's Pages, *optioned by Stephen J. Cannell and Thomas Augsberger;* The Genesis Vault, *in development; winner of eight major screenwriting contests*

If you had ten minutes to do one thing to make a *scene* better, what would it be?

I would read my scene and try to cut all the fat. If I've used three lines of description I try to cut it to two. If two, I try to cut it to one. Same with dialogue. Actually it is more important with dialogue. Less is more. My goal is to leave as much white space on the page as possible.

If you had ten minutes to do one thing to make a *sequence* better, what would it be?

I would look at my transitions. By that I mean that I would focus on where I end a scene and how that then jumps to the next scene. Each scene should end with the reader wanting to know what happens next, and each sequence should end with a kind of emotional jolt that propels the action.

If you had ten minutes to do something for your *career*, what would it be?

I subscribe to *The Hollywood Reporter* email updates. They arrive every morning in my in box and I scan the headlines, then click on the stories that are relevant to my interest/career goals. Knowing what is happening in the industry helps me keep a perspective and avoid diving into a new project that would be DOA because someone else already beat me to the punch.

Ellen Sandler

co-executive producer of Everybody Loves Raymond; *author of* The TV Writer's Workbook, *published by Bantam/Dell*

If you have ten minutes to do one thing to make your *script* better:

Tip #1

Here's a simple adjustment that improves any script: Go through your script (as many pages as time allows) and delete every word that ends in "ly" in the action and description lines. Words like "suddenly," "immediately," "crisply." For example, "He immediately notices the dent in the bumper" becomes "He notices the dent in the bumper." Without "immediately" the sentence is cleaner, sharper.

Or, you may want to tweak the word instead of deleting it. For example, if you've written, "Paul sits in his luxuriously appointed office" cut the "ly" and you've got, "Paul sits in his luxurious office." Do that for every instance and you'll be amazed at how this streamlines your script. It will read stronger and punchier. Guaranteed. Repeat at 10-minute intervals until you've gotten through your script.

Tip #2

Here's another easy trick that improves any action description: Change every verb that has an "ing" ending to simple present tense. "Jennifer starts dialing her cell phone" becomes, "Jennifer dials her cell phone." So easy, but it makes the image sharper to the reader.

You may also find you can get more specific when you get rid of the "is —ing" form. For example: "George is relaxing on the deck, while Jennifer is fixing drinks" becomes "George settles into a deck chair while Jennifer makes martinis." Do that throughout, and your script will feel more active and fresher. Repeat at 10-minute intervals until you've gotten through your script.

If you have ten minutes to do something for your *career*:
Write an email note to someone you want to keep in touch with. Two or three lines are enough to keep a connection going. Something like "Hey Monica, I finally saw that old Steve Martin movie we talked about. Loved it! Thanks for recommending it, I doubt if I would have discovered it on my own."

If you have ten minutes to do something for your career (you really only need two minutes for this one — so no excuses):
Before you go to bed, write down something that made you laugh today. It will sharpen your sense of humor and you might use it in a script someday. But even if you don't, noting it will connect you with your sense of observation and why you want to be a writer.

Michelle Muldoon
2009 Action On Film International Film Festival, Women of Film Award

If you had ten minutes to do one thing to make a *scene* better, what would it be?
As I'm not one to need the perfect environment to write, I often find myself writing in small "time chunks," so sometimes I sit to write a new scene and sometimes I just rewrite a previous one. Often, I look for ways to cut down dialogue and wordy description, other times I'll look at opening and closing of the scene and ask myself if I'm happy with it. I'll re-read it and finish reading at an earlier spot to see if it still works.

If you had ten minutes to do one thing to make a *sequence* better, what would it be?
For me, that means rewriting scene direction. My early drafts are often a tad verbose in that department.

If you had ten minutes to do one thing to make your *script* better, what would it be?

I would look at how I end one scene and start another. Are there connections that can be made to make the scenes flow better? If the scene transitions seem seamless, then I think it's an easier read.

If you had ten minutes to do something for your *career*, what would it be?

Look through my address book of contacts and determine if I've kept in touch. If I've been bad at it and there've been things going on in my career, then sometimes I'll take ten minutes to craft an email newsletter to my "Film Friends and Colleagues" updating everyone on the great things that are happening. No one knows you're successfully moving forward if you don't tell them.

And, if there's anything extra you'd like to add, please do.

Make the Internet your new best friend and read industry websites every morning just like you would the newspaper. If you want to be in the film industry, you should make a point of knowing what's going on in it on a daily basis, especially on the business side of it.

Steve Callen

writer/director of award-winning short You Better Watch Out; *scripts optioned by Piper Films and Tristram Miall Films; script commissions with Duo Art Productions, Bombora Creative and GAM Films*

If you had ten minutes to do one thing to make a *scene* better, what would it be?

Without a doubt, I've written it with too much dialogue so I'd try to imagine the same scene without any dialogue, then try to express the same scene idea through action only.

If you had ten minutes to do one thing to make a *sequence* better, what would it be?

I'd muck around with the scene order. What happens if it's done in reverse? What happens if I take a scene out? What happens if I bring the whole sequence forward?

If you had ten minutes to do one thing to make your *script* better, what would it be?

I'd ask for an extension. Ten minutes wouldn't be enough. But hey, if the extension wasn't granted, I'd probably do a format check and improve readability by making sure there were no paragraphs over four lines long, and all the 'continues' and 'mores' weren't clocking up the pages and I'd do one last spell check. Speaking of which, I'd make sure all words were in U.S. English as opposed to that pesky Queen's English nonsense. After all, Americans won the War of Independence and have earned the right not to spell color without a 'u'.

If you had ten minutes to do something for your *career*, what would it be?
Jump online and book a ticket to LA.

And, if there's anything extra you'd like to add, please do.
Imagine it's opening night of your movie. You're sitting there, nervous as hell, hoping everyone loves it. But you know not everyone will. Some people will have a problem with some bits, others will look at their watches or start Twittering during other bits. Dialogue could've been tighter here. The audience gets ahead of the movie there. The sweat builds on your brow. Someone laughs over a serious line. That scene started too early. God, this is a nightmare. You thought people would forgive that sequence if it was shot well. Which it wasn't. And that actress totally misread that character. Someone gets up to leave the cinema. Then another. They're going to miss your favorite part. They won't be able to appreciate the whole film if they leave now! How dare they?! How dare they trigger this revolt?! You stand up and just as you are about to scream at them, you wake up.

You've fallen asleep at your desk and your cursor is blinking after FADE OUT.

It's time to get back to work and rewrite your movie so everyone is glued to every single bit of your story.

Every. Single. Bit.

Or you could just run it past Pilar when you think you're done.

Stealing Time

I'm writing this section from one of those indoor kid gyms. You know — one of those places with the slides and the jumper and the mermaid wallpaper. In my opinion, places like this were invented so that my kids can play while I work.

Armed with my laptop and a plastic bag of fruit roll-ups, I'm ready to write.

Now, if I were here to brainstorm a screenplay, I'd take advantage of this time in a couple of ways.

First, I'd brainstorm an idea.

And to do that, I'd start with those basic elements presented at the beginning of this book:

A movie is usually about a MAIN CHARACTER with a PROBLEM who engages in an ACTIVITY with STAKES hanging in the balance.

So ...

Who's the *main character*? My kids? Maybe this is a fantasy movie and the kids' gym suddenly becomes an *Alice in Wonderland*-like maze of real-life puzzles and adventures. Then again, *I* could be the main character. Harried mom connects with kids and inner heroine when a natural disaster forces her to protect a kids' gym full of helpless kids and inept parents. Wow, talk about suspending disbelief. Moving on. How about that unappreciated dad in the corner? Nah, he gets to be the hero in lots of movies. Let someone else write that one.

Now I'm seeing her! The young woman behind the desk; the one who checks kids in and reminds parents to take their shoes off. Man, she looks bored. I'm going to wake her up by making her my main character!

So, what *problem* occurs? Aliens land? A kid turns into a monster and terrorizes the kids' gym? Too lifelike. Well, what would be the worst thing that I could imagine? I go through my long list of paranoid-mom, worst-case scenarios. A-ha! I've got one. Hostage situation!

Looks like I've got a contained thriller on my hands. And the environment really lends itself to this kind of movie. Innocent kids, parents with competing personalities, and lots of hiding places.

Clearly my main character is going to have to take the lead. And I imagine her *activity* might fall into a couple of categories: establishing trust with the parents, protecting the kids, teaming up with the parents (among them a cute, single dad, of course), and ultimately fighting off the bad guys.

What makes my main character the right woman for the job is her knowledge of the environment and her natural skills as kids' gym manager: She knows the surveillance system, what toys can be used as weapons, and how to trap the bad guys in the jumpy thing. And, in terms of connecting with the other characters, who else would know how to handle an irate dad or a scared kid more than someone who deals with them every day?

So, putting everything together I've got ….

A main character: My kids' gym manager.

A problem: Hostage situation.

Activity: Establish trust, take the lead, team up with cute dad, battle bad guys.

Stakes: Those sweet-faced little kids.

OK, my ten minutes are up. I know this because my own sweet-faced little kid has asked me for a snack fifteen times and insists that fruit roll-ups taste like leather. And my older sweet-faced kid is screaming "look at me look at me look at me" while doing a death-defying stunt off of a rope ladder that makes me scream out "be careful be careful be careful."

Like I said: end of creative time.

But, in those ten minutes, I accomplished something. I came up with a movie idea. And that's a pretty good start.

Film, TV and Webisode List

Quickie film education: Watch and read the movies and shows mentioned in this book!

(500) Days of Summer. Written by Scott Neustadter, Michael H. Weber. Released 2009.

A Beautiful Mind. Screenplay by Akiva Goldsman, from the book by Sylvia Nasar. Released 2001.

A Bug's Life. Story by John Lasseter, Andrew Stanton, Joe Ranft. Screenplay by Andrew Stanton, Don McEnery, Bob Shaw. Additional writers, story: Geefwee Boedoe, Jason Katz, Jorgen Klubien, Robert Lence, David Reynolds. Released 1998.

A Few Good Men. Screenplay by Aaron Sorkin, from his play. Released 1992.

Adam's Rib. Written by Ruth Gordon, Garson Kanin. Released 1949.

Aliens. Screenplay by James Cameron, story by James Cameron, David Giler, Walter Hill, characters created by Dan O'Bannon, Ronald Shusett. Released 1986.

All About Eve. Screenplay by Joseph L. Mankiewicz, from a story by Mary Orr. Released 1950.

Amadeus. Screenplay by Peter Schaffer, from his play. Released 1984.

American Beauty. Written by Alan Ball. Released 1999.

Animal House. Written by Harold Ramis, Douglas Kenney, Chris Miller. Released 1978.

Anywhere But Here. Screenplay by Alvin Sargent, from the novel by Mona Simpson. Released 1999.

Apocalypse Now. Screenplay by John Milius, Francis Ford Coppola. Narration by Michael Herr. From the novel *Heart of Darkness* by Joseph Conrad. Released 1979.

As Good As It Gets. Screenplay by Mark Andrus, James L. Brooks. Story by Mark Andrus. Released 1997.

Avatar. Written by James Cameron. Released 2009.

Away From Her. Screenplay by Sarah Polley, from a story by Alice Munro. Released 2006.

Baby Mama. Written by Michael McCullers. Released 2009.

Big. Written by Gary Ross, Anne Spielberg. Released 1988.

Blade Runner. Screenplay by Hampton Fancher, David Webb Peoples, from the novel *Do Androids Dream of Electric Sheep?* by Philip K. Dick. Released 1982.

Blood Diamond. Screenplay by Charles Leavitt. Story by Charles Leavitt, C. Gaby Mitchell. Released 2006.

Bloodborne. Written by Matt Harris, 2007.

Body Heat. Written by Lawrence Kasdan. Released 1981.

Bombs Over Brentwood. Written by Steffen Phelps, 2007

Break A Leg. Written by Vlad Baranovsky, Yuri Baranovsky, Justin Morrison, 2007.

Breaking Bad. Created by Vince Gilligan, 2008.

Brick. Written by Rian Johnson. Released 2005.

Casino Royale. Screenplay by Neal Purvis, Robert Wade, Paul Haggis, from the novel by Ian Fleming. Released 2006.

Cast Away. Written by William Broyles Jr. Released 2000.

Citizen Kane. Written by Herman J. Mankiewicz, Orson Welles. Released 1941.

Close Encounters of the Third Kind. Written by Steven Spielberg. Released 1977.

Crash. Screenplay by Paul Haggis, Bobby Moresco. Story by Paul Haggis. Released 2004.

Crouching Tiger, Hidden Dragon. Screenplay by Hui-Ling Wang, James Schamus, Kuo Jung Tsai, from the book by Du Lu Wang. Released 2000.

CSI. Created by Ann Donahue, Anthony E. Zuiker, 2000.

CTRL. Written by Robert Kirbyson, Bob Massey, 2009.

Curb Your Enthusiasm. Created by Larry David, 2000.

Dark Pools. Written by Carole Ryavec, 2009.

Die Hard. Screenplay by Jeb Stuart, Steven E. de Souza, from the novel *Nothing Lasts Forever* by Roderick Thorp. Released 1988.

Double or Nothing. Written by Karen Nation, 2002.

Election. Screenplay by Alexander Payne, Jim Taylor, from the novel by Tom Perrotta. Released 1997.

Entourage. Created by Doug Ellin, 2004.

Erin Brockovich. Written by Susannah Grant. Released 2000.

Eternal Sunshine of the Spotless Mind. Screenplay by Charlie Kaufman. Story by Charlie Kaufman, Michel Gondry, Pierre Bismuth. Released 2004.

Fargo. Written by Joel Coen, Ethan Coen. Released 1996.

Four Weddings and A Funeral. Written by Richard Curtis. Released 1994.

Friends. Created by David Crane and Marta Kauffman, 1994.

Frost/Nixon. Screenplay by Peter Morgan, from his play. Released 2008.

Garden State. Written by Zach Braff. Released 2004.

Gilfs. Written by Chip James, 2008.

The Graduate. Screenplay by Calder Willingham, Buck Henry, from the novel by Charles Webb. Released 1967.

Grey's Anatomy. Created by Shonda Rhime, 2005.

Groundhog Day. Screenplay by Danny Rubin, Harold Ramis. Story by Danny Rubin. Released 1993.

Harry Potter and the Sorcerer's Stone. Screenplay by Steve Kloves, from the novel by J.K. Rowling. Released 2001.

Heat. Written by Michael Mann. Released 1995.

I Was a Teenage Werewolf. Written by Herman Cohen, Aben Kandel. Released 1957.

In Bruges. Written by Martin McDonagh. Released 2008.

In The Bedroom. Screenplay by Rob Festinger, Todd Field, from a story by Andre Dubus. Released 2001.

It's A Wonderful Life. Written by Frances Goodrich, Albert Hackett, Frank Capra. Released 1946.

Jaws. Screenplay by Peter Benchley, Carl Gottlieb, from the novel by Peter Benchley. Released 1975.

Jukebox Zero. Written by Keith Armonaitis and Lynne Christensen, 2009

Juno. Written by Diablo Cody. Released 2007.

Kill Bill, Volume 1. Written by Quentin Tarantino. Character: The Bride by Quentin Tarantino, Uma Thurman. Released 2003.

Knocked Up. Written by Judd Apatow. Released 2007.

L.A. Confidential. Screenplay by Brian Helgeland, from the novel by James Ellroy. Released 1997.

Legally Blonde. Screenplay by Karen McCullah Lutz, Kristen Smith, from the novel by Amanda Brown. Released 2001.

Liar Liar. Written by Paul Guay, Stephen Mazur. Released 1997.

Life On The Inside. Written by Robb Padgett, Steven Rowley, 2007.

Little Miss Sunshine. Written by Michael Arndt. Released 2006.

Little White Lies. Written by Heather Ragsdale, 2008.

Lost in Translation. Written by Sofia Coppola. Released 2003.

Magnolia. Written by Paul Thomas Anderson. Released 1998.

Memento. Screenplay by Christopher Nolan, from a story by Jonathan Nolan. Released 2000.

Michael Clayton. Written by Tony Gilroy. Released 2007.

Mission: Impossible. Screenplay by David Koepp, Robert Towne. Story by David Keopp, Steven Zaillian. From the television series created by Bruce Geller. Released 1996.

Monk. Created by Andy Breckman, 2002.

Monsters, Inc. Screenplay by Andrew Stanton, Daniel Gerson. Additional screenplay material by Robert L. Baird, Rhett Reese, Jonathan Roberts. Story by Pete Docter, Jill Culton, Jeff Pidgeon, Ralph Eggleston. Released 2001.

My Best Friend's Wedding. Written by Ronald Bass. Released 1997.

My Cousin Vinny. Written by Dale Launer. Released 1992.

No Country For Old Men. Screenplay by Joel Coen, Ethan Coen, from the novel by Cormac McCarthy. Released 2007.

Ocean's Eleven. 2001 Screenplay by Ted Griffin. 1960 Screenplay by Harry Brown, Charles Lederer. 1960 Story by George Clayton Johnson, Jack Golden Russell.

The Office. Created by Greg Daniels, Ricky Gervais, Stephen Merchant, 2005.

Old School. Screenplay by Todd Phillips, Scot Armstrong. Story by Court Crandall, Todd Phillips, Scot Armstrong. Released 2003.

One Flew Over The Cuckoo's Nest. Screenplay by Lawrence Hauben, Bo Goldman, from the novel by Ken Kesey and play by Dale Wasserman. Released 1975.

Philadelphia. Written by Ron Nyswaner. Released 1993.

Pink: The Series. Written by Mike Maden. Released 2007.

Pirates of the Caribbean: The Curse of the Black Pearl. Screenplay by Ted Elliott, Terry Rossio. Screen story by Ted Elliott, Terry Rossio, Stuart Beattie, Jay Wolpert. Released 2003.

Pleasantville. Written by Gary Ross. Released 1998.

Precious: Based on the Novel 'Push' by Sapphire. Screenplay by Geoffrey Fletcher, from the novel by Sapphire. Released 2009.

Primal Fear. Screenplay by Steve Shagan, Ann Biderman, from the novel by William Diehl. Released 1996.

Prison Break. Created by Paul Scheuring, 2005.

Project Monarch. Written by Jessica St. James, 2009.

Psycho. Screenplay by Joseph Stefano, from the novel by Robert Bloch. Released 1960.

Pulp Fiction. Written by Quentin Tarantino. Stories by: Quentin Tarantino, Roger Avary. Released 1994.

Rosemary's Baby. Screenplay by Roman Polanski, from the novel by Ira Levin. Released 1968.

Saving Private Ryan. Written by Robert Rodat. Released 1998.

Seinfeld. Created by Larry David, Jerry Seinfeld, 1990.

Sex and the City. Created by Darren Star, 1998.

Shrek. Screenplay by Ted Elliott, Terry Rossio, Joe Stillman, Roger S.H. Schulman, from the book by William Steig. Additional dialogue by Cody Cameron, Chris Miller, Conrad Vernon. Released 2001.

Sideways. Written by Alexander Payne, Jim Taylor. Released 2004.

Slumdog Millionaire. Screenplay by Simon Beaufoy, from the novel by Vikas Swarup. Released 2008.

Spider-Man. Screenplay by David Koepp, based on the Marvel Comics series by Stan Lee and Steve Ditko. Released 2002.

That Other Me. Written by Leslie Lawson, 2007.

The 40-Year-Old Virgin. Written by Judd Apatow, Steve Carell. Released 2005.

The Bad News Bears. Written by Bill Lancaster. Released 1976. 2005 screenplay by Bill Lancaster, Glenn Ficarra, John Requa.

The Big Bang Theory. Created by Chuck Lorre, Bill Prady, 2007.

The Big Chill. Written by Lawrence Kasdan, Barbara Benedek. Released 1983.

The Bourne Identity. Screenplay by Tony Gilroy, William Blake Herron, from the novel by Robert Ludlum. Released 2002.

The Closer. Created by James Duff, 2005.

The Curious Case of Benjamin Button. Screenplay by Eric Roth, Robin Swicord, from a story by F. Scott Fitzgerald. Released 2008.

The Dark Knight. Written by Christopher Nolan, David S. Goyer. Batman created by Bob Kane. Released 2008.

The Departed. Screenplay by William Monahan, from the screenplay by Alan Mak, Felix Chong. Released 2006.

The Devil Wears Prada. Screenplay by Aline Brosh McKenna, from the novel by Lauren Weisberger. Released 2006.

The Fugitive. Screenplay by Jeb Stuart, David Twohy. Story by David Twohy. Characters by Roy Huggins. Released 1993.

The Guild. Written by Felicia Day, 2007.

The Hangover. Written by Jon Lucas, Scott Moore. Released 2009.

The Ice Storm. Screenplay by James Schamus, from the novel by Rick Moody. Released 1997.

The Informant! Screenplay by Scott Z. Burns, from the book by Kurt Eichenwald. Released 2009.

The Insider. Screenplay by Eric Roth and Michael Mann, from an article by Marie Brenner. Released 1999.

The Lord of the Rings: The Fellowship of the Ring. Screenplay by Fran Walsh, Philippa Boyens, Peter Jackson, from the novel by J.R.R. Tolkien. Released 2001.

The Lovely Bones. Screenplay by Fran Walsh, Philippa Boyens, Peter Jackson, from the novel by Alice Sebold. Released 2009.

The Queen. Written by Peter Morgan. Released 2006.

The Reader. Screenplay by David Hare, from the novel by by Bernhard Schlink. Released 2008.

The Shawshank Redemption. Screenplay by Frank Darabont, from a story by Stephen King. Released 1994.

The Silence of the Lambs. Screenplay by Ted Tally, from the novel by Thomas Harris. Released 1991.

The Sixth Sense. Written by M. Night Shyamalan. Released 1999.

The Sleeper Agent. Written by Ryan Boyd, 2009.

The Strikeout King. Written by Geoff Alexander, 2006.

The Wild Bunch. Screenplay by Walon Green, Sam Peckinpah. Story by Walon Green, Roy N. Sickner. Released 1969.

The Wild Rose. Written by Stephen Cowan, 2007

The Wizard of Oz. Screenplay by Noel Langley, Florence Ryerson, Edgar Allan Woolf, from the novels by L. Frank Baum. Adaptation by Noel Langley. Numerous uncredited ghost writers. Released 1939.

The Wrestler. Written by Robert D. Siegel. Released 2008.

Thelma & Louise. Written by Callie Khouri. Released 1991.

There's Something About Mary. Screenplay by Ed Decter, John J. Strauss, Peter Farrelly, Bobby Farrelly. Story by Ed Decter, John J. Strauss. Released 1998.

Three Days of the Condor. Screenplay by Lorenzo Semple Jr., David Rayfiel, from the novel *Six Days of the Condor* by James Grady. Released 1975.

Three Days, Three-Thousand Miles. Written by Suzanne Keilly, 2009.

Tootsie. Screenplay by Murray Schisgal, Larry Gelbart. Story by Don McGuire, Larry Gelbart. Uncredited dialogue by Robert Garland, Barry Levinson, Elaine May. Released 1982.

Toy Story. Screenplay by Joss Whedon, Andrew Stanton, Joel Cohen, Alec Sokolow. Story by John Lasseter, Pete Docter, Andrew Stanton, Joe Ranft. Released 1995.

Tumbleweeds. Written by Gavin O'Connor, Angela Shelton, from a story by Angela Shelton. Released 1999.

Two and a Half Men. Created by Lee Aronsohn, Chuck Lorre, 2003.

Up. Screenplay by Bob Peterson, Pete Docter. Story by Pete Docter, Bob Peterson, Thomas McCarthy. Released 2009.

Up In The Air. Screenplay by Jason Reitman, Sheldon Turner, from the novel by Walter Kim. Released 2009.

Wall-E. Screenplay by Andrew Stanton, Jim Reardon. Story by Andrew Stanton, Pete Docter. Released 2008.

Weekend Warrior. Written by Bill Birch, 2007.

When Harry Met Sally. Written by Nora Ephron. Released 1989.

Willy Wonka and the Chocolate Factory. Screenplay by Roald Dahl, from his novel *Charlie and the Chocolate Factory*. Uncredited dialogue by David Seltzer. Released 1971.

Acknowledgments

T his book could not have been written without the support and infinite patience of my "dream team": Jude Roth, Elisa Wolfe, Elena Zaretsky, and Abby Anderson, who helped me with proofing, researching, and general nudging when distractions with work and family threatened to spin me off course. Jude, Elisa, Elena and Abby also happen to be four of the most talented screenwriters with whom I have worked. (If you're reading this section, represent or hire them immediately!)

Doug Abrams, brilliant novelist, killer book agent, sometimes-client and always-friend, gets a very special "thank you" for smiling through the phone and gently reminding me that, when I finally got my act together, he'd be there to help. And he was.

Special thanks go to the *On The Page* writers who contributed to this book: Bill Birch, Brendan O'Neill, Carole Ryavec, Chad Diez, Chip James, Geoff Alexander, Heather Ragsdale, Jessica St. James, Jocelyn Seagrave, Karen Nation, Karin Gist, Keith Armonaitis, Leslie Lawson, Lynne Christensen, Matt Harris, Mike Maden, Nick Johnson, Paul Pender, Ryan Boyd, Stephen Cowan, and Suzanne Keilly. It was without any hesitation that I included their writing alongside that of some of the most well-known and accomplished writers in the business.

Thanks to Ken Lee, who calmly pushed me to double my page count and, in doing so, sparked ideas for a whole new set of writing tools and exercises.

And finally, I cannot leave this acknowledgment page without an extra thank you to my family. My daughters, Sara and Rita Dodson, lived through Christmas '09 with their mommy's head buried in her computer ... even more than usual. My husband, Patrick Francis Dodson, did double-dad duty and also put up with my constant requests to check IMDb. And my mom, Sydelle Pittas, ran her practiced eye over anything legal, while trying her best *not* to give her two cents about content — something that was very, very difficult for her.

Author Biography

 **PILAR ALESSANDRA** is the director of the Los Angeles-based writing program *On The Page* (www.onthepage.tv), which has helped thousands of writers develop, write and refine their screenplays and television scripts.

She's worked as Senior Story Analyst for DreamWorks and Radar Pictures and covered projects at ImageMovers, Saturday Night Live Studios, Handprint Entertainment, Cineville Productions and The Robert Evans Company. She's trained writers at ABC/Disney, MTV/Nickelodeon, the National Screen Institute, the Los Angeles Film School and The UCLA Writers Program.

In demand as a speaker and guest teacher, Pilar has traveled extensively, presenting classes at Film Training Manitoba, The American Screenwriting Association, The Chicago Screenwriters Network, The Great American Pitchfest, The Northwest Screenwriters Guild, The Organization Of Black Screenwriters, The Rhode Island International Film Festival, The Screenwriting Expo and more.

Her weekly *On The Page* podcast features writing tips and interviews with writers and producers from within the industry.

Pilar's students and clients have sold to Disney, DreamWorks, Warner Brothers and Sony and have won prestigious competitions such as the Austin Film Festival, Open Door Competition, Disney Fellowship, Fade-In Competition and Nicholl Fellowship.

Pilar's *On The Page*® writing studio is based in Sherman Oaks, California. She lives in Woodland Hills, California, with her husband Patrick Francis Dodson (a writer and comedian) and their two girls, Sara and Rita.

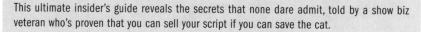

THE WRITER'S JOURNEY
3RD EDITION

MYTHIC STRUCTURE FOR WRITERS

CHRISTOPHER VOGLER

BEST SELLER
OVER 170,000 COPIES SOLD!

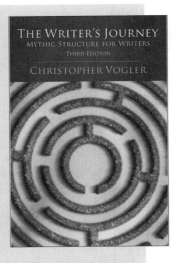

See why this book has become an international best seller and a true classic. *The Writer's Journey* explores the powerful relationship between mythology and storytelling in a clear, concise style that's made it required reading for movie executives, screenwriters, playwrights, scholars, and fans of pop culture all over the world.

Both fiction and nonfiction writers will discover a set of useful myth-inspired storytelling paradigms (i.e., "The Hero's Journey") and step-by-step guidelines to plot and character development. Based on the work of Joseph Campbell, *The Writer's Journey* is a must for all writers interested in further developing their craft.

The updated and revised third edition provides new insights and observations from Vogler's ongoing work on mythology's influence on stories, movies, and man himself.

"This book is like having the smartest person in the story meeting come home with you and whisper what to do in your ear as you write a screenplay. Insight for insight, step for step, Chris Vogler takes us through the process of connecting theme to story and making a script come alive."
> – Lynda Obst, Producer, *Sleepless in Seattle, How to Lose a Guy in 10 Days;*
> Author, *Hello, He Lied*

"This is a book about the stories we write, and perhaps more importantly, the stories we live. It is the most influential work I have yet encountered on the art, nature, and the very purpose of storytelling."
> – Bruce Joel Rubin, Screenwriter, *Stuart Little 2, Deep Impact,*
> *Ghost, Jacob's Ladder*

CHRISTOPHER VOGLER is a veteran story consultant for major Hollywood film companies and a respected teacher of filmmakers and writers around the globe. He has influenced the stories of movies from *The Lion King* to *Fight Club* to *The Thin Red Line* and most recently wrote the first installment of *Ravenskull*, a Japanese-style manga or graphic novel. He is the executive producer of the feature film *P.S. Your Cat is Dead* and writer of the animated feature *Jester Till*.

$26.95 · 300 PAGES · ORDER NUMBER 76RLS · ISBN: 193290736x

THE HOLLYWOOD STANDARD

THE COMPLETE AND AUTHORITATIVE GUIDE TO SCRIPT FORMAT AND STYLE

CHRISTOPHER RILEY

BEST SELLER

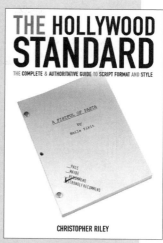

Finally, there's a script format guide that is accurate, complete, and easy to use, written by Hollywood's foremost authority on industry standard script formats. Riley's guide is filled with clear, concise, complete instructions and hundreds of examples to take the guesswork out of a multitude of formatting questions that perplex screenwriters, waste their time, and steal their confidence. You'll learn how to get into and out of a POV shot, how to set up a telephone intercut, what to capitalize and why, how to control pacing with format, and more.

"The Hollywood Standard *is not only indispensable, it's practical, readable, and fun to use.*"
— Dean Batali, Writer-Producer, *That '70s Show*; Writer, *Buffy the Vampire Slayer*

"*Buy this book before you write another word! It's required reading for any screenwriter who wants to be taken seriously by Hollywood.*"
— Elizabeth Stephen, President, Mandalay Television Pictures;
Executive Vice President Motion Picture Production, Mandalay Pictures

"*Riley has succeeded in an extremely difficult task: He has produced a guide to screenplay formatting which is both entertaining to read and exceptionally thorough. Riley's clear style, authoritative voice, and well-written examples make this book far more enjoyable than any formatting guide has a right to be. This is the best guide to script formatting ever, and it is an indispensable tool for every writer working in Hollywood.*"
— Wout Thielemans, *Screentalk* Magazine

"*It doesn't matter how great your screenplay is if it looks all wrong.* The Hollywood Standard *is probably the most critical book any screenwriter who is serious about being taken seriously can own. For any writer who truly understands the power of making a good first impression, this comprehensive guide to format and style is priceless.*"
— Marie Jones, *www.absolutewrite.com*

CHRISTOPHER RILEY, based in Los Angeles, developed Warner Brothers Studios script software and serves as the ultimate arbiter of script format for the entertainment industry.

$18.95 · 208 PAGES · ORDER # 31RLS · ISBN: 9781932907018

SAVE THE CAT! GOES TO THE MOVIES
THE SCREENWRITER'S GUIDE TO EVERY STORY EVER TOLD

BLAKE SNYDER

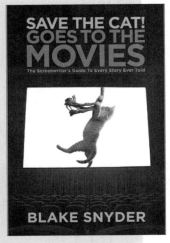

In the long-awaited sequel to his surprise bestseller, *Save the Cat!*, author and screenwriter Blake Snyder returns to form in a fast-paced follow-up that proves why his is the most talked-about approach to screenwriting in years. In the perfect companion piece to his first book, Snyder delivers even more insider's information gleaned from a 20-year track record as "one of Hollywood's most successful spec screenwriters," giving you the clues to write *your* movie.

Designed for screenwriters, novelists, and movie fans, this book gives readers the key breakdowns of the 50 most instructional movies from the past 30 years. From *M*A*S*H* to *Crash*, from *Alien* to *Saw*, from *10* to *Eternal Sunshine of the Spotless Mind*, Snyder reveals how screenwriters who came before you tackled the same challenges you are facing with the film you want to write — or the one you are currently working on.

Writing a "rom-com"? Check out the "Buddy Love" chapter for a "beat for beat" dissection of *When Harry Met Sally...* plus references to 10 other great romantic comedies that will make your story sing.

Want to execute a great mystery? Go to the "Whydunit" section and learn about the "dark turn" that's essential to the heroes of *All the President's Men*, *Blade Runner*, *Fargo* and hip noir *Brick* — and see why ALL good stories, whether a Hollywood blockbuster or a Sundance award winner, follow the same rules of structure outlined in Snyder's breakthrough method.

If you want to sell your script and create a movie that pleases most audiences most of the time, the odds increase if you reference Snyder's checklists and see what makes 50 films tick. After all, both executives and audiences respond to the same elements good writers seek to master. They want to know the type of story they signed on for, and whether it's structured in a way that satisfies everyone. It's what they're looking for. And now, it's what you can deliver.

BLAKE SNYDER, besides selling million-dollar scripts to both Disney and Spielberg, is still "one of Hollywood's most successful spec screenwriters," having made another spec sale in 2006. An in-demand scriptcoach and seminar and workshop leader, Snyder provides information for writers through his website, *www.blakesnyder.com*.

$22.95 · 270 PAGES · ORDER NUMBER 75RLS · ISBN: 1932907351

SELLING YOUR STORY IN 60 SECONDS

THE GUARANTEED WAY TO GET YOUR
SCREENPLAY OR NOVEL READ

MICHAEL HAUGE

Best-selling author Michael Hauge reveals:

- How to Design, Practice and Present the 60-Second Pitch
- The Cardinal Rule of Pitching
- The 10 Key Components of a Commercial Story
- The 8 Steps to a Powerful Pitch
- Targeting Your Buyers
- Securing Opportunities to Pitch
- Pitching Templates
- And much more, including "The Best Pitch I Ever Heard," an exclusive collection from major film executives

"Michael Hauge's principles and methods are so well argued that the mysteries of effective screenwriting can be understood — even by directors."
> – Phillip Noyce, Director, *Patriot Games, Clear and Present Danger, The Quiet American, Rabbit Proof Fence*

"... one of the few authentically good teachers out there. Every time I revisit my notes, I learn something new or reinforce something that I need to remember."
> – Jeff Arch, Screenwriter, *Sleepless in Seattle, Iron Will*

"Michael Hauge's method is magic — but unlike most magicians, he shows you how the trick is done."
> – William Link, Screenwriter & Co-Creator, *Columbo; Murder, She Wrote*

"By following the formula we learned in Michael Hauge's seminar, we got an agent, optioned our script, and now have a three picture deal at Disney."
> – Paul Hoppe and David Henry, Screenwriters

MICHAEL HAUGE, is the author of *Writing Screenplays That Sell*, now in its 30th printing, and has presented his seminars and lectures to more than 30,000 writers and filmmakers. He has coached hundreds of screenwriters and producers on their screenplays and pitches, and has consulted on projects for Warner Brothers, Disney, New Line, CBS, Lifetime, Julia Roberts, Jennifer Lopez, Kirsten Dunst, and Morgan Freeman.

$12.95 · 150 PAGES · ORDER NUMBER 64RLS · ISBN: 1932907203

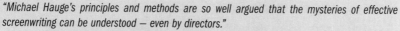

24 HOURS | 1.800.833.5738 | WWW.MWP.COM

MASTER SHOTS
100 ADVANCED CAMERA TECHNIQUES TO GET AN EXPENSIVE LOOK ON YOUR LOW BUDGET MOVIE

CHRISTOPHER KENWORTHY

Master Shots gives filmmakers the techniques they need to execute complex, original shots on any budget. By using powerful master shots and well-executed moves, directors can develop a strong style and stand out from the crowd. Most low-budget movies look low-budget, because the director is forced to compromise at the last minute. *Master Shots* gives you so many powerful techniques that you'll be able to respond, even under pressure, and create knock-out shots. Even when the clock is ticking and the light is fading, the techniques in this book can rescue your film, and make every shot look like it cost a fortune.

Each technique is illustrated with samples from great feature films and computer-generated diagrams for absolute clarity.

Use the secrets of the master directors to give your film the look and feel of a multi-million-dollar movie. The set-ups, moves and methods of the greats are there for the taking, whatever your budget.

"Master Shots *gives every filmmaker out there the blow-by-blow setup required to pull off even the most difficult of setups found from indies to the big Hollywood blockbusters. It's like getting all of the magician's tricks in one book.*"
— Devin Watson, Producer, *The Cursed*

"*Though one needs to choose any addition to a film book library carefully, what with the current plethora of volumes on cinema,* Master Shots *is an essential addition to any worthwhile collection.*"
— Scott Essman, Publisher, *Directed By* Magazine

"*Christopher Kenworthy's book gives you a basic, no holds barred, no shot forgotten look at how films are made from the camera point of view. For anyone with a desire to understand how film is constructed — this book is for you.*"
— Matthew Terry, Screenwriter/Director, Columnist
www.hollywoodlitsales.com

Since 2000, CHRISTOPHER KENWORTHY has written, produced, and directed drama and comedy programs, along with many hours of commercial video, tv pilots, music videos, experimental projects, and short films. He's also produced and directed over 300 visual FX shots. In 2006 he directed the web-based Australian UFO Wave, which attracted many millions of viewers. Upcoming films for Kenworthy include *The Sickness* (2009) and *Glimpse* (2011).

$24.95 · 240 PAGES · ORDER NUMBER 91RLS · ISBN: 9781932907513

{ THE MYTH OF MWP }

In a dark time, a light bringer came along, leading the curious and the frustrated to clarity and empowerment. It took the well-guarded secrets out of the hands of the few and made them available to all. It spread a spirit of openness and creative freedom, and built a storehouse of knowledge dedicated to the betterment of the arts.

The essence of the Michael Wiese Productions (MWP) is empowering people who have the burning desire to express themselves creatively. We help them realize their dreams by putting the tools in their hands. We demystify the sometimes secretive worlds of screenwriting, directing, acting, producing, film financing, and other media crafts.

By doing so, we hope to bring forth a realization of 'conscious media' which we define as being positively charged, emphasizing hope and affirming positive values like trust, cooperation, self-empowerment, freedom, and love. Grounded in the deep roots of myth, it aims to be healing both for those who make the art and those who encounter it. It hopes to be transformative for people, opening doors to new possibilities and pulling back veils to reveal hidden worlds.

MWP has built a storehouse of knowledge unequaled in the world, for no other publisher has so many titles on the media arts. Please visit www.mwp.com where you will find many free resources and a 25% discount on our books. Sign up and become part of the wider creative community!

Onward and upward,

Michael Wiese
Publisher/Filmmaker

FILM & VIDEO BOOKS

SCREENWRITING | WRITING

And the Best Screenplay Goes to... | Dr. Linda Seger | $26.95
Archetypes for Writers | Jennifer Van Bergen | $22.95
Bali Brothers | Lacy Waltzman, Matthew Bishop, Michael Wiese | $12.95
Cinematic Storytelling | Jennifer Van Sijll | $24.95
Could It Be a Movie? | Christina Hamlett | $26.95
Creating Characters | Marisa D'Vari | $26.95
Crime Writer's Reference Guide, The | Martin Roth | $20.95
Deep Cinema | Mary Trainor-Brigham | $19.95
Elephant Bucks | Sheldon Bull | $24.95
Fast, Cheap & Written That Way | John Gaspard | $26.95
Hollywood Standard, The, 2nd Edition | Christopher Riley | $18.95
Horror Screenwriting | Devin Watson | $24.95
I Could've Written a Better Movie than That! | Derek Rydall | $26.95
Inner Drives | Pamela Jaye Smith | $26.95
Moral Premise, The | Stanley D. Williams, Ph.D. | $24.95
Myth and the Movies | Stuart Voytilla | $26.95
Power of the Dark Side, The | Pamela Jaye Smith | $22.95
Psychology for Screenwriters | William Indick, Ph.D. | $26.95
Reflections of the Shadow | Jeffrey Hirschberg | $26.95
Rewrite | Paul Chitlik | $16.95
Romancing the A-List | Christopher Keane | $18.95
Save the Cat! | Blake Snyder | $19.95
Save the Cat! Goes to the Movies | Blake Snyder | $24.95
Screenwriting 101 | Neill D. Hicks | $16.95
Screenwriting for Teens | Christina Hamlett | $18.95
Script-Selling Game, The | Kathie Fong Yoneda | $16.95
Stealing Fire From the Gods, 2nd Edition | James Bonnet | $26.95
Talk the Talk | Penny Penniston | $24.95
Way of Story, The | Catherine Ann Jones | $22.95
What Are You Laughing At? | Brad Schreiber | $19.95
Writer's Journey, – 3rd Edition, The | Christopher Vogler | $26.95
Writer's Partner, The | Martin Roth | $24.95
Writing the Action Adventure Film | Neill D. Hicks | $14.95
Writing the Comedy Film | Stuart Voytilla & Scott Petri | $14.95
Writing the Killer Treatment | Michael Halperin | $14.95
Writing the Second Act | Michael Halperin | $19.95
Writing the Thriller Film | Neill D. Hicks | $14.95
Writing the TV Drama Series – 2nd Edition | Pamela Douglas | $26.95
Your Screenplay Sucks! | William M. Akers | $19.95

FILMMAKING

Film School | Richard D. Pepperman | $24.95
Power of Film, The | Howard Suber | $27.95

PITCHING

Perfect Pitch – 2nd Edition, The | Ken Rotcop | $19.95
Selling Your Story in 60 Seconds | Michael Hauge | $12.95

SHORTS

Filmmaking for Teens, 2nd Edition | Troy Lanier & Clay Nichols | $24.95
Making It Big in Shorts | Kim Adelman | $22.95

BUDGET | PRODUCTION MANAGEMENT

Film & Video Budgets, 5th Updated Edition | Deke Simon | $26.95
Film Production Management 101 | Deborah S. Patz | $39.95

DIRECTING | VISUALIZATION

Animation Unleashed | Ellen Besen | $26.95

Cinematography for Directors | Jacqueline Frost | $29.95
Citizen Kane Crash Course in Cinematography | David Worth | $19.95
Directing Actors | Judith Weston | $26.95
Directing Feature Films | Mark Travis | $26.95
Fast, Cheap & Under Control | John Gaspard | $26.95
Film Directing: Cinematic Motion, 2nd Edition | Steven D. Katz | $27.95
Film Directing: Shot by Shot | Steven D. Katz | $27.95
Film Director's Intuition, The | Judith Weston | $26.95
First Time Director | Gil Bettman | $27.95
From Word to Image, 2nd Edition | Marcie Begleiter | $26.95
I'll Be in My Trailer! | John Badham & Craig Modderno | $26.95
Master Shots | Christopher Kenworthy | $24.95
Setting Up Your Scenes | Richard D. Pepperman | $24.95
Setting Up Your Shots, 2nd Edition | Jeremy Vineyard | $22.95
Working Director, The | Charles Wilkinson | $22.95

DIGITAL | DOCUMENTARY | SPECIAL

Digital Filmmaking 101, 2nd Edition | Dale Newton & John Gaspard | $26.95
Digital Moviemaking 3.0 | Scott Billups | $24.95
Digital Video Secrets | Tony Levelle | $26.95
Greenscreen Made Easy | Jeremy Hanke & Michele Yamazaki | $19.95
Producing with Passion | Dorothy Fadiman & Tony Levelle | $22.95
Special Effects | Michael Slone | $31.95

EDITING

Cut by Cut | Gael Chandler | $35.95
Cut to the Chase | Bobbie O'Steen | $24.95
Eye is Quicker, The | Richard D. Pepperman | $27.95
Film Editing | Gael Chandler | $34.95
Invisible Cut, The | Bobbie O'Steen | $28.95

SOUND | DVD | CAREER

Complete DVD Book, The | Chris Gore & Paul J. Salamoff | $26.95
Costume Design 101, 2nd Edition | Richard La Motte | $24.95
Hitting Your Mark, 2nd Edition | Steve Carlson | $22.95
Sound Design | David Sonnenschein | $19.95
Sound Effects Bible, The | Ric Viers | $26.95
Storyboarding 101 | James Fraioli | $19.95
There's No Business Like Soul Business | Derek Rydall | $22.95
You Can Act! | D. W. Brown | $24.95

FINANCE | MARKETING | FUNDING

Art of Film Funding, The | Carole Lee Dean | $26.95
Bankroll | Tom Malloy | $26.95
Complete Independent Movie Marketing Handbook, The | Mark Steven Bosko | $39.95
Getting the Money | Jeremy Jusso | $26.95
Independent Film and Videomakers Guide – 2nd Edition, The | Michael Wiese | $29.95
Independent Film Distribution | Phil Hall | $26.95
Shaking the Money Tree, 3rd Edition | Morrie Warshawski | $26.95

MEDITATION | ART

Mandalas of Bali | Dewa Nyoman Batuan | $39.95

OUR FILMS

Dolphin Adventures: DVD | Michael Wiese and Hardy Jones | $24.95
Hardware Wars: DVD | Written and Directed by Ernie Fosselius | $14.95
On the Edge of a Dream | Michael Wiese | $16.95
Sacred Sites of the Dalai Lamas– DVD, The | Documentary by Michael Wiese | $24.95